TOTAL ACCESS

Other Works by Regis McKenna

*The Regis Touch: Million Dollar Advice from
America's Top Marketing Consultant* (1986)

*Who's Afraid of Big Blue? How Companies Are
Challenging IBM—and Winning* (1988)

*Relationship Marketing: Successful Strategies
for the Age of the Customer* (1991)

*Real Time: Preparing for the Age of the
Never Satisfied Customer* (1997)

Regis McKenna

TOTAL ACCESS

Giving Customers What They Want
in an Anytime, Anywhere World

Harvard Business School Press
Boston, Massachusetts

Requests for permission to use or reproduce material from this book should be directed to permissions@hbsp.harvard.edu, or mailed to Permissions, Harvard Business School Publishing, 60 Harvard Way, Boston, Massachusetts 02163.

Library of Congress Cataloging-in-Publication Data

McKenna, Regis.
    Total access : giving customers what they want in an anytime, anywhere world / Regis McKenna.
        p. cm.
    Includes index.
    ISBN 1-57851-244-1 (alk. paper)
        1. Customer services. 2. Customer relations. 3. Consumer satisfaction. I. Title.

    HF5415.5 .M3855 2002
    658.8'12—dc21

                                                        2001051536

The paper used in this publication meets the requirements of the American National Standard for Permanence of Paper for Publications and Documents in Libraries and Archives Z39.48–1992.

To Dianne

Contents

Preface

IT WAS LATE NOVEMBER and I was driving from the Kona airport to the north end of the island of Hawaii with my father-in-law, Bill Page, and two of my grandchildren, Molly and Maddy. I asked the girls what was on their Christmas lists. Both of them said, "An Apple iBook." I had just read an article on the plane comparing the software availability between the iMac and the PC, so I mentioned that they might not be able to get all the software they wanted for the iBook. Six-year-old Molly said, "I don't need software—I can go on the Internet and get everything I need." Bill smiled at me. "Dummy," he whispered, as Molly and Maddy started talking about their favorite Web sites.

In today's modern society, a child's experience is one of total access: cell phones, fast-food outlets, jet travel, satellite TV in the SUV, portable DVD players, superstores, computerized classrooms, the Internet. And Mom and Dad stop for lattes at a convenient Starbucks or treats at a Baskin-Robbins, then shop at nearby superstores or specialty shops that display dazzling arrays of groceries, books, clothes, computers, toys, and sundries. Computers reply to customers instantaneously with human-styled responses twenty-four hours a day, and a small plastic card helps you fulfill every want or need. Anything and everything appear to be within reach.

Consumers aren't the only ones living in a world of total access. Access goes both ways: Online or offline, transaction data go into networks where CEOs, sales office managers, and production engineers have everything at their fingertips. Customer and retail transactions, current sales, pricing options, inventory and shipping data—all those and more are sliced and diced any way they want it. The connected manager can check a factory's daily production or inventory in Guangzhou, China, or Eranger, Kentucky, monitor changes in sales just hours after launching a new promotion, and track the ten top customer complaints today or this week. Any businessperson, from the chairman of the board to the shipping clerk, can obtain information about almost anything and everything seemingly at will. The distance between producer and consumer is vanishing into a direct exchange of information, and thanks to the computers, software, networks, and other new technologies underlying the changes in the producer-consumer relationship, our understanding of what we call "marketing" is changing too, right before our eyes.

In the past, marketing has been divided into various responsibilities, over time becoming more specialized and focused on image and branding. Brand became a specialized function all its own, and brand "experts" had little or no understanding of the company's products, competition, or business dynamics. When brand and image are considered independent creations and are only referentially related to the tangible competencies of a business or competitive technology, they lose all meaning and relevance—and marketing is often reduced to vapor.

As a corporate function, marketing today is becoming more separated from product development and management, sales, distribution, business development, and other functions. It continues to focus largely on one-way, broadcast messages and other promotional techniques to convince consumers that they need or want a particular product or service. In the process, it has been consumed by its role of manipulating consumer behavior, buying media, and gaining attention amid the rising competitive noise.

I believe this approach has been ineffective in building long-term customer relationships and loyalty. In our total access world, communication has become interactive and marketing vanishes into the network of relationships and responsibilities. When computers and software do much of the customer interaction and relationship management, the traditional marketing function loses power. As the CEO, the CIO, and new functional roles, such as vice president of operations or logistics and vice president of business development, assume more responsibility for strategy and overall resource integration, the function of marketing is marginalized to the purely promotional aspects of the business.

Writing a book about the future of anything is precarious. Perspective is important. The future of marketing touches on many different issues and responsibilities—the role of marketing as a whole, brand, advertising, computer-mediated customer relationships—which give rise to numerous points of view and endless case studies. But if marketers are to progress and survive, they must challenge their traditional beliefs and assumptions. The traditional roles and responsibilities throughout the enterprise are being reinvented in the light of the new shared intelligent network infrastructure, and while marketing is evolving, marketplace events often bring on accelerated change.

I began researching and writing *Total Access* in the midst of the dot-com mania and stock market boom of 1999–2000; as I completed the manuscript, high-tech earnings declines and layoffs filled the news, and the Nasdaq hit a twenty-eight-year low. Despite the changes in the world around me, my views on branding, dot-coms, and companies such as Webvan did not change from the first draft to the last. While many of my views have evolved over the years, one hasn't: I continue to believe that most of the marketing we see today is all too wed to the past.

Current market conditions reinforce the viability of the concepts this book presents, chiefly that numerous technology- and market-driven factors are unalterably changing the function of marketing:

- The increased efficiency of design, production, and distribution sets the pace of global competition, forcing all businesses to compete on the basis of constant change or novelty and price.
- Technology, competition, and cost management drive the nature of marketing and brand more than promotion or broadcast does.
- The decline of loyalty in general, and brand loyalty specifically, is continuing and will not be abated by more messages delivered through increased numbers and forms of media.
- The drive to be more efficient by automating people-intensive services is shifting many functions, roles, and responsibilities—including marketing—to a number of interconnected enterprise functions and responsibilities.
- Distribution or logistics efficiencies, together with information networks, create diverse access points and enable businesses to achieve persistent presence.
- New forms of information media enable both producer and consumer access, changing the nature of that relationship and also the traditional roles and responsibilities of marketing.

Despite the highs and lows of the market, the fundamental driving forces of marketing remain a constant: Economic progress in the face of increasing competition demands that businesses apply new technology to achieve ever higher productivity goals. We consumers see evidence everywhere—*More for less*; *Lowest prices*; *New and programmable*; *Have it your way*; *Shop and go*; *FREE!*; *Your order is confirmed*; *Enter PIN or password*; *To schedule a pickup, say or press one*; *Compare prices*; *Everything you need in one convenient location*—presented in a kaleidoscope of entertaining and time-distracting experiences.

We speak glibly of "technology disruption," but that disruption most often occurs subtly and gradually. We see it reflected in the world around us: children going to school with computer bags rather than book bags, laborers with hard hats and cell phones, cars with GPS and other wireless features, lower prices for increasingly powerful computing or entertainment products, banks in grocery stores, software engineers designing marketing programs, bigger and bigger superstores, and more FedEx, UPS, and DHL trucks in our neighborhoods. Inside the enterprise, the changes are equally diverse and subtle: the rise in the strategic nature of information networks, customer relationship management, changes in management's roles and responsibilities, distribution of and access to business information at home or in foreign lands, increasing value given to the corporate asset value of intellectual property, and more and more CEOs under pressure because of a lack of a coherent competitive strategy.

I don't know exactly how the enterprise will evolve over the next quarter-century, but I am sure that marketing will become increasingly more integrated into the network. As a result, it will turn into a *direct* dialogue between the consumer and the producer, and the producer will need to respond directly to the competitive demands of the marketplace and develop the specific functions necessary to provide an appropriate response. Clearly, computers and software will play a bigger and bigger role in the producer-consumer dialogue and relationship. Computers will become smarter, faster, and more humanlike. How the humans apply this increasingly powerful technology, and whether consumers will respond favorably, depend on marketing's perception of itself. Some businesses will use these technological tools to broadcast messages and to try to manipulate consumer behavior. But marketers must stop being a megaphone and instead become a customer services integrator and mediator. That way, marketing would take the initiative of creating and sustaining the customer dialogue. If it shrinks from this task, market executives will find their roles abrogated by computers, software, the CIO, and other networked functions—they'll end up with small functional assignments with little corporate power.

Working in Silicon Valley and the global marketplace for forty years has allowed me to witness the new replacing the old as powerful microsized technologies have transformed institutions and human behavior. That transformation has come about not only through the forces of technology, but also through the application of good business judgment, wise cost management, the relentless pursuit of improved productivity, and the wisdom gained by interacting and learning with customers.

I define marketing as a corporate learning experience and, like technology and its applications, we learn through use and experience. Total access extends and expands the customer's experiences to many more times and places. To respond to this new marketplace, marketing will become part of the definition of every manager's responsibility because everyone is now engaged in a network of direct relationships. Brand then becomes the presence and ease of access in the daily patterns of human experience; its humanlike interface; the responsiveness of the service; and the information systems sustaining knowledge of the relationship.

Total Access is about marketing in the future. But the book touches only the surface of what I believe will be a revolution in the producer-consumer relationship. I begin by looking at marketing, past and present. I examine how technology has turned the marketplace into an uninterrupted learning experience for consumers, who have become savvy shoppers and whose preferences change constantly. I also look at how technology will continue to reshape both producer and consumer, and how laws of the new marketplace undermine the old notions of brand and customer loyalty.

The increasingly competitive marketplace is driving management to find new ways of engaging consumers; nothing works quite as well as being "present" all the time. As a result, we now see two direct customer channels: one that delivers information and services, and one that provides tangible fulfillment. Marketing is becoming an architecture of services and relationships that businesses must synchronize and manage with an eye both to understanding the customer as well as understanding the technology. The global corporation, as both a supplier as well as a marketplace, is rapidly being integrated into the information-advanced world through advanced telecommunication and the World Wide Web. If corporations continue to pursue productivity gains and ensure that demand for their products and services will continue to grow, they must see developing countries as opportunities for investment in local infrastructures and people. Otherwise businesses will be engaged in never-ending price battles for overpursued consumers in developed countries.

Marketing must go well beyond what we see in most marketing departments and organizations today. All these changes have already changed many of the perceptions of responsibilities inside and outside the enterprise. While I well understand that many marketing people are actively engaged in building direct customer relationships as well as in the deployment of network and interactive strategies, others in the management structure are finding that they too are much more engaged with the customer and the marketing strategy. I believe that the market leaders of the future will come to see the inefficiencies of past practices from the viewpoint of both the customer and the enterprise, adopt the new total access marketplace as reality, apply imagination and creativity, and develop a new understanding of marketing.

Acknowledgments

During the three years I researched and wrote *Total Access*, I called upon many friends and associates to help me think through my point of view, contribute ideas, read and edit my drafts, and resolve real and imagined conflicts. My partners at The McKenna Group contributed their time, ideas, critiques, and commentary. In particular, CEO Geoff Mott was an invaluable source of ideas and cases studies; most of the subjects addressed in these pages were worked out in discussions during our monthly dinners. MKG Director of Research Brian Miller and consultant Laurel Neale were especially helpful with chapter 10 and other case examples throughout the book. MaryAnn Gutoff assisted me with early research and writing, as did Lauren Barack and Brian Kelly. Bo Caldwell worked with me the last six months, advising me and organizing, editing, and shaping the book as it now reads. Her help was invaluable. (Bo recently published her first novel, *The Distant Land of My Father*.)

My longtime good friend Ann Dilworth advised me on the manuscript, giving me valuable suggestions and just good advice. My agent, Rafe Sagalyn, initiated the original book concept and was immeasurably helpful in resolving major issues. The people at Harvard Business School Press have been very supportive over the years, particularly my editor, Kirsten Sandberg. And while I quote many people throughout the book, I'm especially grateful to Bill Campbell, Bill Crowell, Jim Gosling, Jim Cates, Ali Kutay, and Robert Morris.

Finally, special thanks go to my wife, Dianne, for her help through the process of writing and rewriting this book, help that included everything from critiquing chapters and suggesting ideas to contributing references from the many books and papers she reads. Most of all, I'm grateful for her patience and forbearance during this long project.

TOTAL ACCESS

Chapter One

Introduction

The Idea of Marketing

In today's brave new world of endless innovation, competition, and expansion, marketing is undergoing a complete redefinition and in the process taking on a whole new role in today's corporations. "What comes next?" is the question business must ask.

MARKETING AS WE KNOW IT is disappearing. Today software is assuming the role of listening and responding to customers. Customer relationship management (CRM) may be the most obvious example, but in essence everything the producer or consumer touches is absorbed into an information network where both computers and people store, recall, access, and act upon it. Caught in an interlacing web of interrelationships, traditional marketing is vanishing for the simple reason that its *tasks are being automated and assumed by the mysterious and hidden power of computers, software, and networks.*

This book attempts to frame a discussion of what marketing is becoming, and to explore a new vision and a language for the emerging marketing paradigm. In this new paradigm, computers and the network do most of the work, such as data gathering, decision making, customer response and care, and much more; total consumer access to, and interaction with, the marketplace replaces the old broadcast model and makes us rethink our old notions of brand development; and the marketing function disappears into a network of relationships and responsibilities throughout the value chain—customers, producers, and producers' business partners. Based on my years of experience working with start-ups and mature businesses alike, talking with executives of both leaders and laggards, and observing the relationship between technology and business, I believe that the largely hidden infrastructure of computers, networks, and software will change us more rapidly and more reliably than the content will. Yet "old" marketing, operating as it does on the venerable model of trying to sell through a vague notion of brand, promotion, entertainment, and consumer manipulation, is unprepared for this change.

Driven by new technology, marketing first arose in the collective consciousness with the commercial exploitation of mass production. The development of mass media, particularly television, reinvented it. Its third renaissance—which is where we find ourselves today—has come about because of the following five factors that drive the global competitive marketplace:

1. Production capacity is outpacing demand. Over the past twenty years or so, production systems have undergone vast improvements, to such an extent that almost every manufacturing-based industry can outproduce their market demand.
2. Programmable design and production tools, capable of rapid change and adaptability, supply an infinite array of product choices and novelty at no penalty of cost to the customer.
3. Logistics networks today are efficient, information-managed distribution systems that move and track an enormous diversity of products through an increasing variety of customer access points. These systems are the infrastructure so vital today for delivering low-cost fulfillment and customer satisfaction.
4. New digital information networks and media are dynamically altering the nature of the producer-consumer conversation. Easy, low-cost entry to a communications network to obtain, provide, or otherwise exchange information is changing the producer-consumer relationship from one of broadcast to one of access.

5. Competition is global, continuous, and more intense. Armed with the same technologies and driven to expand growth and market share, corporations are lowering prices, consolidating, and battling for the loyalty of the same (targeted) disposable-income customers. As a result, marketing is charged with keeping the factories churning. More and more of the budget is aimed at trying to create customer demand in an oversaturated, overdistributed, and overstimulated marketplace. Competition and technology are driving lower-cost products and more efficient operations, as well as two of the increasingly costly functions of an enterprise: marketing and customer support services.

To address these five factors, businesses are looking to the new, lower-cost network technologies to connect with their suppliers, channels, and customers directly. To be efficient, responsive, and timely, businesses are connecting their internal information networks with supplier, channel, customer, and other alliance information networks. Within the enterprise, businesses are directing information flow and assigning responsibilities in accordance with their customers' stated needs or wants; as a result, they are developing a qualitatively unique infrastructure to support their customers.

Building, deploying, maintaining, and adapting work processes to this new infrastructure can be complex, costly, and people-intensive unless systems and software take on the task by assuming the workload—which is essentially what's happening. As systems and networks evolve, computers are taking on more and more of the customer interface, relationship dynamics, and support functions. As a result, marketing is radically changing and disappearing into ubiquitous software applications, which are embedded in almost everything consumers touch or use.

Marketing's place within the enterprise is changing as well; businesses are now distributing traditional marketing tasks throughout the enterprise. And as technology creates new tools and new ways of doing things—as computers, software, and networks automate marketing functions and infrastructure—marketing and information technology appear to be rapidly converging, forcing practitioners of the old reach-and-push traditions of marketing to take a smaller strategic role.

A Look at Marketing's Genetic Heritage

Marketing is an invention of the twentieth century, and for most of that century—the last eighty years or so—its goal was to infiltrate consumers' minds and to change their thinking. Marketers tried to influence consumers in a positive and directed manner through a combination of brand identification, promotion, entertainment, and manipulation. To support this goal of customer influence, marketing research didn't mine for new service methods for delivering customer satisfaction, automating services or ways to directly build customer loyalty; instead, it simply tried to discover the subtleties of how consumers think and behave. Even today, much of marketing strategy is driven by behavioral research methods such as focus groups, lifestyle analysis, and anthropological analysis derived from observations of consumers in "real" and staged situations.

Marketing has yet to figure out how to keep customers happy using these methods or how to become a contributing and vital connecting force within the enterprise. Its tactics, I fear, are leading only to more market noise and increasing customer dissatisfaction. A July 2001 *Economist* cover story editorial said it best:

> *Being a customer can be baffling these days. All that choice, all those special deals, all those companies eagerly telling you (as you wait on hold, listening to ghastly Muzak) that "your call is important to us." On the face of it, companies seem keener than ever to sell you their stuff— as, in these leaner times, they should be. But why do you so rarely feel that you are getting special service, or that the company knows the faintest thing about who you are or what you want?*[1]

The kind of marketing we're seeing today is a descendent of past practices. It evolved along with twentieth-century mass-production mentality, and it has become something of a pseudopsychological propaganda machine. Today it is at once a corporation's most assertive public face and its most undefined and elusive activity. Marketing, like total quality management, is becoming a distributed and shared responsibility within the enterprise. We can no longer view it from a single perspective, just as it no longer operates through only one medium.

These changes occurred for several reasons. For one, marketing hasn't kept up with the evolution of technology and business processes, causing it to fall into a malaise with its reliance on the pure broadcast model. While technology has become more and more transparent and adaptive, many marketing strategies have remained static models of a bygone era. Brand, now the center of all marketing activities, has been misinterpreted as attention, showmanship, events, and celebrity—even market valuation. In addition, consumer means and methods of interaction are changing, as is the whole marketplace, thanks to cultural, social, and economic forces. The result of all these forces? Let's take a look.

The Phenomenon of Hype: Tactics over Strategy

Everywhere I travel, I hear that marketing is more important to business today than ever, but the only thing I'm aware of is an increased noise level. There's a lot of hype out there, partly because the marketing function is too often equated with promotion and with the idea that branding is best achieved through awareness. Marketing people deny this assertion, but they continue to spend the largest portion of their budgets on advertising and various forms of promotion. Hype dominates the very idea of marketing, and despite some vibrancy, much of marketing has become obscure and even ridiculous. Thanks to the deafening noise of hype, we no longer know what is real, what is effective, or what common set of principles should guide the marketing process.

One thing that's clear is that tactics have replaced strategy. For example, buzzword solutions, promoted as brands themselves and dispensed by branding consultants, proliferate. Terms such as "viral marketing" and "buzz" itself are some of the latest marketing "buzzword brands" used as new tactics for gaining the customers attention. And while the terms may be new, the concepts are old. The original ideas behind these terms have merit, but such terms reflect tactics that usually rely on traditional forms of broadcast tactics in an attempt to manipulate consumer behavior. Consequently, once those ideas are implemented, they usually end up as programs that generate more junk e-mail.

In the past twenty years, marketing has become associated with increasing awareness and hype, relying on famous personalities, entertaining content, and clever tricks that gain media attention, tactics that have dominated marketing to such an extent that they've become ends in themselves. I've heard people call U.S. presidential candidates "competing brands." Religious organizations, universities, and other nonprofit groups are now analyzing and hiring "brand consultants," and British Prime Minister Tony Blair speaks of "branded politics." But what does *brand* really mean? We at The McKenna Group asked this question of 100 company executives and found no common thread other than a vague notion that brand equates with awareness.[2] The term has lost its meaning in much the same way that *marketing* has. That isn't the only problem; brand is no guarantee, thanks to fleeting customer loyalty. Nevertheless, many businesses are still spending considerable sums of money on branding campaigns, ignoring the new technological and social realities that are shifting the marketplace from broadcast to access.

Hype presents two problems: It has a short-lived effect (and isn't really marketing), and it belongs to the past era of push marketing. That said, it's unrealistic to expect traditional media to vanish anytime soon, if at all, and I doubt that the term *brand* will fade from use or stop tripping so easily from the lips of marketers and marketing consultants. Much of the $460-plus billion worldwide advertising industry rests on the belief that a repeated message can change people's opinions and their behavior, and that it can keep them coming back for more as long as they see or hear that message often enough.[3] That belief may have held some truth when fewer media channels existed, when competition was less intense, when access to information was tightly packaged and controlled, and when product choices were more limited, but things were different in the past. Image making and promotion dominated marketing, and consumers had to work to get information.

More than 1.5 billion people will have access to the World Wide Web within the next decade. We know very little about how this wide access will affect marketing or consumer behavior, largely because all we've seen on the Web to date has been market experimentation. Digital content and programming are still highly unrefined and random, and consumer use of this new medium and its content is highly variable. Broadband, which gives us the capability to communicate human expression and experience more realistically, is available to only a small percentage of the market.

What we do know is that interactive consumers are not passive, as past marketing supposed. They are not anesthetized couch potatoes mindlessly absorbing images and messages. They're proactive, but they're also overwhelmed, oversaturated, and, for the most part, passive to mass media advertising. As broadcast media converge with the Internet, radical changes will take place in the economic and social interplay between the interactive consumer and interactive responding producer. Consumers will have tools for managing broadcast commercial messages, which will change marketing people's long-held assumption that millions of viewers are absorbing their messages and responding appropriately. With an interactive digital medium at their disposal, proactive consumers are powerful. The Internet is proving to be the perfect match for these proactive consumers, almost surreptitiously awakening them and drawing them into active participation. This awakening is the Internet's most significant effect on consumers, an effect that has yet to be fully realized.

The Agent of Change: Technology

Technology is the greatest catalyst for change in marketing. Technological innovations have had a huge effect, so much so that anyone would find it hard to overstate their repercussions on this part of business. This shouldn't surprise us; technology has always been the driver of change in marketing. From railroad to automobiles, from radio to TV to computers, marketing takes advantage of new technology and applies it to new methods of marketing. Although the technology may change, its role never does: It's always the agent of economic and social change. In marketing's short history, we've seen only a few truly revolutionary changes, but almost every significant change has resulted from the emergence of new technologies.

Changes in the marketplace fostered by the prolific advances in computer-aided design, production, and distribution systems, as well as information and communication networks, are too often overlooked as fundamental marketing assets. Marketing is either empowered by or limited by the operational competence of a business. Today's logistics systems represent one of the most radical innovations in business, with benefits to both producer and consumer. Supply and distribution chain systems are creating faster and more efficient ways of moving products and information between suppliers, distribution centers, and consumer access points. Logistics is a transparent customer-satisfying service that has the great power of being responsive to customers and thus increasing customer loyalty. From research and development (R&D) to production and distribution, these highly efficient systems allow information, knowledge, ideas, and novel new products to flow in a constant stream.

The convergence of digital technology and media with new ways of communicating catalyzes changes in marketing by increasing consumers' reach and range of choices, as well as by developing new vehicles to turn advertising into engaging customer communications. Imagine, advertising that listens and responds! Digital technology is improving customer access to myriad product and service choices, as well as to the information for deciding where and what to buy. As personal access technologies become more powerful, the consumer's needs, wants, and demands— not the behavioral models of back-room researchers—will program responses from producers.

The "old" concept of marketing as mass message distribution arose when businesses were rapidly exploiting technologies of mass production. Mass production brought about the concept of mass marketing. New production methods and means of distribution—radio, television, and computers—significantly influenced the evolution of marketing over the course of the twentieth century. These same technological innovations have been the driving forces behind social change as well. New technologies don't simply replace old ways of doing things; they also replace old models of thinking.

Marketing's goal has always been to build the relationship between buyer and seller; its reason for being has been to extend and sustain that relationship. And that's still true. In fact, that relationship is more important now than ever. Technology isn't doing away with that relationship; it's just changing how it's nurtured and sustained. The new tools of marketing are technological, network-based, enterprise solutions that help foster a direct, engaging, sustained buyer-seller relationship. These tools include supply chain integration and management, customer relationship management (CRM), logistics, Internet-based self-service and customer feedback solutions, database synchronization and access, as well as other software solutions.

A Marketing Renaissance

Digital information and network technologies are reinventing just about every business process, and marketing is by no means an exception. As a result of information technology (IT), the whole marketing organization is changing, losing its centrality within the enterprise. As more and more marketing functions are absorbed into the enterprise-wide information network and shared across all business functions, we will see that expertise diffuse. Information technology is now such an integral and essential component of responding to market changes and satisfying customers that executives from many areas of the corporation are making marketing decisions and executing marketing plans.

Although affected by these changes, marketing appears to want to remain a separate and different breed of corporate animal. But it can no longer do so. The marketing organization is becoming increasingly fragmented. The creative functions of promotion and advertising have broken off, and piece after piece of the marketing function—including some key responsibilities like logistics and distribution, business development, strategy, supply chain management, Web site development, infrastructure management, value creation, partnering, and alliances—have been lopped off and allocated to different functional areas in the corporation. And while we continue to cloak marketing in conceptual terminology, using words like *corporate identity, image, integrated marketing,* and *brand equity*—chances are that the company's identity, reputation, competitive position, and value are more in the hands of the CEO, CIO, and the vice president of R&D than in the hands of anyone in a marketing position.

In addition, IT is absorbing marketing functions that can be codified and put into software. Even the process of sustaining customer relationships—what some would call the very heart of marketing—is disappearing into the network and is no longer under marketing's purview. Direct network contact with the customer is creating constancy in those relationships. When a consumer orders from a company online, that communication initiates an interactive response. Information and communication move simultaneously inside the enterprise and interactively with the customer. The information is now stored and readily accessible by both producer and consumer.

Whether marketing is a science or an art has been the subject of a long-running debate. I believe it's neither. Marketing is becoming a technology. The following comparison illustrates this metamorphosis. The left column lists the functions that are slipping away from the marketing organization and moving to IT. The right column lists the functions that are IT operations automated through software.

TRADITIONAL MARKETING FUNCTION	REPLACED BY
Distribution	Logistics, supplier networks
Pricing	Networked consortia, barter and auctions, and value-matched decision systems
Forecasting	Computer simulations from market transactions database
Segmentation	Data mining, self-defining during database access
Research	Daily transaction data analysis, intelligent search tools
Service	Self-service—personalization software and logistics
Competitive analysis	Context search engines and daily market monitoring
Customer relationship management	CRM

Once under the domain of marketing, all the functions in the right column are being transported across the enterprise by networks allowing direct interaction with those who have the responsibility and resources to respond. As you can see, this marketing renaissance is the subtle yet progressive movement of marketing functions and process from centralized control into the shared network community. It engages many old and new players in the marketing processes as active participants with shared responsibilities. Each of these functions will become part of an enterprise marketing architecture.

The Marketing Architecture

A marketing architecture laces together the relevant players in the producer-consumer support system, adding content, services, value, and continued novelty as it matures. The goal of a marketing architecture is total access for both the customer and supporting services infrastructure. It aims to be not simply efficient but also creative. To achieve persistent market presence, companies today must sustain novelty and choice, an endeavor that requires them to generate a constant flow of new products and services in a variety of formats. Because providing customers with such a never-ending cornucopia of novelty is intellectually demanding, costly, and complex, companies need a marketing architecture to interweave the talent and resources within a continually learning, networked community that grows and expands as it engages customers, reacts to competition, and adds capabilities, new players, and scales.

This business concept is not new, particularly to American corporations. To gain market advantages, U.S. companies have long developed alliances—for example, big companies with small ones, and universities with corporate R&D operations. The new wrinkle is the addition of facilitating networks and the newfound capability to evolve goals and objectives through continued interaction. In other words, the architecture learns as it matures.

The goal of much of the partnering and alliance building we see today in all businesses is to achieve economies in time and costs in order to expand existing products and services, or to address new markets. A marketing architecture is essential for building a persistent presence in diverse geographic and cultural market segments. The information network adapts to the functional need of the person accessing it. Consumers want information, price, and availability, while retailers and suppliers want current transaction data categorized by outlet or region. Engineering and manufacturing may want information on returns and service demands or new product rate of acceptance, while logistics may want supplier or volume demand information. A marketing architecture is an evolving set of relationships, internal and external to the enterprise, that act in concert to supply services, products, and customer satisfaction. The systems are scalable so that they can be adapted to the size and growth of the product line or business. Integrating these functions into the enterprise network has many benefits. It improves marketing productivity and the reliability of information, and it reduces the costs of managing and maintaining customer relationships. Above all, it enhances creativity. And customers are happier because the support systems are direct, responsive, and always available.

Human-to-computer communication today is not at all adequate from the consumer's viewpoint. Much of it is every bit as irritating as TV commercials. Market size and cost efficiency, however, will drive the means and methods of interacting and supplying services.

As services become more and more a value-added part of businesses' revenues, those costly, people-intensive functions must become more automated. When labor began to consume a large percentage of production costs, automation changed the economics of manufacturing. Now, service costs are rising in all business categories. With over 80 percent of American jobs currently related to the service sector, the pressure to be cost competitive will hasten self-service automation. The reliability and responsiveness of both the products and the information generated, although seemingly mechanical, are in fact critical to the long-term customer relationship.

Marketing is increasing as a corporate cost, and for that reason IT will continue to absorb most of the marketing activities that sustain a business over the long haul. Soon the IT infrastructure will have more to do with sustaining a brand and customer loyalty than with repeated advertising. The marketing function as we know it is increasingly losing control over the tangible means of addressing consumers' wants and needs. Who is responsible for developing and implementing the infrastructure for this e-marketplace? Not marketing. Software entrepreneurs and the CIO are driving most of these innovations.

As a result, human involvement in marketing is diminishing. Even as marketing's image is being celebrated, marketing practitioners are on the verge of feeling massive repercussions from these far-reaching organizational changes. But while marketing practitioners are losing their former authority and reach into organizational strategy, the marketing functions themselves have not ceased to exist. Rather, marketing techniques for influencing people are being embedded into software and back-end support systems.

An IT-Centered Marketing Organization

Information is at the very heart of any marketing activity. Not only that: It's also the basis on which a company's marketing either succeeds or fails. As customer service solutions continue to be integrated into everything the consumer touches, the software and the network will also become the means a business uses to build and maintain its customer relationships. It is unlikely that the task of managing this complex IT infrastructure will be in the hands of the marketing department. The network is now such an essential part of the enterprise that it is interweaving all business functions.

As a result, marketing executives will have to become far more IT-conscious and competent—which is a challenge, because so far marketing hasn't kept up with technology. True, marketing software has undergone some new developments. In fact, just about all of today's marketing innovations are in the software area, so much so that you could say that software is doing more for marketing than marketing is doing for itself! (That said, much of this new software just automates the old ways, simply improving efficiency without forcing people to think more creatively about new forms of distribution or presence.) But in effect, marketing as we know it is unprepared to manage the IT-enabled marketing processes of the future enterprise. For marketing to be effective, not only will it have to move more of its activities into software, but it will also have to become IT-centered.

As an integral part of the enterprise network, marketing will become ingrained in the management fabric. In the marketing renaissance, "marketing is everything"; many more participants inside and outside the enterprise share in marketing tasks. Networks provide an efficient interchange between all the relevant players in the producer-consumer community. As those interchanges occur, marketing will flow in an infinite network of interactions. Managing that network of relationships will become the key to sustaining not only customers but also the innovations and responsive character of the business. Today it takes the whole extended enterprise to do that.

The Breakup of Marketing

Organizationally, marketing will most likely split into two distinct functions. One will include advertising and promotion, while the other will be responsible for building the sustainable IT and network infrastructure required to provide a persistent presence to consumers, however and wherever they choose to access your business. The budgets for each function and their profitable outcomes will become more visible and comparable. Both will require people to have one foot in marketing and one foot in information systems. The latter group will be responsible—probably to the CIO or directly to the CEO—for such things as the following:

- *Scalable, self-sustaining marketing architecture:* Infrastructure development and deployment, as well as the merging of resources, logistics, and feedback systems, and the integration of multiple functions and resource partners with a single interface to customers.
- *Database management and application development:* Customer care, market simulation, and new market modeling, which means modeling all players from concept, development, design, production, and fulfillment, as well as customer transactions.
- *Web environment development:* Building systems that work across multiple access media, allowing total customer access, yet operating as one synchronized network. The network is far more valuable as a resource-integrating and information access tool than as yet another channel for broadcast.
- *Customer engagement:* Interactive interface, real-time response and feedback systems, customer modeling and self-service programs, such as online ordering and online self-help.
- *Marketing strategy systems:* Using databases and networks to analyze consumer and competitive trends, perform various simulations, compile current information, and communicate it to everyone in the company who must adapt and respond. The network

changes the whole nature of who participates in the strategy process. Using the network, game plans can be more inclusive, monitored constantly, and adapted with instant communication.

This list included only a few examples of a networked marketing architecture, but even here we can see that this kind of endeavor will demand talent and expertise well beyond the kind of marketing we've come to know and love. The emphasis is on fundamentals, not image creation, and on sustaining a continuously adapting network of resources that will support an intelligent, persistent presence in the marketplace. This sounds like work, not fun! This kind of approach to marketing will enable customers to access services while businesses keep in touch with their customers' current activities.

Marketing Disappears into a Totally Accessible Network

The new marketing will both demand creativity and enable an infinite process of change, responding and adapting to the market machinations. Enterprises that are slow to adapt to the new marketing paradigm will vanish, and those that do adapt will become market leaders. How else can a business respond to millions of customers in a dynamically changing environment, with infinite combinations of habits and behaviors? How else can a business keep its customers engaged amid the din and novelty of the marketplace? And how else can a business react quickly to changes in the business cycle, respond to competitors, and learn how to apply the new tools of information technology distinctively? Certainly not by broadcasting more messages through an increasingly noisy environment over increasingly diverse channels. (Television now has an average of about 90 channels; the Internet has 90 million.)

What's Next? Where Marketing Is Headed

So what's next? Variations in the economy may hasten or slow the pace, but I believe that certain trends are clear. What follows is a brief look at them; in later chapters I will discuss them in detail.

First, the digital network–based technologies will continue to transform the marketplace and marketing. And like all other aspects of business, marketing will continue to evolve as part of the enterprise multifunctional network. This transformation will have far-reaching consequences on how companies develop and maintain relationships with customers, how they develop brand, and even how they perceive and accomplish marketing tasks.

The "human element" is certainly vital and will increase rather than diminish as technologies become basic essentials for any business. As John Chambers, president and CEO of Cisco Systems, reminded me, "Someone still has to look at the information, interpret what it means and make the right decisions for the business." We can have all the information in the world at our fingertips and still make bad decisions. In this new, connected, information-intensive marketplace, executives will be responsible for broadening and intensifying their learning in several areas.

In the future, marketing creativity will come from people who understand the realities of the present market and the capabilities of the new digital technologies. It will come from those who bring together the resources necessary to sustain customer satisfaction and loyalty. These people also need to know when and where to apply the new tools of information and interactivity in an imaginative yet unobtrusive way, to expand customer access and engage customers in a continuing service relationship.

The task for marketing today, as it will be in the future, is to integrate and manage the complexity of network relationships necessary for planning, implementing, and running a marketing enterprise. The continuing challenge will be to do so imaginatively enough to create a competitive advantage. Business organizations too often divide tasks between those who think and plan (strategy) and those who implement (tactics). The IT director of a large automobile company once told me, "You tell me what to do and I can put in the pipes." This approach to information systems can work only when the technology, competition, and the marketplace stand still. Strategy has to come from a real-world environment, and it must evolve and learn from its application. In this "get it done now" world, strategy and tactics are working hand in hand, changing and adapting as they go. The Internet revolution is continuing, and customers' attitudes, opinions, and behavior are evolving along with the technology. The practice of applying digital information technology is not simply a tactical activity; it's a moving target that requires an overall strategic approach to a marketing architecture capable of adaptation, change, and constant renewal.

Looking back at the incredible changes over the past quarter-century, we can only imagine the progress and pace of the marketplace in the next quarter-century. I believe that a vision of that time centers on a marketing paradigm in which computers and networks do most of the work, including data gathering, judgment, customer response, and customer care. In this new paradigm, consumer access replaces broadcast, transforming the old notions of brand development. And the function of marketing disappears into a network of relationships and software responsibilities. I believe that we'll be amazed at how much and how well computers and networks directly interface and manage producer-consumer relationships.

In the new model of total customer access, marketing will be distributed across the enterprise, becoming a shared responsibility. The CEO will drive strategy, and the CIO will be largely responsible for implementation. The businesses that invest in a continuous network of services, adapting, responding, and creating new and persistent ways of maintaining presence in the marketplace and interacting with—and providing total access to—their customers, will become the market leaders.

Chapter Two

The Three Stages of Marketing

Reach, Push, and Access

New technology, whether it's the radio or the automobile, the computer or the ATM, always seems to be an intrusion at first. Today, however, consumers aren't faced with abrupt technological change. Instead, they are gradually learning to adapt as they use the evolving technology. All forms of access will become as transparent as the telephone has become.

THE TECHNOLOGY has long been the catalyst of change in marketing, first by increasing the reach to consumers, then by pushing virtual needs and wants through messaging, and now by providing total customer access. Two distinct phases of marketing—what I call the Age of Reach and the Age of Push—were ushered in by the introduction of disruptive production and communication technologies. Today, we see a new phase emerging: the Age of Total Access. Marketers are searching for new definitions and meanings to give this new age a firm foundation. Before we look at the present, however, let's take a brief look at the past.

The idea of marketing as a discrete practice originated in the early twentieth century, but its roots reach back over 200 years, when the Industrial Revolution stimulated an all-encompassing disruption in the relationship between producer and consumer. In the late nineteenth and early twentieth centuries, marketing played a central role in commercial strategy and market development. Specifically, it was an integral force expanding the reach of producers through innovative retailing networks and developing financial mechanisms for consumer credit. In the early phases of market development, establishing sales and distribution systems was crucial to creating a competitive presence in new markets, as well as to ensure a continuous flow of goods to new consumers.

The Age of Reach

The machinery of standardized mass production drove down the cost of products such as sewing machines, toasters, cars, and cameras, as well as an array of new applications of electricity, making their sale possible to an ever-expanding, widely dispersed, and growing middle class. In the United States, the emergence of a large consumer market resulted from a liberal immigration policy and the higher incomes offered by urban factories, which drew people from farms and foreign lands. Soon these new workers began acquiring the goods they were making, becoming the progenitors of the vast U.S. consumer marketplace.

By 1913, with abundant land and natural and human resources, a diverse and growing population, and a stable government, the United States was the world's leading producer of manufactured goods. Entrepreneurial ideas flourished. The spreading web of rail lines and free rural mail delivery created a revolutionary marketing tool: the mail-order catalog. Where local shops had once controlled price, quality, and selection, a new nationwide retailer, Sears & Roebuck, leveraged an infrastructure built by the railroads and U.S. Post Office. Two entrepreneurs, Richard Sears and Alva Roebuck, had launched their company in 1893 to provide goods for rural areas. As the Sears Web site tells us, "Sears, Roebuck and Co. and other mail-order companies were the answer to farmers' prayers. Thanks to volume buying, to the railroads and post office, and later to rural free delivery and parcel post, they offered a happy alternative to the high-priced rural stores."[1] Today, the

U.S. catalog and mail-order business, Sears & Roebuck's descendant, is a $1.5 trillion market.[2]

By 1919, Henry Ford's invention of the Model T enabled the traveling salesman, who had already moved from horse to train, to move to horseless carriage, allowing him to cover more territory in less time. An old-line company founded in 1837 by entrepreneurs William Procter and James Gamble saw the value of that new mobility, and launched a self-directed, mobile sales force. Salesmen peddling everything from anvils to soap could send orders, prices, and delivery schedules anywhere copper telegraph wire could be strung. The information moved fast (operating at the speed of electrons), but it routinely took weeks and even months actually to fill orders.

Around the same time, management innovators began to conceive of business as more science than art, drawing distinctions among engineering, production, and management. Frederick Taylor began writing in 1895, and by 1910, students at leading universities were hearing his ideas about scientific management.[3] Soon businesses began applying Taylor's ideas to systematic planning and production processes giving rise to the discipline of scientific management. Taylor's ideas influenced the development and benefits of functional specialization in all areas of business.

Business courses at universities in the early twentieth century did not use the term *marketing*; they addressed subjects such as trade and distribution, and wholesaling and retailing.[4] No one knows exactly who first coined the term *marketing*, or when, but we do know that it began to take hold after 1910. The term *marketing* originally referred to a variety of corporate activities performed prior to selling or promotion. It was even viewed as "a highly refined system of thought and practice" necessary for the development of a market economy.[5] Indeed, over the course of the last century, the definition of marketing has gone through several transformations, from economic theory to an extension of production, and finally to behavioral sciences in action.

While marketing became more abstract in the universities, it became increasingly pragmatic in the marketplace. Radio was the first major technology to create a perception that an ill-defined business function called "marketing" had significant influence on consumer behavior. Early in its history, radio advertising was highly controversial. In its May 1924 issue, *Radio Broadcast Magazine* announced a $500 contest soliciting the best essay on the topic "Who Is to Pay for Broadcasting—and How?"

The existence of this contest suggests that the magazine didn't believe on-air advertising was a suitable solution to the funding issue. In 1932, though, the solution became evident when Procter & Gamble, the manufacturer of Ivory Soap, sponsored a serial radio show called "Ma Perkins" and gave birth to "soap operas." Radio advertisers amplified the consumer's imagination with stories that drew on homemakers' fantasies and dreams. Mass-marketing theater became a tool for creating consumer demand for not only soap but products as diverse as appliances, cigarettes, and automobiles.[6]

Radio's undeniable power flowed from its ability to do something that until then only a door-to-door salesman had been able to do: elicit a relationship with the listener. Historian Michael Kammen quotes a 1930s media observer who said, "The thing you were able to achieve with radio was involvement. Participation. Because you didn't have all the pieces of the puzzle. The person coming to the radio set had to bring some of the pieces to fill in." Kammen notes that "despite the sheer size of the audience, live broadcasts created at least the illusion of intimacy: the voices were speaking to you in your home."[7]

By 1931, some 608 radio stations were broadcasting to over 12 million people, or 40 percent of American homes.[8] Radio's reach broadened the influence of a new breed of super-celebrity salesmen. Fred Allen, Arthur Godfrey, Jack Benny, Tom Mix, and Bob "Walk a Mile for a Camel" Hope hawked brands and closely identified themselves with their sponsors. One study by a New York advertising agency at the time claimed that radio had pulled in $36 million by the end of 1931, causing a drop in newspaper advertising revenue. Despite the Depression, radio made money.[9]

Radio's singular influence spanned only two American generations. After World War II, television came into the picture, and the avenues for marketing radically changed once again. The convergence of the well-established web of distribution technologies with a widely accepted broadcast medium launched an expansive and powerful retail marketplace. Marketing became a more consciously directed effort. Improved productivity, new products, and better distribution methods gave rise to increasingly imaginative marketing programs, stimulating the growth of a consumer society. At this point, however, technology was still limited to an all "push" marketing world.

The Golden Age of Push

In the 1920s and 1930s, legendary marketers like Edward Bernays, the nephew of Sigmund Freud, drew on popular psychology and symbols to manipulate customers' behavior based on research-directed messages, events, and promotions. Known today as the "Father of Public Relations," Bernays was a master at arranging sponsored events that looked like they arose from public concern. For example, in an attempt to increase the number of women smokers for his client Lucky Strike, Bernays devised the "Torches of Freedom" campaign. Knowing that society generally frowned on women smoking in public and that some women considered smoking to be symbolic of personal freedom, Bernays decided to stage a march in protest of women's inequality. Ten debutantes marched down Fifth Avenue, proudly hoisting cigarettes as their personal "torches of freedom." In a further effort to promote Lucky Strike with women, Bernays suggested that the cigarette maker change the packaging from green to a more neutral color in order to blend with women's clothing. When management balked at the suggestion, Bernays actually persuaded a number of Parisian fashion designers to design their new lines in green. Then he urged Lucky Strike owner George W. Hill to anonymously sponsor a charity ball, whose theme centered around the color green. The event was a success, and green became a fashionable color. Bernays demonstrated that manipulating events and information could influence the public's opinion and behavior. His legacy remains with us today.[10]

For the first few decades of the twentieth century, marketing was integrated with sales and distribution. Things began to change in the late 1920s, when Procter & Gamble established the "brand management system" dedicating teams of executives to manage the company's competing brands. In a memo written in early 1931, Neil McElroy, a Procter & Gamble executive with a mind for organization, defined the role and responsibilities of the "brand man," suggesting that the brand man study the shipments of his brand carefully and look for the combination of things that worked so he could expand them to other regions. If he discovered any weaknesses, he should prepare a plan to address the "sore spot," including a financial plan with expected results. The brand man, McElroy stressed, should gather and analyze information, and should take full responsibility for all forms of advertising, as well as for the "printed word copy" and packaging.[11]

The concept of brand management steadily took hold at P&G, becoming the standard not only in that company but also in the consumer products industry. According to David Aakers and Erich Joachimsthaler, "The process of managing a complex system—often involving R&D, manufacturing, and logistics in addition to advertising, promotion and distribution channel issues—required management skills and a get-it-done ethic."[12]

Although attempts to systematize marketing had been in progress for many years, Procter & Gamble's success in rolling out killer market-share leading brands such as Ivory, Tide, Crest, and Pampers made the company—and the branding process—a model for other consumer companies. The brand management concept gave marketing the equivalent powers and responsibilities of other management functions and was the defining idea behind what came to be identified as "consumer marketing." (In the high-tech boom of the 1990s, high-tech companies recruited P&G executives with the express purpose of transferring P&G's branding skills to information technology businesses.)

In the 1950s and 1960s, several market forces—the postwar economic boom, the geographic shift of one generation and the birth of another, the rise of suburban communities, and television—came together to align brand and advertising with lifestyle marketing research. Companies that had developed production know-how and machinery during the Second World War needed new products and markets to capitalize on those assets. People moved from the crowded cities to the new, spacious suburban communities and parented a new generation. Between 1946 and 1964, 75 million Americans were born and eventually became the most homogenized group of consumers that marketers ever targeted: "the Baby Boomers."

During this same period, television became the fastest-growing consumer product ever in the United States, with just 6,000 sets in use in 1946 to 85 million sets by 1960. The new network of highways interlacing cities and suburbs allowed for efficient distribution of goods to the new centers of population development. Living in crisp, suburban homes, most Americans began to shop at retail centers that have become a shopping cliché—malls. This aggregation of retail outlets under one roof was a marketing innovation comparable to that of the mail-order catalog. The merchandise was simply following the consumer.

This period produced marketing's equivalent of the Ten Commandments: the Four Ps. The Four Ps—product, pricing, place, and promotion—were introduced in the 1950s and popularized in business schools over the next forty years, reducing marketing to a generic set of theoretical principles that focused more on managing marketing's organizational and functional activities rather than on serving or satisfying customers.

Since the 1950s, marketing's creative public manifestation, advertising, took off, reflecting marketers' love affair with mass media. Ad expenditures in the United States grew from $2 billion in 1950 to $250 billion in 2000. Thanks to television and hugely successful brand awareness campaigns, advertising made Volkswagen, Tide, GE, Crest, Playtex, and Marlboro household names. And despite all the attempts to codify marketing into Four Ps, no one had the magic formula to assure the success of a brand or ad campaign. Significant quantities of money have been spent on advertising and promotional campaigns, but a quantitative, definitive method for how much or what style of advertising and brand promotion contributes to a company's revenues remains elusive. The old story about advertising still rings true today: "Half my advertising dollars are wasted," lamented an executive, "but I don't know which half!" Advertising and marketing campaigns continue to be judged as successful today when they achieve high levels of public awareness or awards bestowed by their own profession rather than by the financial and market success of the company.

Advertisers relied on television, the new push medium, to influence millions of viewers with a repetitive, consistent, and entertaining message delivered more cheaply to millions of viewers than any other media could. Marketers now set out to influence consumer behavior with the technology of mass theater. Instead of "I need" being the motivating consumer factor, the power of television as a marketing tool spawned the "I want" factor. Marketers used behavioral research to dig into consumers' habits and hidden desires so that they could construct entertaining images projecting lifestyles that consumers could identify with and aspire to achieve by simply acquiring the product advertised.

Television even played a role in promoting computers. Apple Computer ran its classic "1984" commercial during the 1981 Super Bowl.

Although Apple had been advertising on television since 1980, this single advertisement elevated the personal computer to consumer product status—until then, the general public hadn't seen the PC as a mainstream consumer item—and marked its debut in the magic realm of consumer marketing. This and subsequent ads by Apple changed the focus of computer marketing from one of building industry support and distribution infrastructure to that of building brand via advertising. (The "1984 ad" might have done more for personal computing than for Apple itself. The company slid into the diminished role of a niche player in the following decade while the ad continued to win awards.)

Technology companies—selling computers, software, and telecommunications—followed Apple's lead, using television as a springboard for building brand and expanding their markets. Competitive blood rises for almost anything a competitor does in the high-tech business, and TV commercials were no exception. Many companies dived headlong into electronic media. Hewlett-Packard, Digital Equipment Corp., Silicon Graphics, Sun Microsystems, Intel, IBM, and others launched national broadcast media campaigns. Digital Equipment, once the second-largest computer company in the world, lost market share and was acquired by Compaq Computer, which was subsequently acquired by HP in 2001. Silicon Graphics fell from fame with dismal losses and has struggled for more than five years to regain its former luster. HP and IBM have had varying degrees of success selling directly to consumers. Sun, on the other hand, was early to recognize the power of the network and became the leading supplier of servers (computers) to Internet businesses.[13] The reasons for success or failure are complex, particularly in technology-based businesses, for which innovative technology, price/performance, industry-setting standards, and third party software alliances play more of a role than advertising.

Although TV advertising messages did improve reach by gigantic numbers, this new medium actually moved the relationship between producers and consumers farther apart. Advertisers began to see consumers in statistical terms of "rating points" and "cost per millions." They began using computers to segment markets, using terms such as *demographics* and, in the behaviorist mode, *psychographics*. The terminology itself reflects marketing's adhesion to mass culture and the lack of a customer-centric marketing model.

Despite the lack of consistent evidence to prove their theories, companies became convinced that they could persuade consumers to buy their products by exposing them repeatedly to skillfully crafted messages designed from abstract research and delivered in a staged mini-theater. Businesses saw mass production and mass marketing as the most efficient and profitable ways to succeed in business. Individualized consumer services and direct interaction with large numbers of customers were simply too expensive to implement without major advances automating those services. Originating with production technologies, the concept of mass culture became embedded in our society and extended to education, society, government, and marketing. This quest to create "national homogeneity," complains author Stuart Ewen, was creating a stifling political and cultural conformity.[14] The golden age of marketing was rapidly tarnishing for consumers and producers alike. They just didn't realize it yet.

The Age of Total Access

While the Ages of Reach and Push are marketing's legacy, the Age of Total Access lies ahead of us. Just as in past marketing eras, new technology, a new competitive marketplace, and a new consumer are initiating the era, which will change all our assumptions and all the canons of marketing by opening a direct dialogue between the customer and the producer. The president of a leading global business software company recently said, "Twenty years ago, we told our customers how to solve their problems and what they needed for solutions. Today they tell us what they want us to do."

His comment reflects the flip we've seen in the marketplace in the last two decades. The cause is access and new media technologies enable direct and continuous interaction between producers and customers. This changes the center of marketing gravity because the customer has the power to initiate the contact and make purchase decisions based on a whole new set of market-induced preferences. Today consumers tell producers what they want, not the other way around. Total access is not a broadcast model. Rather, it is an environment where the consumer experiences multiple and simultaneous competitive buying opportunities—an experience that is reinforced every day in our cornu-copia of choice marketplace. For consumers, total access means choice, an unrestrained doorway to variety, price, novelty, and service. It gives them the tools to gather information and check out the competition, to compare one product to another and one supplier to another, trans-forming shopping from an impulse buy to a considered purchase, for even the lowest-cost item. Access is location-independent and comes in multiple varieties—home or office delivery, shopping online or at retail centers, and self-service. It is an expectation of being conveniently con-nected to the marketplace.

Networking and connecting are becoming an important part of today's consumer culture. This consumer mind-set carries an implied right, demand, and expectation for response, satisfaction, convenience, and service when and where the customer wants or needs it. The con-sumer, however, may not consciously acknowledge their new power of access until it is made inconvenient or unavailable.

Total access is affecting business in a variety of ways. For one, busi-nesses are realizing that "getting closer to the customer" means more than gaining proximity. It means connecting and exchanging information as well. It means responding to regular customers with benefits at the check-out counter, or allowing those same customers to check the availability of an item in a company's database.

This kind of comprehensive access turns the tables on broadcasters. Instead of the broadcast media delivering homogenized messages to an undefined mass audience, customers are sending individualized mes-sages back into the system with an expectation of response. Where the media of the past used the airwaves and cable to send messages and information to a waiting, often passive audience whose response was only indirect, the new media is engaged in a direct and reciprocal rela-tionship with an active audience. Not only are *users* capable of talking back—so are the connected computers! Yet most executives haven't yet changed their thinking—they are still looking inside out rather than outside in. They haven't figured out how to "win friends and influence people" outside the broadcast paradigm. I can only conclude that sales-manship must be buried somewhere deep in our collective genes.

The Internet is the connecting medium for all forms of access. By and large, it is qualitatively different from other media. For one, the user initiates communication and has the power to move around from site to site and to get instant feedback. Online consumers are in perpetual motion, not resting at any one site for a long period of time. This is why some online businesses used the term *stickiness* (and not *brand loyalty*) to talk about their marketing strategies: They aim to create "sticky" Web sites that will help them retain customers. Even that term has now largely been abandoned. Because the Internet is not a passive medium, it's not a good vehicle as yet for TV-like broadcast.

The Internet is the medium through which customers and businesses communicate, but it's the access devices we communicate through—the computer, the cell phone, wireless device, or kiosk—that deliver the experience and establish a customer's mind-set. The interactive exchange of information may be transparent, such as when you use a digital "smart" card or credit card containing the information you need to supply, or it can be direct and conscious, such as when you engage in a transaction over the Internet.

While access is relatively inexpensive for the customer, it can be very expensive for the company that is not well versed in automating the details of customer communications and transaction management. I've spoken with executives in many different industries who agree that the volume of direct and indirect inquiries their companies process each year is growing substantially. The numbers of people gaining low-cost access are also growing; companies can expect that managing day-to-day information seekers and customers will become ever more expensive unless they automate the process.

For marketers, total access is both an opportunity and a risk. The access medium—Web site, retail store, or kiosk—carries the consumer's message, which the producer/supplier must acknowledge and address with a response the customer deems satisfactory. The response can vary from assuring delivery by maintaining inventory in local markets to offering prepurchase assistance with information or expertise in a particular area. The marketer has to use the network to catalyze and coordinate the supporting infrastructure to respond appropriately and to build the relationship with the customer. The Internet can connect producer and consumer in many ways and through a variety of devices—computer, wireless device, cash register, ATM, gas pump, smart card, or global positioning system (GPS) device. Gathering customer information from any location or device can be value creating if it is then used to offer supporting services that sustain the relationship. Too often marketers use customer information to target audience's customized messages rather than customized services.

Planning, building, and maintaining a state-of-the-art customer response system is not inexpensive, but in the long run it will pay for itself by realizing cost efficiencies, by attracting new customers, and by engendering more customer loyalty. A customer-responsive information system is a valuable contribution to a company's ability to sustain customers, profits, and brand because it efficiently manages the commitments between producer and consumer.

Sending and receiving customer information and records digitally, interacting with various suppliers for inventory management, distributing customer access points to multiple locations, and increasing awareness of information on customer transactions are all valuable—both as a service response and a planning tool. Customers may not see the support and services infrastructure, but they experience the benefits of the interaction in the service itself.

The Internet allows that "listening process" to be independent of place and time, as well as economically sustainable. As distributed computing and database technologies have progressed, retailers such as Wal-Mart have "listened" to their customers through the "smart" cash register. Sam Walton put it this way:

> I'm told we have the largest civilian database in the world. What I like about it is the kind of information we can pull out of it at a moment's notice—all those numbers! We keep a 65-week rolling history of every item we stock. This means I can pick anything I want and tell you exactly how many of them we've sold . . . not only overall but in every region, district, or store. It makes it tough for a supplier to know more about how his product is doing in our stores than we do. . . . It gives us the power of competitive advantage.[15]

Near-instant knowledge of what customers are doing, and not simply what they say they want, translates to one of Wal-Mart's key competitive advantages. In effect, Wal-Mart has the most sophisticated "customer listening system" of any retailer in the world. Since Wal-Mart "sells what sells," consumers get the message that they can find what they want at the prices they are willing to pay. The result? Customers support Wal-Mart's brand.

A Global Connect

Low-cost communications, improved logistics systems, and multiple points of market presence all contribute to the rise of increased access, but it's the continued evolution of democracy and market economies that create the fertile environment for the technology that drives the progress of low-cost communication. Technology—in particular, communications technology—is more prolific when an open political, economic, and social environment supports its advances.

For years, pundits have claimed that technology has the potential to address the world's ills. But today's rise of global information networks is happening coincidently with the rise of market economies. The phenomenon of access is more universal than you might think. Today 68 percent of the world's population lives under various forms of democratic self-government, an increase of only 30 percent from 1950. Democratic countries become market economies: They seek trade to improve the standard of living, lower tariffs, develop open communication infrastructures, and improve trade relationships; and they seek to enter the World Trade Organization. From 1990 to 1998—less than a decade—the number of United Nations member nations with cellular infrastructures grew from 50 to over 150 countries. "Poor countries," reports the *New York Times*, "had about 40 percent of the mobile phone lines in 1999, up from 20 percent in 1995." The number of cell phone users in the United States is growing at about 24 percent a year, while the growth rate in Africa is 116 percent! Although the cost of making a cell call is more expensive than making a call from a fixed line phone, wireless costs everywhere are rapidly declining.[16]

The cost of mobile-to-land line for all areas of the world has dropped to less than one cent per minute. The variety and reach of the new interactive communication media is expansive. More than 200 communications satellites circle the earth; there are plans to triple that number in the next decade. Satellites have been highly efficient at distributing content, such as broadcast TV events, to both urban and remote areas, and they are now capable of providing World Wide Web access services as well.

Broadband optical fiber is also moving across oceans and continents to compete for customer access. These technologies will enable distant and remote places such as Manaus, Brazil, and Ulaanbaatar, Mongolia, to have the same voice and information access as people in Silicon Valley.

Saying that everyone—or even almost everyone—now has total access would be naïve. Because the cost of enabling technologies continues to decline, however, eventual total access for everyone does seem likely. In 2000, for example, 214 countries had Internet access, up from 60 in 1993 and just 8 in 1988.[17] In a market economy, access both increases the availability of competitive choice and empowers consumers by providing alternative forms of information. The result is positive: When people exercise their right to equal access, and when the price of entry is low, human and civil rights become stronger. In addition, market economies encourage the creation of wealth and viable markets. The first order of business for emerging economies is to upgrade and improve telecommunications infrastructure. With infrastructure in place, countries can rapidly deploy wireless technologies and quickly put revenue-generating cell phones on the market. In 1999, *The Economist* noted that 900,000 new subscribers were joining the world's mobile-phone services every three days.[18] The technology will continue to offer hundreds of millions of people around the globe inexpensive, information-rich access. My bet is that consumer expectations for choice, novelty, service, and customer-specific preferences will increase as access expands.

Responding to Total Access: The Marketing Nerve Center

Telephone access in marketing began long before the Internet arrived on the business scene. And the advent of toll-free numbers gave consumers free access to order, obtain information, or complain. As a marketing technique, toll-free calling worked so well that all the 800 exchanges soon were gone. Adding more exchange networks (888 and 877) helped expand the toll-free system from 2.5 million numbers in 1983 to 15.7 million by 1998.[19]

Today you can see toll-free numbers on everything from Pepsi cans to M&M's packages, and you can get information and directions from toll-free call centers and help desks at many major corporations. Many centers today still employ a great many people to answer customer calls to order products, expedite and track orders, check inventories for availability and prices, and answer complaints and questions. Those employees take the calls and access internal databases for information on products, prices, and availability. Federal Express achieved significant early market differentiation by relying on information systems and call centers, which gave them a distinct competitive advantage. DHL, UPS, and other shipping companies followed. FedEx pioneered many of the advances in access devices and customer support centers and has helped accelerate information logistics as a key marketing function.

Customers show they like toll-free calling by enthusiastically responding and asking for more. Dennis Kyle, vice president and general manager of XO Communications, a market leader in supplying broadband communications services, put it this way:

> *Toll-free numbers and live operators used to be sufficient for all customer service tasks; now customers are asking for more answers, more choices, more hours of business, more speed and more satisfaction. In short, they are demanding more self-service capabilities. Satisfying these escalating demands can be expensive and inefficient, impacting the ability to stay competitive and build relationships with customers.*[20]

The Internet created huge increases in the number of consumer queries and service requests. Customer access suddenly got cheaper and easier and companies had to respond with a more economical and efficient way to respond. Established call centers used to handle telephone requests, catalog sales, scheduling, and other customer services evolved rapidly to fill the need. Today call centers are computerized customer network managers, receiving and integrating all the various access means—including phone, fax, and Internet requests—and then orchestrating and directing the appropriate responses. They are becoming the information nerve center of a company's total access marketplace. Because customers want to gain access from anywhere by any means, the IT goal for most savvy companies is to synchronize all customer or prospect information and response in the same information database. Computer-generated decision making and response will provide instant database search and customized response for many repetitive transactions, replacing rooms filled with people trying to interpret what the customer wants and what the computer screen is presenting.

Real people will, of course, still be necessary to handle complex issues and requirements. Computers aren't perfect, but the rising costs of providing services customized to each request and the declining cost and increased performance of computerized networked management systems will push businesses to adopt automated ways of handling standard and repetitive transactions. Cost management may be the initial motivation, but once the systems and process are in place, the motivation quickly turns to one of marketing. Efficient, responsive service is good marketing, and the connection allows direct communication with the customer, permitting feedback on new products, adding value to the existing customer's purchases, and quickly solving problems or addressing complaints.

Today's systems are far from ideal and, from the consumer's view point, they are frequently more time-consuming and intrusive than the old human-to-human methods. Consumers have high expectations for all service providers: They want rapid, reliable, 24/7 response. Thus to meet those expectations efficiently, companies will increasingly depend on computer-generated response systems. As these systems become more advanced, reliable, and humanlike, the customer will rely on and trust them more.

Total Access: Convergence of Hot and Cool Media

Technology designers are often so enamored with the performance, features, and cost of their products that they pay too little attention to the customer experience at the point of access. Designing the customer interface takes the talents of software and human factors engineers and industrial designers, but also much more. Apple Computer's iMAC, AOL's easy setup software, and DoCoMo's Internet services integration exemplify much more than the design of a device or service. In each case, the company effectively integrated its understanding of the new media and its knowledge of its audience. These companies recognized that new media give soul to what is otherwise a metal container.

Marketing executives will need to shift their thinking from trying to capture customers with entertaining commercials and junk e-mail to developing and distributing interactive, easy-to-use services using the new access media. To design a "don't-give-it-a-second-thought" customer interface will require not only a creative approach and an understanding of the customer, but an understanding of the capabilities and limitations of software and the Internet as well. Today's computer access to the Internet allows the user to obtain volumes of information, but to use that information, the user must apply his or her own knowledge and skills. While this customer interaction is important, the interface programs and information services available must become more engaging and transparent.

Any physical or informational point of customer contact is part of the total access market environment. The total access, connected marketplace came about over the past two decades but the influence of these technologies and resulting social and consumer revolution has only just begun. We have a short-term historical perspective with this new Internet technology—one that has rapidly become expansive and complex. Effective use of this new interactive medium will require a more thorough understanding of communications as a social activity and a better understanding of how new technologies influence and change human behavior. Marshall McLuhan, renowned communications theorist of the television era, introduced the concept that different media inherently carry different qualitative (behavior changing) messages. McLuhan categorized the different media as either *hot* or *cool* dependent on the human affect created by the interaction.[21] Radio, for example, is a *cool* medium of low definition. While a small amount of information is communicated, the listener quickly "gets it" by applying his or her imagination and knowledge to fill in what's missing. Cool media is engaging and experiential. *Hot* media, on the other hand, leaves nothing to the imagination. Movies and television are a hot media because they require low levels of interaction. Thus we use such phrases as "mind rotters" and "couch potatoes" to describe the human experience with much of the hot media. A fast-food cash register is an example of a high-definition, low-participation medium. The cashier presses a picture of the menu item, and the charge rings up—a computer does all the work transparently. The computer and Internet are cool media but can quickly become hot with the addition of a DVD or high-bandwidth, streaming video.

Many marketers mistakenly make the assumption that the Internet is a passive medium (hot) used and responded to by consumers in the same manner as they do to television or movies. Cookies, broadcasting e-mail messages, and banner ads are examples of this thinking. The Internet is essentially a different type of media because it is *interactive*, allowing the user complete control over the nature (hot or cool) of the content. The hot and cool media concept is valuable for marketers to understand, as both modes of interaction can play an important role by combining customer attention and engaging dialogue.

As increased bandwidth and digital technologies hasten the convergence of entertainment media with information technology and networks, we will see the digital content streaming through various delivery devices become more engaging and experiential. However, I think it is counter-productive for marketers to think of the Internet as simply another hot medium capable of locking on to consumer's minds and hearts in fixed time and space as did television programming. We know from experience that this approach alone does not engender long-term satisfied or loyal customers.

Understanding the new network technologies as passive (hot) and interactive (cool) media is important for marketers because interactive customer communications must allow for easy access, engaging participation, and feedback without burdening the customer with time-consuming steps or unnecessary information. Apple and AOL have demonstrated that ease-of-use is not incompatible with engaging participation. Total access shifts the notion that brand is the refuge of the ignorant (hot) to one based on reinforced knowledge, long-term relationships, and sustained communications (cool).

Many of the new access technology developers, such as Apple and DoCoMo, seek a convergence of hot and cool—designing and delivering products and services that try to minimize complexity while giving the user high participation. Engaging the consumer in an ongoing dialogue where both producer and consumer evolve together is to respect and acknowledge the customer's value. Such a relationship builds trust—the foundation of a successful brand.

Communication networks will expand over the next decade, linking not only computers and all point-of-sale transaction devices but also many things and places that are not considered part of the information network today. Video cameras, for example, now used in stores primarily for security purposes, can provide visual databases of information, such as measuring consumer traffic patterns in a retail store, comparing traffic activity at different locations, or even monitoring the response to special promotions or sales.

Many commonplace objects, as well as new and unique information gathering devices, will become smarter at gathering data to send across customer support and service networks. Integrating and linking various customer services will become a major task for marketing. Otis Elevator recently connected 100,000 individual elevators via the Internet for remote maintenance. Once connected, Otis plans to put flat-panel color screens above the elevator doors for building owners to display information such as news, sports, and weather headlines, building information (such as announcements for upcoming fire drills), and local traffic reports.[22] We have already seen access devices increasing in the automobile with cell phones, GPS, and entertainment systems. The next step is to expand those access channels by linking information services from both inside and outside the car. For example, my cell phone and my car have many features I've never used because I would need to take the time to program or load data that I've already stored on other devices. If these devices were transparently connected to a network, though, I would be able to access my own database from any device—a kiosk, my car, my computer, or my cell phone. When I can do that, I become more dependent on— or even loyal to—the connecting total access (hot/cool) system and the standards used to interconnect.

We cannot abate the trend toward hot media intended to entertain and absorb the consumer's attention. However, it is important that marketers not lose sight of the value created by the new interactive media— allowing the consumer to consciously engage in the relationship process. Marketers will discover that total access broadens their opportunities to listen, learn, and respond to consumers. The new total access marketplace is filled with risks as well as opportunities. Today, information flows easily between customer and producer and we have seen in recent times the concern for privacy and security increasing. Assuring the integrity of a customer's information may well become synonymous with insuring your brand's integrity. Marketers must respect and use customer information in a responsive manner and responsible way. To do that effectively, they must understand the nature of the medium their customers are now using.

How Customers Adapt to Total Access

With all this new access technology, what's a consumer to do? It seems that customers adapt to new technology in a variety of ways. Specifically, in the past, we've seen the following four approaches: (1) the innovators—those who love to try new things; (2) the early adopters—those who use new technologies or products before the masses; (3) the late adopters—those who need absolute proof that the new item is secure, reliable, and well tested; (4) the laggards—those who join the fold only after everyone else.[23]

Social scientists have applied this process theory to the adoption of any popular activity and its progress toward mass acceptance. Many generally accepted social norms begin as isolated fads. Rock, country and western music, male earrings, casual dress in the workplace, and hairstyles are just a few such fads-turned-norms. Products also follow this pattern, from personal computers and minivans to skateboards and scooters. Accessibility to new trends is limited at first, expanding as the distribution and references broaden.

I began applying the model to new-technology products in the early 1980s and used it to plan the introduction of first-time innovations. Technology products are never born perfect, so a close working relationship with a small group of users must initiate market acceptance. In the early market phases, the new technology's performance and benefits are market-tested, then improved in the succeeding generations. As improvements occur, the product becomes easier to use and justify, opening up the next market category of potential users. The concept relies on the anticipation of an increasingly larger market opportunity, but a market comprising users less technologically sophisticated than the previous group. Personal computers, for example, began with a market of hobbyists, moved into the business market, and finally into the broad consumer marketplace.

That four-stage concept no longer applies today because many of the biggest companies are much more technologically savvy and are considered early adapters. Wal-Mart and FedEx became the models by applying advanced technologies to achieve market leadership. Many technology products today, such as software applications, start in the consumer market and move to the business market. Another reason the four-stage concept no longer applies is that users, both business and consumer, have access to more specific competitive information, and they no longer have the time or investment toleration for an evolving new technology. Another major change today is that the consumers, not the companies, have become the market driver for new technologies. As the population of information-smart consumers grows, they will have access to the world through the Web, and that experience will change them in ways we may not be able to anticipate.

One thing we know is that people adapt to the presence of technology when it has a sustained presence, particularly when that presence is neither intrusive nor demanding. The new age of information and the universality of its appeal strongly influence the way people adapt. For example, my eighty-four-year-old father-in-law, Bill Page, would be defined as a late adopter, even a laggard, according to the old rules. But he's been using an iMAC and AOL for four years now, and he spends about four hours a day exploring the Web, sending e-mails, occasionally making travel reservations, buying books, and tracking the latest PGA scores. He's hardly a laggard. "Don't-give-it-a-second-thought," or "warm," media access changes the way we adapt to new things. With ubiquitous total access, any style, fad, or newly developed idea will simultaneously appear to all who access it, regardless of their age, their economic position, or any demographic definition marketers assign to them. We have seen this sort of activity in the large number of new players buying and selling stocks online (which certainly isn't all good news—more inexperienced people buying and selling securities online as well as the network backbone of securities exchanges adds to the volatility of the market).

Total access has outdated our definitions. We need new ones, new categories describing how we adapt. Access is not a fad or a passing technological phenomenon. It will change and become more powerful for those who use it. Businesses and market executives must better understand this new media, not as a broadcast tool, but rather as a means of communicating within an open market network. Definitions will change as we learn more, but I've come up with a few categories to describe people (and businesses) as they learn and adapt to the new, information-rich forms of access.

The Information Explorers

Information explorers are people who consume gigabits volumes of memory, storing vast amounts of voice, video, music, graphic, and text data. They access the Web for almost every decision, big or small. They like talking and shopping bits and bytes. Most go online to buy securities and download music, and most have used the Internet to either gather information about a car or to actually buy one. The most likely participants in this category are well educated—often well self-educated on the computer—and their ages range from teenage to late thirties. Information explorers seek out ways to get total access, upgrading to every new cell phone, wireless device, PDA, and laptop computer. They are the first to adopt Linux as the new operating system. Some set up their own Internet host servers, but most use an ISP after thorough evaluation and price comparisons. They are easy to sell, but hard to convince. They are an important group because they plant the seeds for the new technologies, set the pace, and educate the next layer of total access consumers.

The Information-Active

Information-active people don't care about knowing everything about the computer or the Internet—they just want to access it and use it every day. They are heavy users, and they want to stay up-to-date with the latest information and use the best and most affordable products to get it. They access the Internet primarily for news and communications, and they enclose Web pages, articles, and documents in their e-mails. Many business executives in fast-paced industries fall into this category, using the Internet mainly for e-mail, news, stock trading, and personal finance management. A large segment of this group ranges in age from the early forties to the late fifties. This group is active in both business and the community at large. Whereas information explorers tend to focus on the technical features of the tools, the information-active are more likely to talk about the information, or content, they find on the Web. For this group, total access is necessary for professional development as well as daily personal and home business activities.

Children are more likely to start out in this category. I am always amazed and encouraged when I watch children in classrooms using computers and accessing the Internet. An increasing number of young people use cell phones. They are enthusiastic and learn so fast that they quickly become the teachers. The children who have total access today are the information-explorers of the future.

The Information Followers

Corporate America is brimming with information followers. They find the computer an intimidating machine, but they are not necessarily timid users. While most users have no problem using various applications, they are not confident enough to address problems that arise, and they do not demand total access. Information followers consider cell phones and ATMs not technologies but rather convenient utilities. This group will attend training classes on Microsoft's Word, PowerPoint, or Excel, or Intuit's Quicken, TurboTax, or QuickBooks, or perhaps Netscape or Microsoft Outlook. They buy their children computers, and if they go online, they do so either exclusively at work or via AOL at home. This group has limited access outside the office or workplace. They recognize the importance and value of total access to future generations, but they are concerned about cost and know-how.

With more than 60 percent of U.S. households now owning a computer, this group is a likely target for greater penetration. Although the children of information followers may be habitual online users, they themselves aren't. Most have access only through one phone line to the home, which both the phone and the computer share. This largely untapped group is capable of becoming increasingly information-active as costs decrease and ease of use improves.

The Information-Passive

The world's population reached 6 billion at the end of the twentieth century, leaving over 4 billion people with no direct access to information technology. The market opportunity here is infinite. There are approximately 1 billion hardwired phone lines worldwide, and the wireless phone user community is expected to hit 2 billion people by 2003. Access is spreading more rapidly than ever before. China, Latin America, and Asia are investing heavily in communications infrastructures, expecting to add tens of millions of new information access users in the next decade.

No digital divide limits total access to certain segments of society. The cost of access and information continues to decline as it has for the past thirty years, bringing new services to ever more first-time users. The divide that exists between those with total access and those without it stems from political, social, and economic factors, as well as from the lack of a supporting infrastructure. Many countries have virtually no middle class, with huge disparities between those who have access and those who don't. Digital technology will meet the price the market is willing to pay for total access, but it must be met halfway by progressive political, economic, and social development agendas. Total access must be seen as a social as well as a technological phenomenon.

Total access for the information-passive is more likely to be transparent. That is, they will obtain access, probably not via computers but rather through simple interfaces such as mobile phones, ATMs, credit cards, and telephone ordering. When they do access online services, they may do so via a computer at their church, school, workplace, community center, or union hall. And they will be prompted to gain access by the dynamic presence of retail businesses that respond to *local* market needs and economies. That infrastructure is already progressing in that direction, as fiber optic, cellular networks, and satellite communications proliferate. The information-passive constitute a huge market for those who create new, low-cost, technology-transparent access devices.

Transparent Access

Imagine a world of interconnected and mobile access where business-people and consumers alike dip into streams of information with nearly unconscious effort, entering with a thought, a desire, a need, a glance, a listen—then just as effortlessly returning to the activity at hand. In this world of continuous and total access, users dive into a stream of "information consciousness" as they use computer-enabled services. Access is rarely purely passive for any length of time. At in-store kiosks, they can do price and feature comparisons; in their cars or homes, they can access a distributed personal database; they can use any wireless device to obtain voice-to-text e-mail; and they can call up digital instructions at any time from their VCRs, computers, cell phones, automobiles, and industry equipment.

The recent developments of Web services by IBM and Microsoft are a big step in this direction. Web services use the very latest network software architecture to organize, publish, locate, and invoke access to simple and complex applications (services) across the Web. For example, a B2B company may want to offer its customers digital signature programs, transaction tracking, or inventory management programs. Web services can help a company offer and manage any number of diverse services, thereby extending the company's product line while making sure that the customer is tied more and more closely within a network relationship. All access devices are gateways to a vast array of services. With Web services, the complexity of choice disappears for the customer, who finds a portfolio of services easier to access and manage.

The Internet is a service medium. Service experiences generally differ from product experiences. Services help people achieve some information and are intangible. Ted Levitt, author and professor of marketing at Harvard, says that with a service "the customer doesn't know what it is they bought until after they have bought it."[24] Trust is key here. The message embedded in the *experience* of the service overrides all others. As we begin to gain access to the network through almost everything we touch, information begins to take on new shapes, formats, and qualities. We must trust that it's there, that it works time and time again, and that it is reliable. We also trust that it is consistent from device to device and from place to place.

Network service applications are evolving rapidly, and will become only more pervasive, embedded, and transparent. And as that happens, computers as we know them are changing their profile, shrinking in size and fading into the background of daily life.

Within the past five years, we've seen flat computer screens begin to perform better and come down in price. The new Apple G6 super-powerful computer comes in an eight-inch-square box; the IBM NetVista desktop computer is packaged in the base of a flat-screen monitor. By shrinking this way, the PC becomes part of the total access milieu. (Computer interface software, however, lags. The Macintosh revolutionized the ease-of-use principle, but while speed, memory, and software diversity have accelerated, the basic point-and-click of the mouse and pull-down menu have changed little.) Soon the computer will disappear into the network and the customer will perceive only the service application.

The browser was a dramatic means of transparent access to an almost infinite array of information, services, products, and people. I cannot imagine clicking through 500 channels of cable television. But with a browser, I can explore more than 5 million Web pages and more than 550 billion pages of information.

Some forms of transparent access have been around for decades. For example, ATMs began appearing on street corners in the 1970s and at self-service gas stations and retail stores soon thereafter. New access devices take years of modification for consumers to adapt. That said, our access tools in general are pretty primitive because they tend to rely on clumsy hardware and text-only software. They'll become more sophisticated and more user-friendly once designers start taking advantage of the advancing speed and performance of the new processor.

Today producers and consumers alike have many readily available access points to the storehouses and streams of information they need or want. *Need* and *want* are the key words here. We certainly do not want to deal with much of the information we see—a hard lesson learned by online advertisers, who had made very optimistic projections. What the powers behind those online ads didn't count on was fading consumer responsiveness; they didn't realize that open and total access makes information disposable. With billions of pages of information accessible on the Internet (much of it free), a person could spend a lifetime exploring, finding, and buying without ever having to read an ad.[25] In a medium veritably teeming with choices, few people choose to click on ads. In comparison, I have only limited choices while I'm watching TV, reading a newspaper, or listening to the radio.

Total Access Enables Persistent Presence

The mobile phone or information device is the next logical extension of total access to information. Several such information appliances are rapidly evolving into a surrogate services caddy—one means to what I call persistent presence, which businesses can achieve by providing multiple and diverse means of access and experiences for the consumer. A simple example is a book retailer. I should be able to buy a book from the same store online, in my community, or at an airport. Each of the independent locations or points of presence should have information about my purchase history, and I should have the same degree of access and information, independent of location.

Ensuring this kind of access isn't easy, but it will be essential for businesses to create multiple modes of access to their products and services, and to then develop the networks needed to synchronize the interaction among those modes.

We can expect the connections to multiply well beyond the mobile phone, although all the access devices and machines will carry similar capabilities: Internet connection, information storage and communications, as well as many personal programmable features. Another logical access device is the automobile. Many cars have cell phones today, but my daughter's minivan also has separate CD channels for each passenger and a GPS that can locate the vehicle and unlock the doors if she finds herself without keys. The GPS also includes a road emergency locator for service. Some cars even have flat-screen TVs built into the back of the front seats, all of which tells me that the automobile is becoming a new form of medium.

Recognizing this dawning reality, Toyota entered the telecommunications business in 1999 with the formation of a communication division.[26] Masao Yukawa, a senior advisor to Toyota, observes, "The automobile may well be reinvented as new media with value-added communications, entertainment, and streams of information continuously flowing in and out, to and from passengers. Americans spend an average of 80 minutes in their cars every day. That time can be more productive personally or professionally."[27] Toyota understands that eventually those eighty minutes will be used for shopping, information gathering, banking, buying stocks, keeping children entertained in the back seat, talking to friends, and getting reports on the weather. Drivers will check investments, sales, shipments, and bookings. All these applications will be voice-activated and do as many kinds of "information" chores as there are kinds of people.

Digital technology has the power to turn almost anything connectable into an access device, a capacity that's fueled by the insatiable human desire for information and communication. Metcalfe's Law, which we'll discuss in chapter 3, acknowledges the concomitant commercial opportunities by stating that the "value of the network is equal to the square of the number of users." Add a billion wireless phones, a few billion kiosks, a billion computers, a billion cars, and a few billion other miscellaneous devices to the network, and by the end of the first decade of the twenty-first century, the value of the global network enabling total access becomes incalculable. Over the next decade, new generations of microprocessors will deliver more computing power, making it possible to access and use information in ways that are well beyond where my imagination can reach. Suffice it to say that these advances will be the equivalent of the PC revolution, which began twenty-five years ago.

I'm no Pollyanna—I don't buy the outrageous claims that the Internet can be all things to all people. With embedded chips and wireless technology everywhere, though, it seems that almost anything is connectable. Retail outlets can become ever more accessible and can have a constant supply of products and services if they are part of a coherent business network. Many saw the toppling of the dot-coms as a collapse of the Internet, but that is far from reality. The dot-coms fell not because of the technology or because the Internet is not a value-enhancing communicating medium, but rather because they perceived the Internet as a broadcast medium rather than as an infrastructure for delivering value-creating services. As a result, marketing was seen in its extremes: gathering data on the unsuspecting Web surfer to send user-targeted messages. The Internet gives us a technology for dialogue with the customer. Many executives use these same words to describe the benefit of the Internet, but we have seen too few businesses willing to spend the time and money to invest in the difficult task of developing engaging interface programs with useful and needed content. In this new world of total access, consumers are learning how to adapt the novel technologies to their lives while businesses are primarily looking for a means to cut costs. The consumer, I believe, is adapting quickly and will create pressures on product and service suppliers to open a meaningful dialogue. Sustaining the dialogue builds trust, the foundation of exceptional companies. The diversity of input devices and the mobility of locations expected to evolve over the next decade will demand business models that deliver tremendous flexibility, scalability, security, and reliability—along with total access. Most companies will be scrambling to meet those demands, rather than applying innovative solutions to engage and service their customers.

Untethered, wireless access will expand the network of devices exponentially, with all sorts of objects and machines for input and output. More than 1,300 companies, including some of the biggest names in high tech—IBM, Microsoft, and Nokia, among others—are backing a new standard called Bluetooth, which was first developed by Ericsson, a telecommunications company. The new standard, named for a tenth-century Danish king who united warring factions, has the capability of uniting nations of electronic companies and their disparate technologies. Bluetooth, which is embedded in a chip of silicon and buried within each device, will enable practically everything and anything to converse. It promises that any gadget within thirty feet of another gadget or appliance will be able to exchange voice and data, which can then be sent onto the Internet. For example, Bluetooth would allow me to update photos of my grandchildren on my desk by downloading new photo files from the Internet and transferring them wirelessly to a smart photo frame. InStat estimates that some 670 million devices will be on the market by 2005.[28] All this may be a bit optimistic, but the concept and capability for interaction between all sorts of things will continue to evolve and surprise us.

The Open-Door Policy

The information vaults of corporate America are opening to consumers. Databases are now accessible to both suppliers and consumers, and customers can access product and service information, place orders, track progress, and check backorders and order history. Companies can do all this, in addition to responding to e-mail queries and providing self-service for thousands, or perhaps millions, of customers. Doing these things well is good marketing, even brand enhancing—but it's not one of the tasks that the typical marketing department would assume.

How has total access changed the retail business and, in particular, inventory management? We can start by looking at Wal-Mart. Most of its suppliers own the inventory until it's bought. To maintain stock on shelves, major suppliers began collaborating with Wal-Mart to share transaction data under a system called the "vendor managed inventory model" (VMI). According to the *Financial Times*, retailers now allow former adversaries direct access to corporate databases and electronic point-of-sale transaction data. Wal-Mart updates its database ninety minutes after a transaction, providing valuable market and inventory management data on a daily basis to their partners. Not long ago, this kind of data was sold to suppliers.

Business-to-business access is highly pragmatic and motivated by improving productivity and cutting costs. Opening the corporate kimono to consumers is another story. Consumers are typically less forgiving, and they expect technology to work like magic and to perform as envisioned—and often as prematurely promised!

It's difficult to define and segment an audience that doesn't want to be segmented, or one that redefines its needs and wants 24/7. Every business is perpetually "in transition." Yet many executives hold on to past business models and marketing concepts. Even the current Internet "broadcasters" still think in terms of the old media, believing that they can manipulate users' minds with e-mail, cookies, or banners. I know that businesses use these tools almost universally, but the assumption of effectiveness will be challenged by new and innovative methods as well as by old-fashioned relationship building. Future analysis of the market and customers will be based on computer modeling, probability theory, and more reliable interaction with machines rather than on classical segmentation models.

While the digital understructure improves business communications, achieves greater cost savings, and efficiently manages inventories and people, what makes it truly revolutionary is the unprecedented level of access businesses have to information that flows to and from customers. Producers hope to "hook" customers with free devices and charge for services, while customers embrace technology, using it as a tool for amplifying their desires for excellence, value, choice, novelty, and individualized service. Thus, just as broadcast TV was free to consumers in the United States, access to information and services via the Web is mostly free, with revenues from advertising, sponsorship, and reselling of information supporting the new media.

This business model hasn't been very successful for most of the online companies, but it will probably change and adapt over the next decade. Turning the Internet into a money-making channel will mean paying ever more attention to creating true value. That value, I believe, is in being a vital part of a total access architecture. The competition for almost anything online is still viewed as mostly "free," and one thing we've learned is that the market for anything "free" is almost infinite. I did an Internet search for the word *free* using the popular search engine Google and came up with 125 million referenced pages or listings. Producers may like the idea that "quality is free," providing unlimited customer access to their databases. It may even pay for itself by improving customer loyalty and increased revenues.

The result of the intelligent understructure is a marketplace in perpetual motion. It increases total access and interactive communications by presenting a constantly unfolding global panoply of new experiences. Consumers can disconnect just as easily as they can connect. Moreover, user-defined machines and software are making decisions, which leads to the further "demassification" of markets, the fragmentation of audiences, and the rise of individuality. Such prospects pose a danger to businesses built on the legacy inherited from old ways of broadcast marketing, erode the brand value inherent in objects, and foster the reinvestment of trust and identity in an ever-changing array of competing services.

The World Wide Web is at the same time a local market, a personal market, and a truly global mass market. We cannot segment it into channels of broadcast. Users must freely choose to access it and stay with it. But it's a black hole of unpredictability for businesses. Total access removes them from their traditional positions of control, so that to thrive now, businesses must provide many access points to their products and be prepared to engage fully in ongoing conversations with consumers who demand equal footing on the commercial playing field. Businesses today are firmly planted in the "now."

The Future of Total Access

So if this is where we are now, where are we headed? I see some strong indications of where things are going next.

First, search, selection, and decision-making software will be added to access devices, and as a result, the mechanics of consumers' choices of the best product to match their preferences will become transparent.

Broadband will accelerate changes because it will enable more experiential applications and interfaces for the "don't give-it-a-second-thought" access devices. Open, transparent, and inexpensive total access will effect a vast cultural change in the producer-consumer relationship; information systems will continually gather information and assess minute changes in buying habits and behavior. "Attitude"—or a consumer expectation for responsive service mind-set—will continue to exert pressure on all forms of social and commercial interaction.

Consumers will become more familiar with the tools available for screening out unwanted commercial intruders, searching for alternatives, and comparing prices. We can expect to see more demand for information about every public and private institutional activity and at the same time a growing concern for maintaining one's own privacy. This sort of discord is commonplace in American culture. Back in the shops of market leaders, programmable and real-time systems capable of responding to consumer wishes or market changes will be connected.

The demand for total access creates its own market for franchised services. Today, pressed by the growing demand for access and pushed by technology development, the journey traversed by bits and bytes can be traveled over any number of media—copper, ether (wireless/mobile and satellites), or light encased in fiber or cable. The speed of access and capacity for a greater variety of information formats through each medium depends on the physics of the various media as well as the smart devices and software required to manage and present the information to users. As the technology improves, we will see a corresponding decrease in the cost of total access. Market expansion demands those cost reductions, and it does all come down to costs. The cost of Internet access in Japan or Poland is almost twice what it is in the United States.

Over time, most information-wise companies will learn that the way to engage their customers is to develop transparent, less intrusive, secure total access means so that only the services and benefits of use shine through unencumbered by complex technologies. Every kind of access will become as transparent as the telephone has become.

For business, this transparency is both good news and bad news. The good news is that the consumer will become more information-active. That is, each and every transaction will be a source of information and an opportunity for expanding knowledge about that customer. The bad news is that information-active consumers will use this information to change their buying behavior to help them make better, more economical choices. Specialized search engines are already available for locating the best price for any particular purchase. That point was driven home for me when I discovered that consumers could purchase my last book at seven different prices. It's unlikely that producers will be able to use the newly acquired information for anything other than broadcasting "targeted" messages, which will only serve to increase both the noise level and consumers' frustration.

How the emerging peoples of the world will influence world markets as they gain total access is uncertain. Some will certainly become information-active as children of succeeding generations. When 1 or 2 billion people worldwide have access to global information networks, we may well see the greatest business and social disruptions of the twenty-first century.

Chapter Three

New Technologies, A New Marketplace

The Laws

Technology has changed at an unprecedented pace in the past twenty-five years, delivering increased performance and giving us lower-cost ways of working, communicating, and interacting with the world around us. It has enabled farsighted businesses to outpace their competition by creating new products and services, and by managing business processes and operations more efficiently. Certain principles—the laws of the new marketplace—can help us anticipate technology's direction in the future.

NOT ONLY HAS TECHNOLOGY stimulated the general public's imagination; it has also given business new tools for competitive differentiation. In the past, businesses viewed the application of new technology for operational tasks—such as designing, producing, and distributing—as essential for progress in productivity. That's still true, but we now see technological advances as offering new ways to drastically alter the way companies market their products and services as well. Today, for the first time, information technology is shifting management's focus from one of purely internal operational dynamics to the business of interacting with partners, suppliers, and customers. In other words, the network is causing more outside-in thinking, forcing management to think about both the manners and methods of continuously interacting with customers.

This shift in thinking is a whole new thing for marketing, which has traditionally interacted with customers through research organizations, simulated and representative groups of customers, and distribution chains or other filtering agents, while marketing people directly interacted with customers only peripherally and occasionally. In contrast, feedback today is direct, immediate, and continuous, and it will become even more so as total access reshapes both the competitive marketplace and the consumer's behavior.

Business executives, even those from leading-edge companies, have rarely anticipated the disruptive changes new technology brings. Understanding where technology is headed is more difficult than it was in the past, but not impossible. It's also more important to understand the direction of technology because market changes, particularly disruptive changes, are more frequent and harder to foresee than before. Those who develop an understanding of how technology develops have a definite edge. Businesses don't have to adopt every new technology immediately, but if they understand emerging technology trends, they can outpace their competition by being more innovative with the timely development of new products and services, and by adopting new tools for managing business processes and operations more efficiently.

But how do we see where technology is headed, especially today, when it has fallen from grace and appears to be struggling to find growth again? We could turn to market research, but that's an unreliable tool. Focus groups and surveys may provide some information about what customers are thinking at a particular time, but they can't predict the outcome of a consumer's first experience with a product or service, nor can they predict a competitor's move or the surprise of daily market events. Asking customers to predict the future is a waste of time and money. They have a hard time imagining what's possible without first seeing and trying a product or service, and researchers often find an infinite demand for the unavailable. And asking inventors or technologists about the commercial viability of their innovations is likewise unlikely to be accurate. Businesses often take a wait-and-see approach: They delay acting on their visions of the future until they can confirm those visions with convincing market data. History has shown us that new technologies reveal their value when they are applied. For example, it took Thomas Edison twenty years to concede that the main use of his phonograph was to entertain people with music. As Jared Diamond points out, "Invention is the mother of necessity rather than vice versa." He believes that almost every modern invention—from airplanes to automobiles, from the electric light bulb to the transistor—started as a technology in search of a practical use.[1]

We could also look to marketing. One of its goals, after all, is to identify and respond to market changes, and technology is the driver of those changes. But in recent years, marketing hasn't been a reliable rudder. Things are changing so fast that in the past decade, "market-forced" strategy changes at many companies (Compaq, Nordstrom, Lucent, AT&T, Sega, Cisco, Coca-Cola, Campbell Soup, Kodak, Xerox, CBS, and Levi Strauss, to name but a few) left those companies able only to react to the changes around them, rather than to anticipate them. Chances are that things will only speed up more, becoming increasingly complex and competitive—and that marketing will be even less able to predict and respond.

So what's a business to do? How do we predict the future so that we're a little ahead of the game, anticipating change instead of just reacting to it? We need some guidance, and I believe we have it in the form of what I call "the laws of the new marketplace," five principles that help us understand and anticipate technology's progress. These laws forecast and envision the future better than anything market research can offer. While they don't offer specific business or marketing strategies, they do provide a foundation for building future applications by giving us facts about how fast technology is developing, and in what direction.

We know from experience that those who pursue the future by advancing to the edges of the technology learn early and are more likely to succeed. The list of companies that have and haven't done this is long:

Cisco versus Lucent, Wal-Mart versus Sears, Starbucks versus every local coffee shop, Federal Express versus the U.S. Post Office, Sony versus Sega, Nokia versus Motorola, and IBM versus Digital. The driving forces of the laws will continue to reshape the meaning of marketing and market leadership. Grasping concepts behind the laws stimulates the imagination and helps us understand the capabilities, risks, and trends of new technologies. Exploiting them means anticipating what's possible and creating new ways of interacting with customers.

Moore's Law: Transistors on a Chip

The number of transistors on a chip doubles every eighteen to twenty-four months.

The law that sets the basis for the other four laws is named after Gordon Moore, the cofounder of Intel. In 1964, Moore observed that the trend in chip technology was to dramatically increase the power and lower the cost of computing. At the time, he could not have imagined just how prophetic his statement would be—or how prolific the transistor would become. Since the mid-1970s the number of transistors on a chip has increased more than 3,200 times, from 2,300 on the first microprocessor to 7.5 million on the Pentium II processor, so that now we have roughly 1.2 transistors for every ant in the world.

A transistor is hundreds of times smaller than the human hair, yet the integration of transistors onto a chip of silicon cuts the cost of processing information to fractions of a cent per transistor. The result of this trend is an incredible expansion of applications of applied computing power. Evidence of Moore's Law is everywhere. If you use a cell phone, personal computer, ATM, or PDA, you've been exposed to Moore's Law (and perhaps also to Metcalfe's Law, which we'll discuss in a minute). These information access and interactive devices embed unique service-like functions inside products. These days they're everywhere: in automobiles, refrigerators, TVs, fax machines, telephones, toys, pacemakers, hearing aids, vending machines, greeting cards, traffic lights, watches—even your power tools! Each of these devices uses hundreds of thousands, even millions, of transistors integrated onto a chip of silicon. And although not all these devices are digital, they all follow Moore's Law. That is, they keep doing more work: They have more function and features, all at lower and lower cost.

Moore's Law has been in effect for more than thirty years, progressing steadily through the ups and downs of market cycles. In turn, over that same period it has driven IT capital spending in the United States at a phenomenal rate, from just under 20 percent of spending in the early 1960s to almost 50 percent in 2000.[2] Computer, software, and telecommunication companies have seen the complete disruption of traditional notions of pricing and costs, alliances, standards, management processes, and brand leadership, all because of the steady advancement of Moore's Law. The constantly lower price of smart products is reshaping competition, allowing Microsoft to move from a just another PC software company to a major force in enterprise computing.

The entire $3 trillion U.S. retail industry depends on the flow of information from data scanners to inventory management, through distribution-supplier warehouses to the shelf and checkout counter back through the development and supply chain. The process is accomplished through chips encased in computers and adapted by software and various networks of communications. To the consumer, these devices mean the twenty-four-hour availability of hundreds of thousands of different products. Tailoring products or services to an individual customer's requirements or customizing marketing programs would simply not be economically possible without low-cost computer networks and software programmability.

Intel chips very definitely follow Moore's Law, but they're not the only devices that do so. Xilinx, a highly successful $1 billion semiconductor company in Silicon Valley, announced a chip with 210 million transistors diffused into a piece of silicon about one inch square. This chip is another example of how Moore's Law and the underlying technology engender change in the products as well as in the level of dependency of the people who use them. Xilinx chips are user programmable; that is, users decide what they want the chip to do. The chips are used in computers, machine tools, communications equipment, and much more. They allow product designers to make rapid customized changes by adding functions or changing existing programs and services after the products are built, and even after they've been installed on customer premises. The changes can even be made remotely via the Internet. This type of technology embeds services and helps Xilinx customers adapt quickly to technology or market changes.

Embedding digital chips into everything that the consumer touches, relies on, and uses regularly gives new services persistent presence. By designing these chips and service capabilities into user equipment, manufacturers are better able to sell ongoing services and to maintain customer relationships. Equipment producers not only achieve cost savings on services; they also help their customers keep pace with rapid change.

Moore's Law Applied for Diabetics

Forty years ago, I was diagnosed with diabetes. At that time, medical technology chiefly meant test tubes—computers didn't exist. So once every three months or so, I would go to a lab for a glucose blood test, and about a week later, my doctor would call to tell me the results. All either of us knew from the test data was the percentage of sugar in my blood at the moment that the blood was drawn, information that wasn't all that helpful, as blood sugars can and do vary widely from hour to hour and day to day. Testing at any one time of day really doesn't give you much useful information.

All that has changed as a result of Moore's Law. Today I can check my glucose level any place and at any time, and get the results in five seconds, thanks to a small device that I carry with me. The device, which weighs only a few ounces, contains several chips, each with approximately 150,000 transistors that perform precise calculations measuring the glucose level in my blood. The device also keeps records of 150 different tests, along with the date and time of each. The output is a digital representation of the amount of glucose in my blood.

The glucose monitor chips are rather simple, but they illustrate the point. Manufacturers have learned that by practically giving the devices away they establish a "marketing presence" with the customer. Although drug stores sell the monitors for about $50, they carry rebates of $30 to $40. The manufacturers make their money on the test strips (much like razor manufacturers make their money on blades, not razors). The customer keeps buying the test strips and over time may buy added services such as remote storage, formatting, and data management. Today we're seeing new functions as well, which will give the monitor capabilities now available only in a PDA or cell phone. Such devices might even integrate Bluetooth software (discussed in chapter 2), allowing for wireless connection to a computer, an online remote monitor, a data center, and even your physician's computer. LifeScan already makes hospital-use glucose monitors with built-in barcode scanners to identify patients and the attending nurses and send the information via infrared (light wave) to a central computer. The result of all this technology? Better patient care through the availability of more accurate, distributed information that can be recorded, recalled, and tracked over time.

What does all this have to do with marketing? Plenty! The market for glucose-monitoring devices is growing from an estimated 151 million diabetics today worldwide to an expected 400 million in the next decade.[3] More than half a dozen manufacturers compete in this market, each trying to convince a diabetic person to adopt its monitor. Diabetics should test their blood at least three times a day using the appropriate test strips; if they do, they basically ensure that the manufacturer will get monthly revenue. Producers can also add new services and integrate various functions into the monitors, engaging the user in a system of diabetic management. For example, I have five monitors, all the same kind. I keep them in my car, my office, my briefcase, my jogging pack, and at home. Although manufacturers constantly send me various models free for trial use, I use only one model because of its size and portability, because I want the information from one to be consistent with others, and because I can use the same test strips, which are expensive, in every monitor. I also like to be able to connect the monitors to my computer (to gather data) and not to worry about compatibility. And by extending the connectivity of the monitor with secure communications, I can download the data to my doctor's computer or to a data center for comparisons, trends, and new services such as remote self-management. If users agree to be a node on the network, pharmaceutical companies working to monitor the effect of a new drug on blood sugars can also use the data from those users.

It's not hard to imagine embedding chips in products, connecting those products to a network, and maintaining a steady flow of services to the users. In fact, we can expect to see more and more remote applications that will provide new services and enable the rise of the mobile consumer. E-mail and online securities trading were made possible by low-cost access devices and the Internet. Because we can expect to see Moore's Law in effect for the next fifteen years or so, we can also expect to see more and more smart access devices, which will gather and deliver engaging forms of communication and information in all imaginable ways. Thousands of creative mobile applications can bloom from the availability of low-cost chips, increased bandwidth, and Internet connectivity. Banks could provide their customers with wireless devices with built-in customized, connecting applications. Grocery stores and hardware suppliers could scan inventories and order and access accounts from home, car, or workplace.

For marketing, Moore's Law means the continued production of intelligent products with integrated communications. It also means more network connections and more diagnostic self-services. This is good news for marketers. Adding intelligence to any type of medium creates the capacity for some kind of interactivity, and one of marketing's primary responsibilities is to communicate with customers. But applying the kind of imagination and creativity that stimulate dialogue and engagement with those customers across widely distributed points of presence will require more than just message-making. It will require an understanding of how to interface with those customers in this new interactive marketplace in which the value of the network increases dramatically as the number of users rises. That brings us to Metcalfe's Law.

Metcalfe's Law: The Value of the Network

The value of the network increases by the square of the number of users.

Bob Metcalfe, a former researcher at Xerox Palo Alto Research Center (PARC), is the co-inventor of Ethernet, a world-standard technology that now connects more than 100 million computers. When he and I met in 1979, he had left PARC and was setting up 3Com to design and develop local area networks for PCs.

Metcalfe's Law states that the value of the network increases by the square of the number of users. A simple example is the fax machine. One fax machine is of no value until at least one more is connected to it. Connect a million fax machines and the value of the network grows as the square of the number of users. The business community has come to depend on fax machines—which have become very inexpensive—for rapid document communications.

Digital signatures illustrate how a seemingly simple application can change not only a business process but the economics of services as well. A great deal of what is sent by both fax and express mail today is done to obtain pen and ink signatures. On October 1, 2000, digital or electronic signatures became as legal as those signed on paper.[4] Digital signatures can now establish "authentication" of documents sent over the Internet, assuring users of both the identity of the person signing and the integrity of the item signed. Thanks to the legality of digital signatures, sending signature pages on documents via fax or mail will soon seem antiquated. As a result, the value of the network increases, not only by the number of connections but also by the improvements in productivity, particularly in service businesses, resulting from the application of efficient software programs.

Already we have seen the effect of Metcalfe's Law on the software business—in their eagerness to cash in on expanding networks, developers are moving from selling packaged products to selling time. More and more software today is integrated with a service offering because services can be offered via a network. Updates and software components are free online because the developers recognize that by sustaining users' demand for service, they will be better able to keep those users in their camp and sell them higher-value products. In effect, these companies are using networks to build and sustain service relationships.

The network concept has expanded the businesses of those who plan, build, and maintain them as well. IBM, once the largest software developer and supplier in the IT business, is now one of the world's largest service companies, just as FedEx and DHL are much more than package-delivery services. To stay ahead of the curve, Federal Express now sees itself as a "provider of global transportation management services, integrated logistics, consulting and other professional services."[5] The company began by building its own proprietary distribution network, with devices and systems that scanned and tracked packages and allowed customers to access their databases for self-service. Now Federal Express is teaching its customers how to do it.

Metcalfe's Law applies to far more than computing systems and the

Internet. It's really the new paradigm for the marketing renaissance, where everything and everybody are connected within networks of various communities. The Internet and other forms of connectivity won't eliminate gatherings such as business and industry conferences and user groups. Rather, they will better sustain and increase the value of relationships developed in face-to-face meetings. Connecting people builds value, whether that value is social or economic. In this new century, the "network" displaces hierarchy and "mass" as the model, and it becomes the underlying value-added model for organizations, markets, and diverse institutional forms.

Gilder's Law:
The Quality and Efficiency of Information Communications

The bandwidth of communications is growing faster than computing power by doubling every year. It will continue to do so for the next twenty-five years.

I have a file on my computer labeled "Photos," which I created a few years ago to store the increasing number of digital photos that I receive via e-mail from friends and family. And it also stores photos that I take on my new digital camera. (After owning several good 35mm cameras and playing amateur photographer for years, I'm now hooked on taking digital photos.) And my communication of information doesn't stop with photos: I can see movie clips and listen to music; I can even review a music clip from a new CD before ordering it online. These things have become routine for me and for many others, so much so that it's easy to forget that the average PC user has been able to do these things for less than a decade. Only a few years ago, downloading one photograph could take five or ten minutes and consume up to a million bytes of memory (1 MB), which doesn't sound like much until you recall that the standard memory on a computer in 1990 was about 40 megabytes.

The reason for the expansion of these applications in recent years is simple: The cost of storage, computing power, and bandwidth has dropped drastically, while performance has vastly increased. Today the standard hard drive on a computer stores over 20 gigabytes (20 billion bytes), and with a standard computer modem operating at 256 kilobits per second, downloading a full-page color photograph may take only a few seconds, all thanks to increased bandwidth.

A picture is still worth a thousand words; it also requires a lot more bandwidth. Although bandwidth is technically the speed of data through a medium, for the user it is the capability for immediate access to information or dynamic content measured in bits per second (bps). A full page of English text has about 16,000 bits. A fast modem can move about 15,000 bits in one second. Full-motion, full-screen video would require roughly 10 million bps, depending on whether the file is compressed.[6]

Increased bandwidth is valuable in the world of the Internet because the more information that can be transmitted instantaneously, the more dynamic ways of human expression can be conveyed electronically. With more bandwidth, devices can deliver greater emotional and intellectual communication—thus we'll begin to see more live video and film clips on the Internet, things like new product introductions, fashion shows, demonstration selling, instructional seminars, and live visits to travel destinations. BroadWare Technologies, a streaming video start-up in Silicon Valley, has come up with a very practical use for increased bandwidth. It is using continuous live video for the secure monitoring of child care centers and children's hockey centers, allowing working parents to go online and see their kids live, in real time, from wherever they are.

Gilder's Law, which posits the yearly doubling of bandwidth, is named for George Gilder, who promoted broadband and the Internet for many years. (He was also the person who first ascribed Metcalfe's Law to Bob Metcalfe.) Gilder's Law is a direct descendant of Moore's and Metcalfe's laws. By cramming more transistors onto a chip, cost effectiveness rises by the square of the number of transistors. Consider transistors as parts of a microsystem, designed so that each part must communicate with the others in order to do a complete task. The closer together the parts are placed, the faster the communication, and the more efficient the microsystem becomes.

Gilder raises the transistor and the chip to a network systems level by addressing the expanding number of computers connected by fiber-optic networks. By 2000, about 90 million computers were connected via the World Wide Web. The worldwide communications between those computers are increasingly made through the 283 million miles of installed optical fiber cable.[7] In 1999 and 2000, reports the *New York Times*, "100 million miles of fiber were laid around the world at a cost of $35 billion—more than enough to reach the sun."[8] As a result, the capacity of the Internet backbone has doubled every 100 days.[9] The faster data move through the various media, the more information can be sent in less time. Hence, the cost of transmitting a bit of information optically halves every nine months—versus the eighteen to twenty-four months of Moore's Law.[10] It takes a photon, a unit of light, one 20-millionth of a second to cross the United States. We know of nothing that is faster than light.

The number of connected servers, or host computers, on the Internet has risen dramatically, from 1 million in 1993 to well over 115 million in August 2001.[11] That number is flattening, but it will still exceed 150 million in the next few years. Each computer is like part of a relay team, a high-speed participant leveraging all others by increasing the network's performance, bandwidth, capacity, and value. Add wireless phones, cars, planes, and other digital devices to the network, and we approach the infinitude of bandwidth. I'm not talking science fiction; optical networks are replacing the older technologies, and the new light-speed networks will enable the full expression of human communications. A smile, after all, contains a lot more information than e-mail does.

Gilder thinks the older "copper-caged" technologies of communication create a gridlock for information. "Immobile information makes our businesses larger, more static and hierarchical than they need to be. It makes our economies less flexible, our jobs less fulfilling, our lives less luminous with opportunity," he says.[12] But the availability of increasing amounts of bandwidth "changes everything," says Gilder. Imagine that bandwidth will be free. If the law of thrift in Moore's Law was to "waste" transistors on a chip, the law of thrift in the new paradigm will be to "waste" bandwidth.[13] What does Gilder mean by "wasting bits and bandwidth?" Gilder is an economist, and he thinks in economic terms. He rationalizes that the laws of economics operate on the principles of thrift and scarcity: When we have an abundance of inexpensive anything, we waste it. Air, water, and time are examples. Doubling bandwidth every year, then, will lead us to waste it—we will leave our access devices on all the time, twenty-four hours a day, seven days a week. Leaving the TV or cell phone on when no one is watching or talking is wasting bandwidth. Radio background music is wasting bandwidth. A screen saver or game on your computer is wasting bits.

The phrase "wasting bits and bandwidth" gives a somewhat inaccurate representation of the situation. Increased, lower-cost bandwidth actually offers tremendous opportunity. When "bits and bps" are abundant, they make possible a steady stream of services that we see as services, not as technology (e.g., when we exchange photos over the Internet, we don't think about the computer or the monitor or the modem or the miles of fiber-optic cable that make that exchange possible). While the current generation of personal computers and cell phones accomplish an astonishing variety of things, the next big wave may be the reconfiguration of what they do. Applications may become transparent (hidden), which makes the connecting machine, device, or screen even more dynamic, interactive, and engaging. We may no longer have to dial up or log onto the network. The device will deliver the service, front and center.

For example, in Japan, the DoCoMo i-mode cell phone incorporates features of a phone, a PC, and the Internet. DoCoMo didn't want to emphasize the Internet or new technology. It simply wanted to give consumers a technologically transparent way to search, shop, and locate places using the accepted cell phone format. While i-mode's services are highly popular among twenty-four- to thirty-five-year-olds of both sexes, the most frequent users are women in their late twenties, a large consumer group with higher disposable incomes.[14] (As a side note, a major limitation of mobile and pervasive technology is battery life. Much of the advance in battery life we have experienced with our telephones and computing devices has come about through semiconductor technology. The battery itself is improving rather slowly, with efficiency doubling every seven years, and it is slowing its pace according to Dr. Joseph Gordon of the IBM Storage Research Center.[15])

Very little has changed in the personal computer in the past fifteen years. Imaginative ways to present information and capture users' emotions are still lacking, although connecting the computer to the network has begun to remedy that. Thanks to Moore's Law, Metcalfe's Law, and Gilder's Law, we are no longer the captive audience of a few application development engineers. Today we have access to the infinite imagination of expanding users. The PC is becoming a fast, high-capacity, "dumb" access device. Rather than residing on the computer, applications and information are increasingly accessed and available from the network. The whole idea of the PC is changing: We're moving away from a PC that continually has applications being invented and added to it, and toward a PC that is, more than anything, a portal through which intelligent life can express itself from anywhere on the planet.

Gilder's Law tells us that we will see the expansion of networks delivering more and more entertaining and diverse media forms. The sharp decline in the telecommunications and Internet infrastructure businesses in 2001 came about in part by the industry's optimism for unabated market growth. While cell phones and Internet usage continues to expand, much of the fiber optic cable is "dark" or left unused. As yet, consumers have too few reasons to purchase engaging content or time- and money-saving services. Marketing's challenge is to expand its bandwidth of imagination and use this new powerful bandwidth for true consumer interactive communications, rather than as yet another form of broadcast. Unfortunately, Internet marketing has come to be identified with junk e-mail, banner ads, and pop-up sales messages. The expanding bandwidth capability of the network media is an opportunity for marketing to move beyond the push era of the past into a customer-serving total access era.

The Law of Storage:
Inexpensive Storage for an Infinite Amount of Information

For the network revolution to progress, storage and memory performance with corresponding decreases in cost must expand at a rate faster than that in Moore's Law.

The information society is generating an astonishing and growing amount of information, and every form of that information—science and daily business transactions, stock market and tax records, television shows, music, and movies—is stored in some kind of medium. Researchers at the University of California, Berkeley, estimate that "the world's total yearly production of print, film, optical, and magnetic content would require roughly 1.5 billion gigabytes of storage. This is the equivalent of 250 megabytes per person for each man, woman, and child on earth."[16]

Human beings have an insatiable appetite for information, even when it has little value or use. We've become information pack rats. The statistics are just as staggering when you get more specific. For example, look at the Internet: The total amount of information sent out over the Internet is doubling every hundred days. E-mail is a big part of that. Every e-mail message must be stored on at least three different computers: your computer (or whatever computer you send it from), the receiving computer, and at least one computer in the network (usually many more as the network passes the message from node to node). There are more than 440 million corporate and individual mailboxes in the world. AOL's 20.5 million subscribers sent 110 million e-mails in 1999, up from 50 million in 1998. E-mails now outnumber pieces of mail delivered by the U.S. Post Office.[17] And all those e-mails require storage. In one six-month period in 1999, AOL consumed 42 trillion bytes of storage. In the same period, Mail.com consumed 30 trillion bytes in just forty-five days.[18] Estimates say that by 2005 the average U.S. consumer will receive 1,600 commercial e-mail messages and more than 4,000 nonpromotional and personal correspondence e-mails each year.[19]

Storage, or memory, allows us to access and recall information at the tap of a finger. Look at the rapid acceptance and growth of CDs and CD-ROMs, a form of storage that has become so much a part of our lives that we are no longer amazed at the amount of video or music entertainment packed on a small, thin disk. Hard-disk storage holds the information that allows businesses to remember and respond to customers in very personal ways. Amazon.com remembers me better than the bank teller I've dealt with for twenty-five years—while we humans fumble to recall the name of a person we met yesterday, devices and systems have resident memories, which give them instant recall. The people at Amazon don't have to know their customers when their software can do a better job of it.[20]

Generally speaking, we think of memory in two categories: temporary and long-term. The hard disk drive in your computer is used for long-term memory, while the computer's RAM (random access memory) is short term. Information such as documents, letters, and e-mails is stored temporarily on a chip in your computer until you decide to save it to disk permanently. Semiconductor memories are silicon chips, with the most common being DRAM memory. Other types of semiconductor nonvolatile memories store programs, instruction sets, or data when the device loses power or is turned off. There are many different types of solid state memories but because they are semiconductors, they all follow Moore's Law and have seen, in the past twenty years, a dramatic drop in cost along with a corresponding increase in density.

Fortunately, we've seen a rapid evolution of storage technology. IBM recently introduced a 1-gigabyte disk drive the size of a pack of matches. This "microdrive" can hold up to a thousand high-resolution photographs, a thousand 200-page novels or nearly eighteen hours of high-quality digital audio music. Where this device might find new applications is left to the imagination. Robert Morris, storage director of IBM's Storage Research Center, says that disk drive technology has been advancing even faster than Moore's law. The corresponding measure, which is Gigabits per square inch, has been doubling about every year rather than the 18–24 months of Moore's law.[21] Morris further defines the Law of Storage as having information at the right time and place. Since 1956, when IBM developed a new recording-head technology, the bits-per-square inch of storage surface (areal density) has been doubling every year. That is, all the information processed and forwarded by networks has to find a place to be stored, even if only temporarily.

Many people have been responsible for the development of the various memory and storage technologies, but probably no other company or group has driven the technology as far and as fast as IBM's Storage Research Center in San Jose, California, beginning with the introduction of the first magnetic storage over forty years ago. In a 1999 article, Paul Horn, director of IBM research, tells us that the first magnetic disc drives developed by IBM in 1956 took "about a billion billion atoms to store one single bit of information. Extrapolating from that past through today and out to 2025, and you get down to 1,000 atoms per bit of information."[22]

The most dramatic effect of this shrinkage of the bit is the reduction in the cost of storage. The cost to store one megabyte (1 million bytes) in 1956 was $10,000; that has dropped to less than a cent today. Within the next twenty-five years we will be able to store a trillion bytes of storage for less than $0.25.[23]

From a marketing viewpoint, the continuing progress of these technologies provides enormous opportunity for redefining "local presence" to a customer. Robert Morris expresses it this way:

> *Even more important than a cost takedown or a performance improvement is when the technology crosses an important threshold. The technology improvement by itself is just a yawn unless it enables some new phenomenon (or value to a customer). Disk drive storage became revolutionary when about 5 years ago it became cheaper to store and manage data on a disk drive than on paper—that caused a rapid upsurge in adoption and a change in how our back offices operate. We've seen other such effects. Another revolution began to occur just recently when the cost of storing a movie on a disk drive fell below about $20. That is, I can now store 4 or 5 movies on a $100 desktop drive.*[24]

Morris also points out a paradox arising from the acceleration of both Gilder's Law and the Law of Storage. If bandwidth advances to a point where it is fast and free or nearly free, only one document of, say, the *New York Times* will be needed. All subscribers will be able to access and read the daily news as if it were locally present on their computer. So we see two extreme scenarios: an implosion of data to single published copies, or an explosion of data to many replicated copies. Morris comments:

> *But of course, nothing ever becomes free or almost free—demand always arrives to fill the supply. That is why we now have 1,000 times as much storage on our PC, we don't read any faster and it still fills up! Of course there won't be an implosion or explosion of the Internet. But if the relative progress we have seen in the past continues, we'll continue to keep lots of data in our personal computing environment. Wireless communications will become more widespread and ease the availability of data. But just as we are seeing a lot of caching (temporary storing) of data in the Internet today, we'll see a lot of replication of data onto local devices: this will be for the purposes of caching to hide the latencies of the network, for reasons of privacy, and because wireless communications will sometimes be intermittent. This is also why information is being stored throughout the Internet—so it can keep up as the load skyrockets. It is*

also why we are seeing storage appear on digital video recorders and TV set top boxes so that we can watch media when we want to and not when it is being broadcast.[25]

Now let's take a look at the connection between the Law of Storage and marketing. The proliferation of information from what seem to be an ever diverse and omnipresent media has made information disposable. The human memory is overloaded with commercial information and trivia, and yet we continue to be bombarded with more than we can digest. When marketers achieve persistent presence through ubiquitous accessible memory, they will discard the old notion that brand relies on the consumer's memory and recall to sustain repeatable sales. The instant recall of information and experiences from embedded or remotely accessible memories inside counters, shelves, kiosks, automobiles, appliances, computers, phones, and a million other things and places that don't rely on broadcast or human memory will be the means for customer continuity. If the experience isn't available in local memory, it will be accessible over high-bandwidth networks when and where the consumer interacts with a point of presence.

The Law of Software: There Is No Law

Software is difficult to place within a clear progressive framework, as is Moore's Law. It advances rather slowly compared to chips or storage devices, and because it's embedded inside information devices and systems, it tends to follow hardware performance improvements. When new advanced computers enter the market, software applications take a year or more to catch up. Software has progressed by becoming more adaptable and modular, cheaper, and faster to deploy. Operating systems— the programs used to manage a computer's internal instructions and information—have progressed from expensive and unwieldy programs used in mainframes decades ago to small component-like programs used inside network-enabled cell phones to deliver and send information in various formats. From cars and airplanes to stock markets and banks, grocery stores to restaurants—everything the consumer touches today is software-enabled.

Even though no specific law governs the expected progress of software, it is perhaps the most significant technology for marketing executives to understand, for the simple reason that software applications automate producer-consumer relationships, giving "personality" to interface devices, delivering new and imaginative services, enabling new forms of entertainment, and allowing consumers to access, choose, and engage.

A few years ago, after a talk to senior management at Procter & Gamble, one of the vice presidents asked me if I thought P&G's future advertising agency might be a software company. It was a provocative question. Software engineers are the artists of the high-tech community; in fact, many of the software engineers I know are musicians as well. They're the ones who rebel against being contained within standards and are always exploring the outer boundaries of the possible. They're the ones who conceive and develop the new tools of marketing. The only "law" I can offer about software is that it is getting more modular, more network- and user-friendly, more ubiquitous—and, of course, cheaper.

Goslings's Observations on Software

In my search for a software law that was comparable to Moore's, Metcalfe's, Gilder's, and Storage laws, I had an e-mail conversation with Jim Gosling, co-inventor of Java and well-recognized software guru. Java works just about everywhere—from TVs and cell phones to ATMs and supercomputers. It's also the basis for additional e-commerce applications.

Java is an open system, which means that anyone can license it and adapt it to his or her particular needs. It is flexible, adaptive, creative, open, and democratic. It doesn't care what other software the system may be using; it's agnostic and widely regarded as revolutionary, because it's based on breaking software into modular, reusable components that can be plugged together to create new applications. Called "beans," Java's components are, like the Internet, highly adaptable and mobile.

When I asked Gosling if he knew of a "law" governing the progress of software, he sent the following reply:

I wish. The closest I can get is "software is hard." People often have the misapprehension that building a piece of software is like building a chair. It isn't. Software is more about framing human intellectual activity than it is about technology. Unfortunately, humans progress through Darwinism, not Moore's law. Progress through Moore's law is exponential, while Darwinism is essentially a Monte Carlo technique whose progress is logarithmic, the functional inverse of an exponential.

Since human intellectual capacity isn't progressing at an interesting rate, progress in software turns into leveraging what we've got to work with. One form of leverage is to just piggyback on other progress. For example, it's often the case that clever and fast solutions to problems don't exist, but slow brute force solutions do: over time, Moore's law makes brute force solutions usable.

Another form of leverage is tools that make certain intellectual problems go away. For example, in Java, there is a whole area related to the memory model that gives developers about a factor of two productivity increase. To have a parallel to Moore's law, tools would have to be evolving and finding such intellectual levers on a regular basis. But it's been slow.

Another form of leverage is through not solving problems that have already been solved. In a strong sense, this is what building modular systems is all about; build systems so that you can plug in preexisting modules instead of designing new ones. This is the core of the Object Oriented Programming (OOP) methodology.[26] One of the things I'm proud of in Java is that it really makes OOP work. Once you have a market of modular components, they take on aspects of a network where Metcalf's law applies: the value of a OOP methodology is quadratic in the number of available components. [27]

Even though there may be no law that is associated with increased software performance, the technology is moving rapidly, and marketing people must learn to appreciate and understand it. All the other laws rest on a software platform, which underscores that the marketing activities of the future will depend on software in many shapes and forms. Software gives personality, presence, and value to chips, cell phones, computers, glucose monitors, and automobiles. It is the means of engaging the customer, sustaining the relationship, and delivering value. Marketing executives must understand the power of software and help define and maintain its applications for delivering services, engaging and sustaining customer dialogue, and creating value for their business and their customers.

The Five Laws and the Future of Marketing

While certainly we can view these five laws as interesting technical observations that have very little relevance or value to marketing and its future, each of them will continue to affect how organizations are structured, how they compete with each other and engage partners, and how they interact with their market and their customers. By paying attention to these laws, a business will be able to differentiate itself and position itself in the marketplace.

At the foundation of all producer-consumer relationships lies information that, to be communicated effectively, must be constantly interpreted, refined, repackaged, and recreated into new, engaging formats for media. It must also be efficiently managed in the background to meet customers' expectations and to bring them superior satisfaction. Brand is ultimately customer satisfaction; it can take many different shapes and distribution patterns. Envisioning how a business might take advantage of technology to create competitive advantage will require a better understanding of the possibilities not only from marketing executives, but also from all executives.

Let's look now at what lessons marketers can learn from each law:

MOORE'S LAW

- "Make everything you and your customers touch smarter."
- Add entertaining and amusing features to products and packaging with animation, sound, talking instructions.
- Add remote services and monitoring via embedded devices; interconnect everything.
- Add intelligence to any product for instruction, embedded help services, sensing changes and feedback, and diagnostics.
- Incorporate user programmable features—"have it your way."
- Add connectivity for incorporating online access to services. Connect anything back to your Web services.

METCALFE'S LAW

- "Think networks"—of people, places, and things.
- Connect everything and everyone.
- Synchronize data to all points of customer access. Develop a coordinated, uniform services interface with one database of information and multiple points of access.
- Identify "consumer traffic patterns" and connect them. The connection may be physical or electronic; it may be via machine or human, machine-to-machine, or direct or via partners.
- Pattern alliances and points of presence for customer club card identification, extending offers and information for reengagement.

GILDER'S LAW

- "Show and tell" anywhere, anytime.
- Create new forms of uniform access in malls, airports, businesses, sport centers. Retail is a physical, geographic presence.
- Include remote education and training.
- Use company-produced "narrow-cast" programming for announcements, new product introductions, training, and product demonstrations.

THE LAW OF STORAGE

- "Distribute reusable information." Provide the same removable, portable directory database in a phone, laptop, desktop, PDA, or car.
- Embed video, music, recall information, and instructions in portable products and equipment.
- Apply storage to provide convenient, time-saving applications, such as TiVo, in order to allow on-demand viewing of content.
- Store books, catalogs, and magazine archives on miniature disks or devices like the IBM Microdrive or make them available through download services.
- Provide "field support in a box." Give sales and field service people all product, pricing, availability, instructions, standards, and applications in one portable, updatable database.

THE UNWRITTEN LAWS OF SOFTWARE

- Understand that software gives personality to products, devices, services, and businesses.
- Realize that software is perhaps the most tangible and creative technology that marketing can apply to its diverse universe of applications inside and outside of the enterprise.
- Follow the software and apply your imagination.

Technology's Limitations

As someone who has closely watched the rapid changes in technology and social adaptation over the past forty years, I am always amazed by how much people complain about their computers and other information and communication gadgets. This isn't because I am a patient individual— quite the contrary. I just remember how difficult and time-consuming the old ways of doing things were. But as the tools of the Information Age roll out into the hands of customers, we expect them to work reliably and consistently, and when they don't, we expect the supplier to solve the problem by providing whatever help and services we need. Sometimes we consumers do get reliable help and support, but more often than not we get poor response and inconsistent service.

While the popularization of new technology gives us a glimpse of a world where anything is possible, the implementation and support infrastructure behind the technology typically don't back that vision up. Sooner or later, reality catches up with the vision. Don't get me wrong: Dissatisfaction is an important type of feedback. New technology penetrated the market so fast that the infrastructure and technology—and many of the businesses involved with them—haven't had time to develop, let alone adjust to the demands of the market. These things take years, not months. Businesses must receive continuous feedback from the market if they are to change and evolve.

We often hear of market dissatisfaction with the U.S. telecommunications infrastructure, which was long dominated by government regulation of standards and pricing. Since deregulation little more than twenty years ago, new players with new ideas and technologies have entered the market. But the industry hasn't quite shaken off eighty years of regulation, nor has it adjusted to the freedom that comes with an open market. Meanwhile, technology forges ahead, unconcerned with government or business rules that apply to any particular industry.

For example, delivering broadband to the home has become a bottleneck. I still can't get a DSL connection to my home, although people within a few blocks of my house can. I can get the more expensive T1 service, and new players offered high-speed access in my area, but they haven't been able to follow through because they have either to build their own infrastructure or to piggyback on existing ones. Broadband technology is progressing, but in a way that's similar to a stream of water flowing downhill with many impediments in its path: It breaks through in some areas but stalls in others. Eventually, a main stream develops and others feed into it.

Businesses need to develop new business and financial models that can meet competition, broaden the market, and sustain the high cost of services. It took three different technicians three different visits to install a DSL line at my second home. Installing broadband at home is a high-cost service that can't be justified by the old methods of installing phones. Estimates tell us that over half of the installed fiber is "dark"—that is, it's not being used. Unless new applications encouraging frequent online information and entertainment use are developed, available bandwidth will remain a latent capability. John Chambers of Cisco compared this situation to the highway systems: "Unless off-ramps and arterials were developed, freeways would be useless."[28] Consumers expect information and service to be free or nearly so. But "free" doesn't mean free of costs, and many new and old players are struggling today with both adaptation to the new world of partial regulation and a new level of service demand. We need to find creative new service models that offer sustaining customer value and leverage information technology's ever-increasing propensity for improving service productivity.

Information and telecommunications R&D, progressing somewhat independently of business market cycles, drives each of the five laws I've mentioned in this chapter. All the laws in concert have added new capabilities, enormous productivity-enhancing benefits as well as new future visions of opportunity for both business and society. But the revolution is just beginning. And businesses will need to keep their sights on the future opportunities by listening to the technology and the customer, adapting as they learn.

Darwin's Law (Revised)

It's not the strongest of the species that survive, nor the most intelligent, but the one most responsive to change.[29]

Managing the rise of new technologies or the transition to new ways is as important as the adoption of the technology itself. Social, economic, industry-specific, and political factors all play important roles in creating the environment not only for a successful technology, but also for the successful market development. Many businesses have excellent technology but are unable to cultivate the financial or competitive business strategy to pull it off. Marketing, defined as promotion and awareness, is perhaps the least important factor in the success of a business in transitional times. What is most essential is to understand that the dust will settle and the businesses that remain will be those that have built the infrastructure for sustained growth.

Management, customers, and brands will all come and go, but an enterprise built on distributed market presence, customer access, and a flexible IT infrastructure can grow indefinitely. The laws are the foundation of market resilience. Having an appreciation for these technological trends should give management the optimism from future business and market planning. Optimism, after all, is the basis for most forecasts and visions.

Adaptation is the key to survival. Dot-com consultants promoted such shortcuts to success as "first mover advantage," "cyberbrand leader," "gorilla," or "e-category killer," when the long-term success of any business can't be summed up in a simple sound byte. We can never take industry dominance or market share for granted. Market forces that include technological advancement increasingly drive business. There are many stories of businesses that have been forced to change and that have chosen to adopt new ways of their own volition.

Like hidden, subterranean resources, the laws of the new marketplace bubble to the surface, often disrupting the status quo, but more often enabling new ways of doing things. They are the driving forces of market change, and they provide us with tangible, predictable trend data without the rigidity of fixed outcomes. While the laws appear somewhat inevitable, there is still much room left for the exercise of imagination, creativity, and innovation, the essential elements for competitive differentiation. And whereas risk is certainly associated with committing to the investment in new information tools, the evidence is clear: You have to play to win, and the laws help everyone do that. Tracking technology trends is not only appropriate for high-tech companies. Every business in the coming century will need to apply computing power, store and move information, design and deploy networks, and become more "IT smart" in order to command a sustained leadership position.

By understanding the laws of the new marketplace (which are more about economics than they are about technology), you can better anticipate the new tools that will lower costs while improving productivity, customer interaction, and market tracking. And that anticipation gives you a jump on your competitors. Most of all, the laws help us all to understand technology, and the intelligent use of technology stimulates creativity and delivers a unique customer experience. Technology doesn't just change the processes of work; it also changes the people who do the work. And that's worth anticipating.

Chapter Four

Forget about Loyalty

Problems with Branding

Today's consumer exists in a sea of novelty that both attracts and distracts. The erosion of brand and the consumer's trend to disloyalty have evolved from the economic and social fragmentation of society and from the personalization of technology, which gives individuals the tools to manage and control their own choices.

M ANY BUSINESSES have found that today's faster, better technology has helped them improve customer satisfaction and generate more repeat business. Greater customer loyalty should be next on that list, right? Surprisingly, it's not. In fact, technology has fostered not brand loyalty but brand switching. These days, brand loyalty seems to be eroding before our eyes. And because brand—which is, generally speaking, consumers' continuing expression of loyalty to a product, service, or company—is at the heart of a company's vitality, marketing is in for a shock.

What's causing this erosion of loyalty? One of the main causes is the wide variety of choices consumers now have, thanks to technology. As technology has lowered the entry barrier for tens of thousands of new products and services, companies are developing those offerings faster than ever before. Technology has also made it possible to create new channels of supply for narrower segments of the market than was economically possible before. It has also enabled a vast distribution network capable of managing an almost infinite number of products, and it has brought about CAE, "computer-aided everything"—computers help in the design, production, and distribution of an almost limitless variety of products and services.

The automation of the supply chain and the technology of logistics give us flexible and information-laden conduits of supply, and the transformation in means and methods of distribution—all enabled by information technology—is unprecedented. Technology has also given us the Internet, another factor in diminishing brand loyalty. Internet enthusiasts and pundits herald Web technology as a way to sustain customer loyalty, but in fact, just the opposite has occurred.

All that choice is a mixed blessing to consumers, because it attracts as well as distracts. But its effect on marketing is clear: Consumers are becoming less loyal to brand. They know what their options are as never before, and they have a lot more to consider than just brand.

While technology is a major cause in the erosion of brand, it isn't the only one. Society and culture have played roles, too. Not only has consumer loyalty to specific brands diminished but society in general seems to be far less loyal to anything. Factors such as the diversity of media, the variety of forms of entertainment available to us, our personal and work time commitments, and competition for our time have even encouraged a trend to disloyalty. As Harvard professor of public policy Robert Putnam describes it, we're experiencing a lack of belonging that stems from a decline in social capital.[1] Virtually every form of traditional community bonding organization—church attendance, club meeting attendance, citizen participation, voting, and company loyalty—has declined steadily. And while this decline may be more obvious recently, it hasn't happened overnight. It has been developing for decades.

Given change that is that marked and widespread, we shouldn't be surprised that its effects trickle down to consumers and their purchasing behavior. The nonstop novelty we see today, plus the events and media that fill our every waking moment, vie constantly for our attention, distracting us. The traditional notion of brand focused on cohesive social concepts, so it's little wonder that brand loyalty has declined. In a perpetual-motion society like ours, attention to anything is short-lived.

The incredible growth in media has also played a part in the erosion of brand. New media channels bombard consumers' senses every minute of every day. Look at radio. It may seem to have moved to the background, but it hasn't in the least. The average U.S. consumer has 2.5 radios (as well as 2.5 TVs) and can access more than 15,000 stations. Digital satellite radio will further expand the range of choice for radio listeners on a global scale.

Most marketers consider television the premier brand-building medium; certainly it was a driving force behind many consumer brands from the 1950s through the 1980s. But in the 1980s, cable television began to encroach on the major networks, and today, with cable and satellite television, consumers can choose from more than 250 channels. Nielsen Media Research tells us that as of 1997 the average household was receiving 49 channels, up from 19 in 1985. And thanks to the remote control device, these 49 channels have created an audience of channel surfers.[2] Today's consumers have access to more than 180 cable channels; if you have satellite television, the number jumps to 250. New, specialty channels are being added all the time: videos, games, and music—the list seems to grow by the day.

Generational factors come into play here. Approximately 45 percent of those born between 1965 and 1980 are channel surfers, whereas surfers account for only 20 percent of those born between 1909 and 1945.[3] Baby Boomers developed their consumer consciousness as television programming and broadcast advertising matured. Although you might think, then, that Boomers are more susceptible to highly promoted brands, remember that this generation also experienced, and supported, the growth of product diversity, convenience stores, and fast foods. They've also fostered the eager adoption of a vast variety of new businesses and services.

Consumers are gaining more control all the time. ReplayTV and TiVo are two digital video products offering consumer-controlled selection, recording, and programming of TV content. The device—or "black box," as *New York Times* journalist Michael Lewis calls it—is similar to the Internet in that it's linked to a network that can monitor and record changes in consumer viewing behavior. "Eighty-eight percent—88 percent!—of the advertisements in the TV programs seen by viewers of their black boxes went unwatched," reports Lewis.[4] And another factor contributes to the TV viewer's inattention: the remote. I speak from experience here. I don't think I've watched a TV commercial in five years. The second a commercial comes on, I flip to another channel and watch something else, anything else—another football game or some other show—so that I'm not "advertised at."

The biggest player of all in the media game is the Internet, which simply overwhelms all other media. More than 34 million unique domain names (Nike.com, Intel.com, and RedCross.org, for example) are registered worldwide, with almost 400,000 new domain names registered each week.[5] We're seeing more new products, more places to buy them, and more types of media available to obtain information from all the time—and remember, this is still the early stage of broadband Internet communications. Even so, consumers can access millions of sites and hundreds of thousands of products and services from locations around the globe. And because a buyer can access and search the Internet so easily, he or she can be constantly on the prowl for new sources, lower prices, faster delivery, and customizing services. By surfing the Net, a new class of consumer is learning to engage in long-distance information gathering and buying.

What all those media mean to marketing are more and more new, diverse options competing for the consumer's time. Just possibly, businesses are spending more money trying to convince people to switch their loyalties than keeping current customers satisfied and served. With that huge number of media channels seeking attention, a lot of the content gets tuned out. The consumer is at the controls, choosing exactly what he or she does or doesn't want to see. The personalization of technology, which gives individuals the tools to manage and control their own choices, has also contributed to the consumer's control. No more does a mass audience sit eagerly absorbed in the content of a one-minute commercial.

These media and technology influences may vary from culture to culture and country to country. The social and economic patterns within subculture groups vary greatly within megacultures such as the United

States, which is individualistic, and China, which has a collective culture. Management professors and authors Sirkka Jarvenpaa and Noam Tractinsky tell us that "in individualistic cultures, the needs, values, and goals of individuals take precedence over the group's. In collectivistic cultures, the needs, values, and goals of the group take precedence over those of the individual."[6] As we'll see in chapter 8, marketing systems must be sensitive and adaptive to cross boarder reaches of the new global capability of the World Wide Web medium.

The Disloyal Consumer

When we talk about brand, we're really talking about customer loyalty, which brings us to the customer-producer relationship and the use of new interactive technologies such as the Internet. This new consumer access medium, however, may be encouraging only disloyalty. A sort of virtual mobility is allowing consumers to move from one place to another easily, turning today's consumers into new-age hunters and gatherers. They're culturally driven mobile shoppers, unrestrained by time and place, continually seeking novelty and unique experiences that are readily accessible and economically advantageous. Media surfing with devices like the remote control and the mouse contributes to a mobility that in turn causes consumers to grow restless, turning them into entertainment and information nomads. As Robert Putnam explains:

> Anonymity and fluidity in the virtual world encourage "easy in, easy out," drive-by relationships. That very casualness is the appeal of computer-mediated communication for some denizens of cyberspace, but it discourages the creation of social capital. If entry and exit are too easy, commitment, trustworthiness and reciprocity will not develop.[7]

The consumer-producer relationship is becoming more transactional than personal, which fosters a brokerage marketplace in which, according to some experts, "the flow of materials and services through the value chain is coordinated by a decentralized price system. Relationships among firms can be short-lived, since price and net value received on a transaction by transaction basis determine the exchange of economic resources."[8]

In his book *The Loyalty Effect*, author Frederick Reichheld tells us that "on average, U.S. corporations lose half their customers in five years, half their employees in four, and half their investors in less than one."[9] In 1960, the average U.S. company listed on the New York Stock Exchange saw a 12 percent turnover of its shares. That percentage rose to 46 percent in 1990 and soared to 75 percent in 1999.[10] Many years ago, I heard a psychologist here in California say that divorce is prevalent not because people are unhappy, but rather because things are too good. "There are too many other possibilities," he said. We can certainly ascribe the same concept to modern consumers, well-educated employees, and stockholders. Many of us are enjoying the riches of plenty, and the daily passing stream of possibilities will not end soon. There may be variations in the economic cycle, but the new high-speed, efficient, information-abundant, interactive infrastructure is gearing up for more of the same. Increasingly, consumers are jumping ship and finding a whole world of options.

Adapting to and learning how to negotiate this brave new world can't help but change consumer behavior. As businesses learn how to improve the means and methods of delivering choice and novelty, consumers are learning to shop from their newfound social and market experiences. The grocery store is a wonderful classroom. In recent years, shoppers have found not only more diverse products but a massive number of new products in varying shapes, colors, and sizes, as well as new services. Carrefour, Europe's largest retailer and marketing pioneer, offers shoppers services ranging from watch repair to car rental, travel reservations, and wireless phone arrangements. Run out to the market for a quart of milk or loaf of bread and while you're there you can bank, drop off your film and dry cleaning, have your taxes reviewed and paid, buy flowers for that special someone, and take home a hot meal—all with one stop.

Retailers are learning a valuable lesson from this expanded one-stop shopping: that the proximity of services creates loyalty. Has anyone noticed that the grocery store is becoming the mall for consumable products as well as a center for consumer services? An environment like this can't help but build expectations for choice, novelty, instantly accessible services, and competitive prices. John Chappell, president of Nike Japan, told me that Japanese consumers have become so accustomed to novelty that Nike now introduces new models of shoes every three months instead of every six months.[11]

In the United States, consumers can feel overwhelmed when they consciously think about how many choices they have. As Michael Kammen notes, the paradox of the American consumer is that we compromise our values in the face of pragmatic market decisions all the time.[12] While people feel overwhelmed by 200 channels of TV or 100,000 items in a retail store, they continue to support low prices and the diversity of products and services available in the marketplace. They vote every day for diversity by choosing where and how they shop.

Producers are very aware of their customers' fickle nature, which has led to intense competition for viewers in television programming and on the Web. In 1999, cable passed network television in market share.[13] So in order to compete, television programming has become more bizarre and risqué to attract and hold viewers. "Reality TV" and "voyeur TV"—which represent anything but reality—are examples of the desperation that competition is causing. Television networks have reason to panic: Not only are the number of competitive channels increasing; according to a recent study conducted by consumer and media research firm Scarborough Research, people are shifting their "screen time" allotment from TV to the Internet. The study, which examined the changes in traditional media consumption of online users, found declines across all media, but the decline in television was striking: 23 percent of online consumers indicated that they view television less often since they began using the Internet.[14]

The Internet's take on our new consumer might be more realistic. While Internet site owners try to build loyalty by hounding users with banner and pop-up ads announcing cash prizes, free gifts, and trial offers, the executives who run those sites don't talk about brand loyalty. Rather, they talk about "stickiness"—how they can make their site "sticky" enough for the consumer to stay there for awhile, and to come back. The term reflects a break with the brand jargon of the past, but, more important, it tells us that those Internet executives are pretty realistic. They've admitted that Web users will eventually pull away and surf to other sites. With so many possibilities to explore and an infinite array of novelty a click away, who can keep users' attention on any one subject for very long?

Redefining the Indefinable

Brand has traditionally been the emotional glue that binds consumers to products and services. It's also a subject that, like religion and politics, elicits opinion and emotion from just about everyone. We all feel the need to defend or justify it. I have occasion to speak to many groups in many countries, and when I criticize the common perceptions of brand, I can be sure that several members of the audience will approach me afterward, ready for debate. And although I always acknowledge the importance of brand as *everything* a business does to engage, support, and sustain customer relationships, brand enthusiasts hear only my criticisms on the over-emphasis placed on awareness. But with more than half a trillion dollars spent each year worldwide on advertising and promotion to develop and sustain brand, it's easy to see why marketers are so defensive and why producers—not consumers—marry themselves to their brands and lose perspective.

To many marketing people, brand is more of a belief system or even a religion than a science. They don't question the methods and practices of branding today; their gospel is made up of business school case studies along with the latest well-publicized, attention-getting methods of today's hot companies. They assume that brand begins and ends with awareness, name recognition, and perception.

But the task of engaging consumers' intellectual and emotional qualities with the goals of creating awareness and finally changing behavior is complex and little understood. We too often assume that the way consumers behave is consistent with their knowledge, perceptions, and stated opinions. But despite all the focus groups and consumer research, despite the massive advertising and promotion campaigns devoted to new products, we see more product failures than ever. According to Robert McMath, president of the New Products Showcase and Learning Center,

> It is generally agreed that eight out of 10 consumable products don't make it in the long run, and some observers believe the failure rate runs as high as 94 percent. That means 94 percent of all new food, beverage, health and beauty, and miscellaneous household and pet products are not successful—never mind cars, electronics, fashion, and so on.[15]

While the promotions we're seeing may be more entertaining, they're probably not more effective.

What Brand Isn't

The following quote by a design firm executive illustrates the market mumbo jumbo that surrounds brand: "If a product is something that is produced to function and exist in reality, then a brand has meaning beyond functionality and exists in people's minds." Huh?

As you can see, defining brand is tricky. Let's start with an official definition, from the American Marketing Association in 1960: "A brand is a distinguishing name and/or symbol (such as a logo, trademark, or package design) intended to identify the goods and services of either one seller or a group of sellers, and to differentiate those goods or services from those of competitors." Marketers still use that definition today, and I'm certain that many still agree with it wholeheartedly. In fact, that traditional view of brand as a "recognized name" has become the justification for the status quo, giving marketers a rationale for spending unaccountable dollars.

The problem, as Terry Hanby has pointed out, is that the AMA definition is written from the brand owner's perspective, not the consumer's. In addition, Hanby says, the definition "treats brand as an extended product that can be decomposed into its elements without losing meaning." Finally, it suggests that differential pricing rests on a relationship between product differentiations.[16] Yet pricing is based on many factors entirely independent of brand or brand recognition, even pricing of so-called premium brands. Marketers long assumed that sustaining a premium price differential between a leading brand and a competitive one was the primary rationale for brand investment. Yet Mercedes found that it could not hold to its pricing structure in the face of lower-cost luxury cars from Lexus, and Procter & Gamble lost market share in several traditional brands after raising prices in 2000. When AMD (Advanced Micro Devices) introduced a high-performance microprocessor chip that was cheaper than Intel's, Compaq Computer abandoned Intel for AMD. Thus clearly the traditional definition ignores the consumer's experience with the product or service and the fact that the many options offered to the consumer may well be at parity.

It's also been stated by marketers that brand is a "promise" that, when fulfilled, creates trust. This view is the hardest to defend if we base it on the idea of branding as perception.

Traditional notions of brand are based on a certain assumption of consumer ignorance—the thinking is that consumers will trust the company's messages and products to deliver as promised. But studies have shown that most Americans believe that they live in a less trustworthy society than their parents did.[17] As a result, consumers are increasingly skeptical of messages that bombard them endlessly. In February 2001, the *Wall Street Journal* reported the results of research done by marketing research firm Harris Interactive and the research group Reputation Institute. Citing Philip Morris's expensive ad campaign to convince people that they are benefactors of social good, the *Wall Street Journal* states, "While advertising can be effective in getting the message across, it doesn't necessarily change opinions." Philip Morris continued to rank "low" on the trust scale. The article went on to say that "no news is good news." Johnson & Johnson enjoyed the most consumer trust, according to the survey, yet it was also the company that avoided the most limelight.[18]

The disassociation of brand from the new realities of business—technology, innovation, product and service development, networks, software, new forms of distribution, and cross-industry alliances—misleads marketers by suggesting that a brand is a product unto itself. In fact, brand, like quality and marketing, is an integral part of all enterprise activity. In reviewing the many files on brand that I've collected over the years, I find most brand advocates speak in generalities expressing vague notions on the subject. Indeed, I've noticed an increase in the number of articles in both the general and business press on the subject over the past decade.

In 1994, a study by the advertising agency Young & Rubicam showed that "brands are built first by differentiation, that is how brands are perceived; then relevance, or how personally appropriate is the brand; esteem, or how highly regarded is the brand; and familiarity, that is, awareness of the product."[19] To which we might say, "Duh!" Human affinities are obviously essential ingredients of any consumer activity. I can't see how this sort of analysis can help anyone trying to develop or sustain a brand. It's like saying, "To be successful, you must be successful." What's missing is the realization that perception is based on the consumer's experience. The quality, timeliness, accessibility, and immediate applicable benefits of the product or service influence the nature of that experience. Brand advocates tend to assume these attributes are given and that brand can be built independent of them.

What Brand Is

"I think, therefore I am." In the seventeenth century, Descartes's abstraction cut the world into two—one of ideas, the other reality. Over the centuries, as reality either confirmed or denied ideas, we have learned that nothing exists in the mind alone, but always in some relationship to reality.

"I brand therefore I am" was the hallmark of the dot-com's brief era. Every definition of brand that I've encountered tries to give meaning to brand in order to justify expenditures for attention. In 2000, I conducted a survey of 100 executives, in the United States and the United Kingdom, asking them to define what *brand* means to them. The results have led me to believe that there are almost as many definitions of brand as there are products. For example, one CEO said, "Brand is a name or some kind of visual image that strongly represents a company's product and something consumers can readily identify with." Another said, "Brands are mental URLs that point to a cluster of emotional affiliations. A strong brand will defy conscious attempts at reprogramming." Still another: "Brand is a strong and resonant promise which relates to deep human values and aspirations. A relationship of trust and clear parameters."

My own informal surveys tell me that brand has a thousand different definitions, and while no one seems to agree on an exact definition, "perception" seems to be one of the most common characteristics. No one in my surveys has suggested that the distribution infrastructure, innovation, standardization, information access, a pervasive network, consumer experience, or persistent presence was the basis of brand.

Many executives also assume that brand is a shortcut to demand creation. That may have been the case when consumers faced far fewer choices, limited media, and many fewer channels of delivery, but in today's world, where everything is media and information is increasingly disposable, where the marketplace is flush with choice and price is a high preference, the idea of achieving lasting loyalty seems doomed.

Brand may well be indefinable, or it may be definable in an infinite number of ways. And that is its strength. "Branding is, at best, an imprecise art," says *The Economist*. "Most consumers would be hard pressed to explain why, say, Levi's or Nike are losing cachet to such newcomers as Tommy Hilfiger."[20] Brand's primary asset is that it is complex and not well understood. Many consider it a magic solution that drives customers' desires to select one product over another in the face of competitive offerings. But if the matter were that simple, or just a question of awareness, anyone with the right textbook and financial resources could develop a successful brand.

In some businesses, brand depends almost totally on research and development. Pfizer's Viagra and Eli Lilly's Prozac are only two examples. Such revolutionary new drugs can build or change the reputation of a company overnight. Since pharmaceutical companies enjoy such high margins on proprietary drugs, they must invest heavily in getting to market first. As proprietary drugs reach the end of their patent life, the companies try to move the products into the nonprescription category. Johnson & Johnson's Pepcid and GlaxoSmithKline's Tagamet are examples of prescription products that are now sold off the shelf. In prescription pharmaceuticals, for example, a generic can rapidly take a large share of the market once a popular and successful branded drug's patent has expired, a move that has happened so often that "generic" has become a trusted brand in its own right—though what this really demonstrates is that price is a higher preference than brand.

Pharmaceutical companies are recognizing the power consumers yield. In recent years, they have moved drug advertising from technical magazines targeted at physicians to *Newsweek*, *Time*, and other popular magazines, where they address the consumer directly. These days patients are informed: When they visit their doctors, they bring with them printed Web pages, magazine ads on drugs, and questions about whether or not a new product would be right for them. Physicians have told me that often the patients have uncovered some news item or a piece of obscure research, and they turn out to be a step ahead of the doctors, which tells me that doctors are going to have to keep up or lose out to the information age.

The flip side is that consumers can also obtain biased, misleading, and often false information on the Internet. This type of problem will be with us as long as the medium remains and we have an open market-place. Trusted, reliable sources of information must be developed where people can be assured of the reliability of content. This isn't about image or brand; it's about a specific solution for a specific need and an experience that is verified by real-world experience. It seems likely that the pharmaceutical company, hospital, or individual with the most complete, unbiased Web page or easily accessible source of information will become the brand leader. Because the physical product requires a reference channel (a physician) and a fulfillment channel (a pharmacist) who both reinforce the trust experience, more and more of the information and communication will be direct between producer and consumer.

Despite the complexities that surround us, marketers still seem to believe that the formula for brand is simple. Let me give an example. A few years ago, I spoke to a senior management group at a large electronics company in the cellular phone business. Management's concern was the increasing cost of R&D for products that dealers were giving away free as incentives for customers to sign service contracts. I said that competition and pricing pressures would continue to grow as the world market expanded. From 1990 to 1998, more than 100 countries added cellular networks, adding up to a total of more than 160 countries. Soon wireless networks will expand to virtually every country in the world. Moore's Law tells us that costs will continue to decrease for the chips that enable portable devices.

I told this group that their company would have to "forward-integrate," that is, add innovative functions and services, reduce prices, and that they should begin to think of the company as a technology *and* service company. Service, once considered a low-tech operation, is now high-tech with software programs instantly responding to customer's wishes by linking their cell phones to a wide range of network resources any time, anywhere.

After my presentation, the next speakers came forward: They were from Procter & Gamble's Tide marketing team, talking about how P&G maintained the value of the Tide brand. They were impressive, and the company's marketing history brought added credibility to what they said. But I had a difficult time equating a cell phone with a detergent, and I had the distinct impression that most of the telecom executives in the room preferred P&G's promotional approach to mine. As it turned out, the company did miss the next wave of digital cellular technology, and that alone set it back in the market. So far, innovative companies such as Nokia and DoCoMo have assumed the leadership of the cell phone market. Both companies pushed the technology forward while integrating new services into and through their mobile phones. Innovating with technology gave both firms their market leadership position.

Holding onto the old definition of *brand* and thinking that real marketing is "consumer marketing" are dangerous assumptions. Despite fifty years of brand promotion, Tide has lost market share in the past five years. Levi's, another well-known brand, has been unable to use its brand equity to hold back the rush of young consumers to new brands such as Tommy Hilfiger. Microsoft tried to capitalize on its ubiquitous computer label and enter the mainstream consumer market with Microsoft Home and Microsoft Bob; both products failed miserably even though the company spent millions introducing and promoting them. Apple's success when Steve Jobs rejoined the company in late 1996 was due not to its much-publicized advertising campaign, but rather to the launch of the innovative and colorful iMAC product line—along with lowered prices. Levi's, Sears, Tide, Oldsmobile, and Buick all have "recognized" names, but that didn't hold their customers when such things as choice, novelty, technology, lower prices, and new forms of conveyance started hounding the customer twenty-four hours a day.

Despite all the attempts to enshrine brand within a particular formula, the companies that break all the rules seem to be the ones to gain the market's attention. Charles Schwab, for example, launched his very successful financial trading business by becoming a discount broker in a world that believed that people would trade only with established brands, and that they would pay a premium for doing so. Intel owned more than 80 percent of the microprocessor market before running its first "Intel Inside" ad. Had any company other than the established market leader run those ads, the ads would have failed. Likewise, Starbucks became a household word long before launching a national campaign. Can we say that these companies were not brands until they launched their national awareness ad campaigns? Successful company case studies fill the texts in business schools and the pages of the business press. We do learn from others' mistakes and successes, but creating a new brand isn't done by looking in a mirror. It's done by imagining the future.

Information and brand are often in opposing camps. If, for example, consumers knew that many products are the same under the skin—that, for example, car manufacturers use the same engines and chassis with different bodies, simply "branding" the cars as different; or that there is little difference between one PC and another since 80 percent of the products sold use the same components along with an Intel microprocessor and Microsoft software; or that all detergents were basically phosphates; or that generic drugs are basically the same product as the branded version, only cheaper; or that cosmetics companies custom-package the same makeup at specialty counters in department stores that can be bought off the shelf at a significantly lower price—if consumers knew these things, trust would fade rapidly.

Today, brand loyalty is virtual, and many consumers will choose a brand for pragmatic rather than emotional reasons. "Logo lovers, take heart. As the luxury economy sputters and stalls," reports the *Wall Street Journal*, "a boom in high tech fakes is shifting into overdrive. These aren't the old, tacky knockoffs that can be spotted a mile away, but a new breed of look-alikes, born of high tech manufacturing techniques and savvy packaging." The article quotes a woman from the exclusive Boca Raton, Florida, area saying, "I'm not too proud. The women here drive Rolls-Royces, but these days, they have no compunction about buying a copy."[21]

Mistrust of a brand or a company doesn't necessarily affect sales, but it does lead consumers to make a distant and more pragmatic choice. Such a change may not have immediate implications, but it could come back to haunt a brand if a competitor steps up with an equal or better choice. Nike's offshore manufacturing practices seriously eroded public trust, but consumers continue to support and buy Nike's products. After denying any such activities, the company responded by setting up a labor practices department and an ongoing system to independently monitor subcontracted consumer products manufacturing. Bridgestone/Firestone will have a very difficult time regaining public confidence in its tires after all the reports of injuries and deaths from blowouts. And even though "Trump" is one of the most recognized brands in the United States, with Donald Trump flaunting his views and wealth in the media almost daily, Trump Hotels & Casino Resorts ranks 527th—in the bottom ten companies—on *Fortune's* 2001 list of the

"Most Admired" companies. Brand built on trust or a promise is difficult to define, create, and sustain, particularly in a society where every point of view has an airing. And the effect is a more skeptical consumer.

The loss of trust isn't limited to products. Over the past few decades, we've seen traditionally trusted service "brands"—lawyers, congressmen, journalists, reporters, and other authority figures—lose consumers' unqualified trust. Gallup's annual honesty and ethics poll asked Americans to "rate the honest and ethical standards of people" in forty-five professions. Veterinarians scored higher than doctors, clergy, and policemen. While nurses, pharmacists, and doctors ranked in the top five, achieving very high to high scores of 58 percent to 73 percent, TV reporters and commentators dropped from 36 percent to just 20 percent in 1999, bankers dropped from 39 percent in 1981 to 30 percent in 1999, and newspaper reporters fell from 30 percent in the same period.[22]

I may be reaching to infer that the declining social capital and trust in judges and clergy translates to less confidence in advertised promises. But social morés are complex patterns of human behavior, and we often see them transferred from one action to another. For example, the Conference Board's reports on consumer confidence are intended to reflect the influence of consumer attitudes on expected purchase behavior. The release of a report, whether positive or negative, influences people's perceptions of the economy. It's not a leading indicator, but rather a report on people's recent experiences.

We'll find it even more difficult to identify trust as a key factor as information and telecommunication converge with access media, where everything and anything are manipulated and become a subject of discussion and scrutiny. Digital media have no special power to establish credibility with customers as they enable the deliberate manipulation of context and images—the true identity of the singers on a CD branded with a particular pop group's name, the actual location of the correspondent's report. Inventing context to support a particular point of view warps our view of things. Worse, most people are unaware that they are looking through unreliable lenses at what they presume to be reality. Digital media also have the facility to gather information about the behavior of the unsuspecting online user by tracking every click and purchase. While something like junk e-mail is only a minor encroachment on consumer trust, the unintended consequences of such marketing tactics may well escalate to consumer backlash and federal legislation.

Value and quality are perceptions, and they are important from a consumer's perspective. But for those perceptions to be more than just perceptions, a business must make sure that it delivers tangible benefits that are reinforced every time the customer experiences the product or service. Experiences vary with the changing market environment. In the boom market of the 90s, many products and services seemed affordable. However, by mid-2001, those same items may appear luxuries. The reality is that to adjust to the ever-changing desires of the new consumer, brands will have to change constantly. At a 1998 *Fortune* magazine dinner, Peter Drucker told me that he didn't see how any brand could maintain its primacy in the next decade, and that "it is obvious that choice is overwhelming any particular brand."[23]

I already know what the objections to my views on brand will be. "Brand is much more than awareness," the brand experts will say. "It's the uniqueness of the product, the quality and experience of the customer." And I agree. *Fortune*'s "Most Admired" list uses eight indicators of reputation:[24]

1. Innovativeness
2. Quality of management
3. Employee talent
4. Financial soundness
5. Use of corporate assets
6. Long-term investment value
7. Social responsibility
8. Quality of products/services

Although these attributes are the core of marketing, marketing itself isn't an item on the list, and it has very little power or authority to shape these reputation building blocks. Most marketing people would agree that these qualities add up to a company's brand. But my experience with marketing executives across many different industries tells me that the marketer says one thing and spends money doing another. Marketing's power, influence, and budget are increasingly limited to various forms of promotion.

Marketing has been obsessed with image, brand, and message making, and in the belief that such concepts will persuade the customers to respond as desired, companies have devoted sizable budgets to pursue those obsessions. The idea that customers are mutable to marketing-crafted messages is so ingrained in the thinking process that marketing executives have missed the opportunity to take control and responsibility for building and sustaining a communication infrastructure tying their business and customers together into an interactive relationship. Marketing is responsible only for the message or content. And content alone will never be able to sustain long-term customer relationships.

The Challenge for Producers

With the vast changes in the marketplace and in consumer loyalty, producers are definitely facing some real hurdles. Let's look at a few them.

Changing Symbols

Imagery has always been one of marketing's most powerful tools, but when we talk about brand, imagery isn't just a tool—it's part of the foundation. Icons are crucial in communicating the intangible aspects of brand. Businesses use symbols on buildings, letterheads, trucks, packaging, and advertising to tell consumers indirectly about their best features—for example, the quality of the products, the company's reliability, its leadership. But what happens when those symbols vanish?

The banking and brokerage worlds are good places to look at symbols. When I was a kid, my father banked at Brookline Bank, our town's only bank. Its architecture was impressive and quite distinct from other buildings in town. As you entered the doors, the large safe set against the back wall lay open with its thick metal door exposing the gate to the vault. The architecture delivered a message to customers: "Here is a safe, secure place to house your money." Banks once stood in the center of a community, a very powerful symbol in itself.

No more. My bank is a kiosk on a street corner, in an airport, or in a grocery store, a cafeteria, or a business lobby, either near my home or in a foreign country. Its symbol is "ATM." And while I know that ATM means "automated teller machine," which is part of a network of networks operated by a bank or by alliances of participating member banks, I know very little about how financially stable that network is or if it even resides in a building. When ATMs appeared over thirty years ago, the banking community was very cynical about them, just as they were with home banking via the Internet. Many bankers said, "It is too complex," or "People will not remember their PIN numbers," or "Twenty-four-hour service is not necessary."[25] Despite that skepticism, the ATM changed people's behavior because it offered persistent presence for an important consumer service. Consumers use the ATM service because it's always there when they need it. Symbols of trust emerge in the consumer's consciousness as they experience people, places, and things in the daily patterns of living. The ATM is one example but many others have become the symbols of satisfying service experiences—AOL, Starbucks, Wal-Mart, FedEx, Apple's iMAC, or Nokia.

Brand in the Land of Technology

Building brand in the technology business is more a matter of building alliances and relationships than it is of advertising. In technology, your brand is your network, which is why so many technology companies have divested marketing of the "business development" function and the responsibility for alliance relationships. While technology is a big advertiser in consumer media, technology marketing is much more of an industry infrastructure development process. The marketing of more complex technical products is based on establishing standards or compliance with existing standards, aligning with other industry partners, and integrating elements that others may produce into a complete solution.

Most online brands we recognize today will vanish within the next decade. The reason will have far less to do with their name recognition than with their inability to finance and build the global infrastructure necessary to maintain a persistent presence in the marketplace. AOL, on the other hand, is one of a few companies to see that the Web is only one of the many media it must use to reach consumers. Its purchase of Time Warner shows us that AOL envisions its future not as an Internet business limited by that medium, but rather as an entertainment/media company prepared to address the transient and mobile new consumer.

The continuing alignment of partners in the high-tech business illustrates the "shared solution" nature of the business. Marketing people in high tech who do not understand the role standards play in creating markets and market leaders will be ineffective. In technology markets, the standard is the brand. The battle between the U.S. Justice Department and Microsoft illustrates just how difficult it is to determine the difference between a standard and a monopoly. (The fact is that every technology business strives to have its product become the standard so as to enjoy dominance of the architecture and therefore of the market.)

Software developers think in terms of what processor technology to use in order to be part of a particular infrastructure composed of other hardware and software vendors and technologies. "Wintel," a contraction of Microsoft Windows and Intel, is a term used to refer to a particular architecture that dominates the personal computing environment. Software developers must align their technology to be compatible with the standards set by Wintel. Other standards such as Java and Linux compete with Wintel but each standard represents a brand applied to that particular technology market infrastructure. Companies become identified with particular standards and are often judged as successful or not based on their market share of a particular standard. In this case, a brand is a complex set of alliances with a whole network of other software companies, systems integrators, and often hardware suppliers. Users then feel secure in adopting a product because of both its compliance with standards and the company's alliances. We have only to read the daily high-tech news to see the steady flow of announcements of deals, alliances, cross-licenses, investments, and partnering in every segment. It's as though Kellogg's had to form alliances with milk, sugar, and coffee companies to assure consumers of their compatibility at the breakfast table.

For a software company, alliances and standards leadership or compliance are key to the company's branding and position in the marketplace. The relationship between Intel and Microsoft was essential to maintain the standard. And it was their design successes and relationship with IBM that originally gave both companies an architectural lock on the standard and the market. Certainly their customers continue to look to them for new products, and customers like to buy from industry leaders.

But new standards, new technology, and decreasing prices (cf. Moore's Law) must continue. New products in the software market are introduced on average every six months and in the chip market, every nine months. When Intel failed to address the low-priced segment of the microprocessor market, AMD took market share. When Microsoft failed to recognize the Internet as a new medium, it lost out to Netscape. When Sun, HP, or IBM misses an opportunity to take advantage of the next fastest chip or the next emerging technology, the one who does take the opportunity also takes market share. It's little wonder that Java and Linux, the emerging hot computer standards, are commanding so much attention from everyone. They represent "open systems," allowing any- one who can demonstrate compatibility and advantage to make improve- ments and add-ons. As standards, they encourage more industry players and even competitors to adopt them as standards, all of which means that innovations make it to the market faster. But most important, the industry leaders have announced their support of this software. Imagine a beer, soap, cereal, coffee, or automobile company keeping that pace or operating under those rules. In technology businesses, new price/per- formance thresholds are constantly achieved, old standards are revital- ized and new ones emerge, and with these changes, new brands always arise to challenge the current popular brands.

Hidden Choices

Achieving loyalty is a very difficult task in a marketplace of constant novelty and overwhelming choice. The logistics infrastructure for deliv- ering goods is increasingly sophisticated, linking the databases of vari- ous and remote suppliers so that purchase and delivery of a complete product or solution are coordinated from different sources of supply. The consumer doesn't see the multiple and complex interrelationships among supporting players. The browser, search engine, and "go-find" technologies make the decision process easy and transparent. As the various access media are embedded in cars, television sets, phones, appli- ances, shopping centers, and the workplace, choice itself becomes even more ubiquitous and unconscious.

Consumers often don't have any idea which producers they're deal- ing with. For example, Intel delivers more than half a billion chips each month through a diffused network of distributors such as Dell and

Compaq, along with tens of thousands of equipment suppliers. Visa is a diffusion distributor for Bank of America, Yahoo! and AOL are diffusion portals for hundreds of software applications, and portals on the Internet are information distributors through which businesses can supply all kinds of products and services.

Wooing the Disloyal Consumer

How does brand stand a chance in an environment like that? What's a producer to do? Fold his tent? Call it a day? No. Certain strategies do work; the evidence is around us. We'll start with a strategy that has limitations.

When marketing has problems, benchmarking is often viewed as part of, or at least the start of, the solution. The problem with that approach is that marketing is not generic. What works in one industry may not work in another; each one has its own unique market infrastructure that must be approached differently. Because of that, close analysis and in-depth research about the marketing processes and methods in one successful company may not apply to another company. There's just no guarantee that that kind of information is transferable. David Teece of Berkeley's Haas School of Business says, "Knowledge assets are normally difficult to replicate. Even understanding what all the relevant routines are that support a particular competency may not be transparent." He further points out that "some sources of competitive advantage are so complex that the company itself does not understand them."[26] Benchmarking is indeed valuable for executives to measure progress and learn, but they can't view it as a way to imitate "the best." It must become a way to stimulate creative new ways to differentiate your products and business from the competitive pack.

My marketing experience with all types of businesses over the past forty years has shown me that the businesses that succeed are the ones that have the most diffused and ingrained distribution networks with a diversified market presence. Today the information network is akin to the old physical distribution chain. Distribution is information based; it means linking resources and services direct to consumer access.

Early marketing emphasized expanding retail presence as well as adopting new production technologies and leveraging the new media of the telegraph, telephone, radio, and TV. As new ways of establishing presence developed, marketers such as Coca-Cola, Procter & Gamble, and Disney and relatively new marketers such as Microsoft, Starbucks, and Dell took advantage of them. From our rearview mirror of history, those advances appear simple and obvious and even slow to change. But those who did adapt prospered, while many more chose not to recognize the technological and market dynamics of their time and vanished. Gone are the DuMont Television Network, Philco, Dodge, Oldsmobile, Burma Shave, Digital, and Pets.com. Every business failure is the failure of a brand. The reasons and causes of failure are often complex and vary from business to business and industry to industry but the notion that brand is a static trademark or process of creating and disseminating the brand name is shortsighted.

Presence is a necessary ingredient in consumer products, but it alone won't do the trick. Businesses must mix in product innovation, pricing, and loyalty to existing customers. The half-life of a brand has no doubt shrunk from years to months. To keep pace today, marketing must deal with a new order of complexity. The communications and distribution infrastructure necessary to keep a market presence alive twenty-four hours a day, seven days a week, gathering information and closing the loop between consumer desires and consumer satisfaction, requires an understanding of how to apply the new network medium creatively, a task far more difficult than running an ad campaign. Unfortunately, most marketing people aren't up to the task. They still look at the various media as distinct and separate channels for message delivery, rather than nodes of a network connecting and distributing information. Most confuse the medium with the media, and end up blindly thrashing about in the Internet, using it as though it's just another form of TV.

Management must stand back and look at the big marketing picture. Businesses today may face the greatest challenge and opportunity yet seen in the history of marketing since P&G consecrated brand in the 1950s: that of reinventing marketing for the age of networks and the interactive consumer. The Web is the most evident new business phenomenon of our time; as such, it's viewed as a specific form of medium.

In fact, it's not a single entity, but rather a conceptual framework for social and business institutions. Today, people attend social events, for example, in order to "network." Most successful enterprises are not hierarchical, but rather a network of interacting functions and responsibilities. Political and financial networks extend across national borders. Whereas businesses have long had networks linking various operations, the new networks give unprecedented access to consumers as well. This growing ubiquitous consumer access using an increasing variety of low-cost devices will flip the broadcast world upside down.

The consumer network environment is indeed new. Rapid changes in the social, political, and economic climates on a global scale are unprecedented. The global enterprise is not only a reality; it is increasingly an essential aspect of all growth businesses, made possible to a greater or lesser degree by its network capability. Extending the enterprise to new territories and new customers means offering them a choice. As access extends in ways we cannot imagine to billions of consumers beyond the several hundred million online today, we can expect that patterns of behavior will change radically. This change will not result from enticing messages, but rather from the very presence of the new medium itself.

A marketing architecture—incorporating the customer, marketplace interactions, and enterprise-wide support infrastructure—is a crucial part of a successful strategy for dealing with consumer disloyalty. That's probably no surprise, since business networks have been with us for a long time. Coca-Cola, considered the most recognized and successful brand worldwide, delivers a billion soft drinks a day to consumers because in its 130 years of business, it has invested in a network of bottlers, distributors, and retailers around the globe. A Coke is still cheap and accessible. Starbucks also uses an architecture strategy. It has achieved its brand identity by giving consumers access to its products in airports, malls, and neighborhood shopping centers everywhere. Starbucks' presence almost rivals AOL's: I can order the same Frappuccino on Uchisai-wai-cho in Tokyo as I can at the corner of Fremont and Mary avenues in Sunnyvale, California. Without their diffusion network infrastructures supporting a market presence, brand, for all these companies, would be an empty promise.

The Future of Brand, the Brand of the Future

The proliferation of products and resulting increase in consumer choice are not going to slow down anytime soon. Nor should we want them to. Expanding choice is essential for free-market competition to flourish. Today's technology and current production systems are progressively providing more flexibility by improving productivity, mass customization, modularity, and programmability. Computer-aided design and manufacturing, supply chain automation, customer relationship management, and all the various forms of e-commerce, search engines, and other find-and-compare software technologies are evolving to give customers what they want when they want it. Such production systems enable made-to-order products and foster emphasis on services over products. As computers assume more of the process and functions, everything becomes infinitely malleable. Given the nature of diversity, the automation of commerce, and the milieu of the new marketplace, what can we say about brand and the future?

The very nature of who we are and how we participate in this world shows that we are different kinds of consumers. The degradation of brand to that of naming, personality, awareness, recognition, and recall isn't enough to hold today's consumers. It's based on a definition that is too fixed in time and space. Time and space for today's consumers are virtual, relative, and transient, not only because of the Internet, but because our society has taken on the qualities and characteristics of the transactional nature of networking. We live in a society of constant motion. In the connected world, access and persistent presence replace the traditional channels for brand. Geographic proximity will have more to do with establishing a successful product or service than any other form of promotion.

The factors that have contributed to the erosion of brand—technology, social and cultural influences, new media, and a rapidly evolving commerce infrastructure—also play to a more psychologically distant consumer. What all of this tells me is that brand loyalty is a thing of the past, and that in the coming years, you can expect your customer to be virtually loyal, at best.

Chapter Five

The Transformation of Today's Consumer

Preferences

Consumers are changing before our eyes. As easy access to

information and the power of choice it brings continue to grow,

the variety of consumer options increases. Today's consumers

act on self-determined preferences, much like the programmable

preferences in their computers.

CONSUMER SELF-AWARENESS has steadily grown over the past twenty years, owing to oversaturated commercial experiences and the accessibility of information. Today consumers know they're being courted, and they know how powerful they are in a marketplace where business repeatedly comes to them, seeking attention, support, and loyalty. They're more pragmatic than the consumers of the past, and thanks to more available tools for shopping and greater access to diverse products and services, consumers now have power over choice.

So far these changes haven't turned out to be radical departures from consumers' values. In fact, the increased power that consumers have doesn't have much to do with what they value in their daily lives—and many marketing professionals don't realize it. The relentless quest to find the core motivating "values" distracts marketers from understanding consumers' true nature. I don't mean to dismiss values as behavioral influences in people's lives; I'm saying only that understanding the mores of any society is complex and difficult. Historically, marketing has played with these concepts as if they were more art form than science. Values require interpretation; as a result, they are influenced by the interpreter's views of the world.

While consumers move from brand to brand, marketers keep trying to delve inside the recesses of consumers' minds and figure out how to bring them back to the brands they're supposed to know and love. After all, isn't a brand supposed to be a seamless extension of the consumer? Once a no-nonsense Bud man, always a no-nonsense Bud man. The sparkle on your kitchen floor is intimately tied to your self-esteem—and the floor wax that makes it all happen. For a long time, the marketer's premise has been, "Understand how consumers think, and you can influence their behavior."

The bottom line is that trying to understand consumers' buying behavior by understanding their value systems is futile. We don't know what people think until they act. And once they do act, their actions often conflict with what they say. But this is relatively new news; let's back up and see how we got here.

The Evolution of Consumer Consciousness

The twentieth century was a time when, thanks to the influence of Freud, the unconscious became a prevailing influence on all social development and interaction. The idea of values as the unconscious agents driving consumer's purchasing behavior caught on quickly in marketing thought. Researchers tried to uncover people's deep motivation patterns, and marketers treated them as if they were DNA messengers, stimulating and mass-replicating consumer desires, ambitions, and dreams. Even with a lack of empirical evidence, marketers believed—as did many of us—some set of Freudian influences directed the average consumer to purchase certain products according to deep-seated value systems.

The first publicized mention of American's common values came in 1922, with the publication of journalist Walter Lippmann's *Public Opinion*.[1] In 1935, George Gallup introduced his opinion polls, the first surveys to explicitly associate individual values with "public opinion." Although America was already a multicultural society, such observations helped individuals in particular social groups see that other people in this diverse society had common aspirations.

Behavioral psychology entered the commercial marketplace in the 1950s, when some ad agencies hired "motivational researchers" to probe the recesses of the consumer's mind, assist in developing campaigns, and thereby exploit the link between want and need. It was an easy step to align behavior theory with opinion polls, and then with promotional activities, to exploit previously hidden wants, desires, and fantasies.

No one is certain when the idea of associating personal and social values with consumer behavior first appeared, but we do know that Stanford Research Institute's VALS (Values and Lifestyles questionnaire, a type of psychographics research) popularized the concept in the early 1980s. The research focused on trying to pry into the behavior of the American consumer; in so doing, it was a popular form of psyche voyeurism. In 1997, for example, SRI reported that "contrary to the notion that TV-watching is a group experience, at least 50% of Americans frequently or almost always watch television alone. This solo viewing is possible because two-thirds of U.S. households have two or more TVs." The study further found that "online services in general are not yet compelling enough to provide serious competition to traditional television programming. Most online users spend relatively little time online."[2] But just two years later, Nielsen/NetRatings reported that the "average U.S. Internet user went online 18 sessions, spent a total of 9 hours, 5 minutes and 24 seconds online and visited 10 unique sites per month."[3] Nielsen also reported that the average television viewer watched TV 7 hours, 26 minutes a day.[4] I don't expect the Internet to wipe out television; my point is that because research like this is unable to reflect the discontinuous change that alters people's lives, its value is somewhat questionable.

In an effort to uncover the motivations behind consumers' purchase decisions, ad agencies and other marketing organizations subscribed to the lifestyle and demographic studies. In the mid-1980s, Apple Computer retained a well-known national research firm to determine whether consumers would continue to buy personal computers. The resulting research warned that because Americans didn't want more technology invading their lives, the growth of the PC would be difficult and slow. The explosive PC revolution more than proved that prediction wrong. Predictions for the future for a new technology or any new product and the market's acceptance of it are more a matter of vision than science. For marketers to rely on research that attempts to connect consumers' values and opinion with their eventual behavior is risky, and just as likely to fail as succeed.

Even though the theoretical link between consumer desires and buying behavior hadn't been proved, advertising and marketing schemes began to tap theories on how cultural values are expressed in society, and to rely on those theories to attract consumers and influence their behavior. Author and sociologist Juliet Schor has echoed this belief in her book *The New Politics of Consumption*:

> *What is more generally true, I believe, is that many consumers do not understand why they prefer one brand to another, or desire particular products. This is because there is a significant dimension of consumer desire, which operates at the non-rational level. Consumers believe their brand loyalties are driven by functional dimensions, but a whole host of other motivators are at work—for example, social meanings as constructed by advertisers; personal fantasies projected onto goods; competitive pressures. While this behavior is not properly termed "irrational," neither is it conscious, deliberative, and narrowly purposive. . . . The realm of consumption, as a rich historical literature has taught us, has long been a "dream world," where fantasy, play, inner desire, escape, and emotion loom large. This is a significant part of what draws us to it.*[5]

The process of the human mind, translated into behavior and action, is highly complex, involving a host of social interplay that is well beyond the power of any one form of or attempt at manipulation. The more we try to figure out the dimensions of human motivation, the more we find the unexpected, unfathomable, mercurial human being.

At one time we could view values as sets of beliefs and actions that bind communities together. But the word *value* has become almost as overused as the term *brand*. We've come to use it as a prefix or suffix to anything and anyone: social values, corporate values, consumer values, market values, religious values, political values, and value chains. We ascribe *value* to anything to which we want to give transcendental attributes. *Value* can describe the relative worth of something, or it can be an ideal we aspire to and by which we judge others and ourselves. We value honesty, loyalty, fairness, and success. We also value family life, education, and loyalty. Our values remain concealed until we reveal them through our words and actions. Values can hardly be discerned from a questionnaire or focus group. They must be "read into" the things we say and how we say them.

People's abstract associations do indeed drive them to buy certain classes of products and services. But which associations are driving which purchases? Even if we could establish accurate correlative evidence, linking personal or social values with American consumer behavior is fundamentally flawed because we live in a culture that believes and does completely different things. Alexis de Tocqueville saw this dichotomy in us 150 years ago, observing that individualism and idealism were just as characteristic of Americans as were conformity and materialism. American cultural historian Michael Kammen has observed that we seem to be both conformists and anti-traditionalists at the same time. Our values, or high ethical standards, are quite often compromised by the ethos of the marketplace.[6]

From Values to Preferences

Values are difficult to fathom on both an individual level and on a grand social scale. As an individual, I am much more likely to communicate freely and directly about my preferences as a consumer than I am about my values. Consumers change tastes, habits, wants, desires, and behaviors all the time. When I recently asked a teenager why she no longer preferred Tommy Hilfiger jeans, she said, "That was last week." The fad had passed and her preference had changed. But had her values changed? Of course not. She had simply changed her preferences, and both of us knew what she *wouldn't* be buying the next time she went shopping for a pair of jeans.

Instead of values, today's consumers act on sets of self-determined preferences, much like the preferences you can program into your computer—preferences such as which font and type size you want for your documents. For now, I have chosen to file my e-mail in a particular folder and to divert junk mail into a "toss file." Those are two of my preferences—for now, at least. Because preferences are programmable, I can easily change them at any time.

Consumer behavior mirrors this programmable software. Consumers often make a selection based on the preferences of, say, price, novelty, access, and do-it-yourself service before they even consider any particular brand. While some consumers may strongly prefer a particular brand, the preference usually doesn't last. Brand, in fact, is probably not something e-consumers consider when they begin their search prior to making an online purchase decision. And as the power of choice grows, thanks in part to easy access to information, loyalty to any single preference will probably decrease. In other words, as the number of choices increases, loyalty to any one of them will decrease.

In our information access society, consumers' perceptions of products, services, brands, and commercial relationships change all the time. And while we may not be able to forecast the nature of these changes, marketers must become better equipped to adapt rapidly to the consumer changes that do occur, something that marketers can do if they focus on preferences. While values require complex human interpretation, preferences are more pragmatic and directly actionable; thus they can be linked to R&D, new products, features, and services. In this era of rapid and unforeseeable revolutionary change, businesses can use the established information infrastructure to respond to the specific elements of consumer preferences. They can engage in an ongoing analysis of the stream of customer transactions, constantly monitoring and adjusting them to meet their customers' needs in all their permutations.

Consumer Preferences Today: The Top Five

User preferences vary from situation to situation, depending on circumstances. Sometimes price is extremely important. In other situations, being able to choose from and combine many options takes higher priority. Today the top five consumer preferences are, in no particular order, choice, price, novelty, simplicity, and speed. (*Access*, the term I use broadly for physical and virtual market presence, is also a preference; because I discuss it in chapters 2 and 8, I won't dwell on it in this section.) Other preferences may include brand, quality, and self-service, but I will address only the top five, because they have increasing primacy over brand. Depending on the consumer, the buying situation, the time of year, economy or other factors, the order of preferences can change: Sometimes novelty trumps choice, just as price can override choice.

The following list shows how consumer preferences have changed in the last two decades:

CHANGING CONSUMER PREFERENCE PRIORITIES[7]

1980–1985	2000–2005
Brand	Choice
Quality	Access
Convenience	Price
Price	Novelty
References	Speed
Service	Trust/Reliability
Novelty	Simplicity
Utility	Service

Choice

In a 1988 article, I wrote that choice was gaining greater value than brand. I based my thesis on two phenomena: first, "other" was one of the top market share leaders in almost every industry category, ranging from computers to beer; and second, technology was leading to the creation of a wider variety of products and services, as well as to more channels of delivery to willing and increasingly savvy buyers.[8] Brand aficionados vehemently protested my views, saying that brand was still the preeminent reason consumers chose a product or service, and pointing out examples of products and companies with dominant market share.

It's important to distinguish between market share/ownership and the consumer's experience of choice. Even though a company like Procter & Gamble can own a large share of the market, the consumer sees aisles and aisles of an increasing diversity of products, not just P&G products, at the grocery store. Anheuser Busch holds the largest individual market share for beer in the United States, but when beer drinkers in Minnesota shop, they see not just Budweiser and other Anheuser Busch beers on the shelves but a multiplicity of brands, including Grain Belt, Pig's Eye, Grain Belt Premium, Grain Belt Light, Grain Belt Premium Light, Pig's Eye Pilsner, Pig's Eye Lean, Pig's Eye Ice, Pig's Eye Red, Pig's Eye Nonalcoholic, and Yellow Belly. Intel and Microsoft both own the largest share of their respective markets, but their product catalogs are filled with variations and options on any one product. At your local retail computer store, the wide variety of PCs with myriad permutations of software configurations shows you why consumers don't get very excited about who manufactured each operating system or microprocessor. As long as consumers perceive they have choice over the applications, they're happy. We also see this phenomenon in the business-to-business marketplace. Every business struggles with the task of keeping its expanding price list from overtaxing inventory and service costs, but the bigger and more powerful the customers, the more options and variations they demand.

We've seen ever more diverse products and services coming through both old and new distribution channels. Thanks to new design, manufacturing, and logistics systems, the marketplace sees a constant flow of novelty: New names, products, and services enter the market all the time (the U.S. Trademark & Patent Office issues more than twelve hundred new trademarks each week), and many quickly become household names. Think of Starbucks, Yahoo!, Amazon.com, AOL, Intel, Dell, E*TRADE, and multitudinous others. In November and December 2000, my wife and I received almost a thousand catalogs in the mail. Most went straight into the recycling bin, but as I leafed through each day's arrivals, I was awed by the quantity and diversity of products available.

Large retail stores have such a wide variety of products that they might track 300,000 or even more stockkeeping units (SKUs), and well over 50,000 different products line the shelves of the average U.S. grocery store. "Other" still holds a commanding market share in cookies, beer, clothes, software, personal computers, car production, cosmetics, and financial services. Cell phones, free to users for the price of a service contract, are available from thousands of suppliers throughout the world. And in the high-tech world, hundreds of companies manufacture personal computers; the market expands as more and more devices rely on chips to connect machines and people.[9]

Today virtually no product is immune from market innovation, segmentation, and the resulting fragmentation of product lines. Manufacturers themselves help drive the choice preference, and brand extensions and private label business add to the proliferation, sending an experience message more effectively than any broadcast message of differentiation. Look at the choices that Coca-Cola gives shoppers: Its products now include Coke, Diet Coke, caffeine-free Coke and Diet Coke, Diet Cherry Coke, Sprite and Diet Sprite, Lymon, Mello Yello, Mr. PiBB, Fresca, and Fanta and Diet Fanta, among others. PepsiCo and other major suppliers offer an equally diverse and expanding line of drinks. Entrepreneurial regional and niche players such as Snapple Beverage Co. and South Beach Beverage Co. (SoBe), with their selection of "new age" natural drinks, were eventually acquired by the larger suppliers with strong distribution capability. PepsiCo bought the SoBe line and Britain's Cadbury Schweppes acquired Snapple Beverage Co. This one example can be extended and applied to almost every industry—high-tech as well as financial services. It is a business cycle that delivers and supports consumers' ever-expanding preference for choice.

More and more businesses and retailers are also using incentives to attract and hold their customers. More than half of all Americans belong to at least one loyalty program. But are they working? When the *Daily News Record* posed that question to store executives, most were "very reticent to give any quantitative measures of success, giving 'soft' rather than 'hard' answers to the question of bottom-line performance."[10]

Brands may come and go, but the underlying ability to design, manufacture, and distribute a variety of new products, as well as variations of existing products, is increasing. One day many consumer products may be wholly customized, but that day is in a distant future. Consumers will continue to be pursued with new sizes, shapes, colors, variations, permutations, and innovations, with multiple ways to buy and pay. Today, partial customization is the state of the design and manufacturing art.

Price

There are only so many customers to go around, and the competition for their hard-earned cash has intensified in recent years. For some time now, producers have been "buying" their customers by offering them two-for-one discount coupons, rebates, mileage awards, and free software to induce loyalty. Ironically, this practice has been a major factor in creating consumer *disloyalty*.

The Web has reintroduced the old pricing mechanisms of auction and barter. While we may not see all goods and services coming under the rap of a cyber-gavel, Internet auction sites have certainly influenced consumers' views on pricing. In 2000, 29.7 million registered users traded $5 billion worth of merchandise on eBay. In the eBay marketplace, shoppers can trade and bargain for deals on cars, art, jewelry, theater tickets, and myriad other goods and services. eBay is not starting a new trend, but rather picking up on one that has existed in the U.S. marketplace for many years; the Internet just encourages and facilities the shopping and negotiating process. According to marketing professor Indrajit Sinha, "The vast sea of information about prices, competition, and features that is readily available on the Internet helps buyers 'see through' the costs of products and services."[11]

The "better price" phenomenon on the Web has hit almost every industry and business, from legal services to molded plastic parts and fasteners. Forrester Research estimates that the number of online bargain hunters will grow from 3 million to 14 million by 2003.[12] The economic downturn will only serve to stimulate online bargain hunters. And it's not only on the Internet that buyers are looking to save money. A *Business Week* article titled "This Year, It's Chic to Shop Cheap" reported that some high-income consumers have started shopping at discounters such as Wal-Mart, Kmart, and Target.[13]

Are consumers aware that they're choosing low price over brand, and even over what has traditionally been called *quality*? I think they are. During an interview with NPR's *Morning Edition*, Mike Bond, a vice president at an airline seat design and manufacturing company, was asked, "Why are the coach seats so crowded on certain airlines?" His answer was that although passengers complain, time and time again, they choose price over comfort.[14]

Brand no longer provides a pricing umbrella. Marketers have lost their hold on price controls as product information and costs are shared and cross-checked within buying consortia or chat groups across the network. Software brokers now search and find the best deals on car loans, mortgages, books, and medical plans, and from books to cars, consumers go online to check availability and compare prices. We can expect a lot more of this bargain hunting in the future; its full extent will be revealed as more sophisticated "search-and-compare" software becomes available. Price, like quality, has come to mean "the best possible value." But with ever-increasing access, consumers will change the definition of value again and again and again.

Novelty

My wife, who has devotedly driven BMWs for over twenty-five years, recently chose a Lexus SUV because she liked the features better than those on the comparable BMW. "You know what you just did?" I asked her when she'd made her decision. "You just selected novelty over brand."

Today technological progress has translated into perpetual novelty, something consumers and Wall Street have come to expect. In fact, novelty has become commonplace, whether you're talking about fashions or cars, pocket calculators or software. Providers introduce new services, gadgets, and appliances with upgraded built-in features (including features we may never use) every day. More than 31,000 consumer products were introduced to the American public in 2000.[15] And the number of new products and permutations of existing products and services within the business-to-business marketplace no doubt equaled or exceeded the number offered in the consumer market. Every day, customers are bombarded with ads, news articles, direct mail, sales calls, and e-mails about new products. Consumers have come to expect that whatever is coming to market next month will be better and cheaper.

This anticipation of novelty can have a negative effect as well. Many of us hold off buying an automobile, computer, cell phone, digital camera, or software application, assuming that the next new product or series will have more features or better performance. Many high-tech businesses "preannounce" new products, which freezes buying decisions and preempts competitors until the product is actually available. Even though preannounced software is known by the pejorative term "vaporware," software companies still engage in preannouncing and keep consumers on tenterhooks.

The number of new product introductions is doubling every two to three years, creating niches within niches, all crowded with competitors. Most high-tech businesses report that they derive more than half their revenues in any given year from products that are less than two years out of development. All that novelty doesn't mean that customers are dissatisfied with the products they're using when they decide to switch. It just means that something new is always catching their attention and meeting their novelty-seeking preference system.

We fear that change may drive customers away, but in many circumstances the need to pay attention to change only keeps consumers more tuned in. Bob Greene, syndicated columnist for the *Chicago Tribune*, made that point in an article about MTV and its rotating cavalcade of hosts. The cable rock network tossed out the old rules and proved that a network need not be loyal to its stars, their current viewing fans, or industry convention. "MTV made huge stars of young, inexperienced announcers, and got rid of them as soon as they became famous," says Greene. "If you have a star, you must do everything to keep him or her, or your viewers will leave your network. Right? Wrong."[16]

Simplicity

There's a real yearning for simplicity today. You see it everywhere: in home design and architecture, in management and corporate organizations, in Web navigation and devices. Today Amazon.com lists more than 400 titles on the subject of "the simple life."

I understand that yearning. In spite of all the much-ballyhooed technologies that are supposed to make our lives easier and more enjoyable, our lives seem filled with activity and the simplest of things seem complex. Seemingly simple tasks such as getting from place to place by car or plane, getting a bill corrected or an item returned, dealing with the health care system, getting cable TV adjusted, and ordering DSL service can turn into hours-long ordeals. The more gadgets I buy, the more time I seem to spend programming, updating, downloading, syncing, and calling for help.

Case in point: I recently ordered a digital projector online from Compaq Computer. The box arrived on my doorstep within days. After all, we live in the New Age of Retailing: fast shopping, fast delivery. But inside the box were *two* projectors. So much for convenience, I thought, and my feeling of satisfaction evaporated. Have you ever tried to return a product that you didn't order? It takes time, and it quickly becomes a frustrating experience of being put on hold, being transferred to different departments, explaining what happened several times, and then being responsible for seeing that the extra shipment is returned. When charges for two projectors showed up on my American Express bill, I had to spend more time calling to fix that. When I discussed the whole problem with a customer service representative at Compaq, I told her I'd ordered online. "That happens a lot," she said sympathetically. I'm pleased with the projector; getting only *one* of it was the hard part. Perhaps I should have called in my order, or even taken the radical step of just going to the computer store and buying it in person.

This post-technology yearning for simplicity may run in my family. My son, a jazz musician in New York City, refuses to answer his e-mail. Although he's quite computer literate when it comes to composing and arranging music, he says that if he answers his e-mail, the senders will write back again and expect him to enter into a continuous dialogue. This is too much to ask. He doesn't have the time, he says, to take on another obligation, especially when the obligation placed on him is outside his control. He phones a lot.

And my wife's motto is "Keep it simple." One way she does that is not to link too many things together. For example, she doesn't like being on the same network with my computer. "The more things are connected, the more problems come up," she says. And she's right. A pervasive and complex network of interconnections underlies most transactions in the world today. When aberrations occur, that understructure can become visible. Complexity and simplicity exist side by side, more complementary than oppositional, but behind the simplest of interfaces resides a host of complexity.

Flick a light switch and think for a moment about the electrons flowing across thousands of miles of copper wire through transformers, power stations, and generators. A similar kind of infrastructure now ties business inventories into airfreight schedules, truck depots, highways, and grocery shelves. Nobody is worried about—or even sees—the complexity as long as the lights go on and the lettuce is fresh. It's the same with cell phones, which most people hadn't even seen until ten years ago. Users see and touch only twelve buttons. Inside the plastic shell, a few chips, each little bigger than a thumbnail but containing millions of transistors, encode and decode your voice and send it across continents via a network of computers, fiber optics, repeater stations, satellites, and local networks, and back again, all in a matter of microseconds. But the best part is the phone itself: It's become cheap enough that when it breaks, we throw it away. Simple solution, hugely popular item.

From chips to networks, simplicity is always the goal, but when everything is interconnected, incompatibilities enter the picture. Standardization helps immensely, which is why so many technical companies develop alliances and partners. In effect, they're creating a product or market standardization that enables customers to buy without fearing that they'll get a fragmented solution. And standardization simplifies marketing. No matter what business, the concept of "plug and play," or a Lego-like approach to integrating products with others on the market, helps customer adopt and buy new technology because it's simple and easy.

In business, simple product design is far more than a matter of aesthetics and customer eye appeal. Simplicity increases reliability and is necessary for good quality. It's a means to achieve productivity through efficient design of processes and products. Minimizing steps in a process, creating smaller task-oriented teams, eliminating paperwork—each of these strategies helps get things done quickly and efficiently. Fewer components—even though each component may be more complex—mean less trouble. For example, the microchip has vastly increased the reliability and quality of all machines by integrating (through an integrated circuit) many functions into one small piece of silicon. Like the light switch, the chip inside products manages the internal complexity—all the user experiences is the touch of a key or a click of the mouse and the resulting information or action. The typical automobile is made of 14,000 parts, which are divisible into subsystems, but the user need be in touch with only a few to be a driver. A simple interface manages the complexity.[17]

The market revolution for simplicity in computers started with the Apple Macintosh, which exemplified the most differentiation and appeal. My eighty-three-year-old father-in-law uses an iMAC, and so do each of my five grandchildren, all of whom are under the age of ten. Steve Jobs is the one who pushed through the vision of simplicity. He believes that products should be technically elegant and that their design should convey the aesthetic qualities reflecting that elegance (and he's the one Silicon Valley executive who carries this philosophy through in his business and personal life). Until he returned to Apple in 1996 and introduced the iMAC two years later, Apple had been in a ten year innovation drought. During Jobs's absence, Apple's management had not understood that ease of use—simplicity—*was* the company's brand.

Speed

I was relaxing under a beach umbrella in Hawaii, reading and listening to the sounds of my grandkids jumping in and out of the surf, when I heard the buzz of a cell phone. Sitting under the umbrella just a few feet away, a man reached into his beach bag and began a lengthy business conversation. While I don't go quite that far, both my wife and I do check our e-mail every day while we're on vacation. We feel like we need to. The very presence of the medium creates an anticipation of need. The diffusion of digital information alters our sense of time and place by shifting the paradigm from a fixed location to anyplace, anytime. For executives in this "Real-Time Age," ignorance isn't bliss; it's stress. If we're not connected, we don't know what's going on. And with such widespread access to the network, something is always going on. Personal computers, the Internet, faxes, cell phones, and pagers turn any location into an office. Some of us have even come to enjoy being tethered.

Instant cash is available from an ATM almost anywhere I travel. Home diagnostics tests for glucose, cholesterol, blood pressure, and pregnancy provide instant answers for health needs. Credit card verification takes a swift swipe of the card, and tailor-made coupons are presented to shoppers based on their current purchases. More than 400 communication satellites circle the earth, enabling us to access distant events, as well as connecting people and machines around the globe.

While the phrase "time to market" came into common use long before the advent of the Internet—and while time and timing have always been critical factors for business success—technology's tendency to "speed up" time creates serious challenges for business. Executives today—indeed, all of us—sense an internal ticking of the clock that never lets us forget that goals and objectives must be achieved within a finite period that passes all too quickly.

Technology has decreased the time it takes to acquire and use information, make decisions, initiate action, deploy resources, and innovate to nearly zero. We live in a "real-time" world that is synchronized by the functionality of high-speed computers capable of assimilating information and responding virtually simultaneously. The marketplace is the classroom for studying the consumer, and what we have learned is that this technology has created the "never satisfied customer" (which is the subject of my book *Real Time*).[18]

Fortunately, the same technologies that lead us to expect real-time fulfillment also give us tools for conducting real-time business. Executives can and must learn to use these new tools and to become completely comfortable with their applications. To make the best-informed judgment and the best possible decisions anywhere, anytime, they have to have the very latest information.

And while it's true that the sound of a beeper or cell phone can shatter the serenity of a remote beach, the feeling of being connected does give us a sense of security. When I'm on vacation, I spend an hour or two each day answering my e-mail and forwarding important tasks to others so that issues or clients receive immediate responses, not because I feel forced to, but because doing so lets me to relax. I know that problems are being addressed, and I don't have to worry about being engulfed by an e-mail tsunami upon my return—a situation that would almost instantly reverse any feeling of renewal that I got from my vacation.

Preferences are consumer responses to the economic and social environment. We expect human values to have a certain permanency or overriding effect on society as the environment changes, whereas, preferences are pragmatic consumer responses to the current marketplace.

Perhaps the events of September 11, 2001 will have far-reaching consequences for our society. While the nation's response increased the public's expression of our long-standing values, this catastrophic event will not change the consumer's ability to chose and change their preferences. One change may well be the increased preferences for security and privacy. Occasional stories appeared in the news concerning executive kidnappings or worse, raising concerns but implying that such incidents were relatively few and isolated to certain politically volatile regions.

Throughout the last decade, most consumers experienced the freedom of mobility, both physically as well as virtually. Executives and tourists traveled about the world filling the airplanes and hotels to capacity. The supporting travel services grew rapidly as well as the information and communication infrastructure connecting travelers with their office or home anyplace at any time. The mobility and freedom across the World Wide Web reinforced the consumer's mobile experiences of the physical world.

Catastrophic and unexpected events, however, interceded and are now causing a change in our expectations and behavior. For the business or vacationing traveler, security, or personal safety, has become the highest priority. Price and time have now moved down the list of preferences. Governments and businesses will require (and some will demand) more personal information in order to assure everyone's security. Privacy is assurance of information—personal or business—confidentiality. The sharing of medical records without the patient's permission is an invasion of privacy. However, in the new networked world, the rules of personal safety and personal security are interrelated. In hindsight, the debate about personal information privacy and security using the Internet now appears as an interesting academic discussion. Suddenly, it has all become very personal.

Trust: Security and Privacy as a Preference

Trust is not simply a human-to-human requirement for building a relationship; it's an attribute that we expect from inanimate things as well. I trust my car brakes to work reliably when I need them, and I trust my ATM to keep others from accessing my money and personal information. As we rely more and more on machines and networks for maintaining commercial relationships, we also trust that the connecting systems will ensure privacy and security.

Although these concerns are somewhat latent in business and consumer commerce today, the breach of electronic trust can have a significant negative impact on business. In 1994, a young Russian hacker, along with several accomplices, gained unauthorized access to Citibank's cash management system and transferred $10 million to the bank's accounts around the world. The initial monetary loss was significant, but the loss of trust was far more costly to the bank. The subsequent loss of business resulting from customer concerns and competitive poaching "has been estimated as being as high as some billions of dollars."[19]

Privacy is a major issue and concern for marketing—at least it should be. But many marketing programs today gather customer information and use it without the consumer's knowledge. Not only when you make an online purchase but every time you visit a Web site or touch an electronic connected device, someone is collecting information. When you sign up for a credit card or subscribe to a magazine, chances are the sponsoring business sells your address to a list broker. You can track this kind of activity by misspelling your name on a subscription order form and then noting the junk mail you receive addressed to your misspelled name. Few Internet users realize that when you click on a Web page, a "cookie" is often downloaded to your computer memory. It acts like a locator beacon, sending a signal back to the Web site originator when you go back to that site. And the tools for cross-referencing various customer databases with various forms of access are getting more and more sophisticated. The new embedded electronic media are far more subtle and surreptitious than broadcast media. And because these systems are so sophisticated and complex, they are fraught with potentially huge marketing issues. One is privacy.

Consumers and producers have shown less enthusiasm for demonstrating concern over privacy and security than you might expect, even though viewing these two concerns as anything less than a priority may be a "brand accident" waiting to happen. Each year hundreds of millions of people go online to engage in text conversations, buy products, and sign up for information services, all with little concern for privacy—or so it seems. There's certainly a nagging concern in the back of people's minds as to the integrity of the network and the privacy of personal information they provide during any type of online transaction, but when it comes to taking prohibitive measures, most consumers have no idea what to do or how to go about protecting their personal information. And most companies address the issue only when a problem arises or a hacker gains unauthorized access. According to Bill Crowell, president of software encryption company Cylink and former deputy director at the National Security Agency, "Business models before the

Internet accepted a certain amount of fraud as part of the cost of doing business. But with the Internet, fraud may be repeatable on such a large scale that it may no longer be possible to pass costs on to customers."[20]

Users seem to feel that privacy and security, two distinct issues, are embedded and *expected* services. After all, I don't sign up for a separate "connect via a secure server" when I use an ATM. Business-to-business hasn't been very aggressive about security, either. Microsoft itself had its databases invaded by hackers in 2001. But businesses and consumers may awaken and become more scrupulous about these issues as more and more electronic interaction takes place directly between producer and consumer. If brand is the embodiment of trust in the producer-consumer relationship, as many claim it is, then privacy and security must become major concerns for marketing. I suspect that every industry will find growing concerns from customers and employees as commercial and private interactions via networks flourish. They may find that proactively addressing these latent concerns is a means to build genuine trust. In the long run, they may also save money by avoiding lawsuits and the necessity of crisis management advice.

Preferences are not the same as values. Rather than attempt to analyze a set of vague concepts, business can both tune into and rapidly address changing consumer preferences. Every day, retailers collect data in intricate detail on consumer preferences. And once they identify your preferences, they can monitor and qualitatively address, measure, and even influence those preferences through interactive dialogue. And in so doing, they must make sure that the transaction is secure, to protect consumers' privacy.

Preferences will change over time and will vary widely depending on the social and economic context of a particular market. Stepping into the market today with a new product, service, or change in price is precarious. The present methods of forecasting how consumers will respond to anything new are inadequate; marketers must ultimately rely on human judgment and experience. Aside from actually spending more direct time in front of customers, marketing executives must shift their attention to better understanding and use of the information generated and gathered from daily purchase transactions.

Experience, along with current customer activity information, is the best way we have of making judgments about customers' potential behavior. At best, doing so is still a high-risk activity. Rather than prejudge consumer motivations and behavior, businesses would do well to engage their customers in a continuous dialogue in order to gain better insight into their preferences. They must then translate those preferences into new products and services addressing choice, price, novelty, simplicity, proximity, and so on.

In the future, marketing will wholly depend on machine-to-machine interaction, eliminating the need for sociological interpretation and relying instead on real-time transactional information and rapid response within a trusting relationship. The concepts of mass customization and self-service are the future; they are what the huge investment in the e-commerce infrastructure is all about. Such systems enable any preferred attitude, value, want, belief, or desire to be addressed in real time. The objective is to eliminate the risk, cost, and complexity of doing commerce in an entirely unpredictable marketplace.

Chapter Six

The Customer Experience

Persistent Presence

Persistent presence is a consumer's consistent and reliable experience with a producer at any time and in any place. It comes from a combination of factors enabling sustained consumer access and repeatable experience through multiple formats and media. The logistical infrastructures that sustain a consistent contact experience lie at the foundation of persistent presence.

THEOLOGIAN PAUL TILLICH REFERRED to *presence* as the ever-moving boundary between past and future. In an ever-changing, competitive marketplace, consumer preferences and their perceptions are always in flux. The new information and communication tools give marketers the means to monitor and respond to consumers as they cross the boundaries of change. When a business has persistent presence, the consumer enjoys a consistent and reliable experience with that business at any time and in any place—over time. The concept of persistent presence relies on an intelligent information infrastructure enabling a continuous dialogue between the marketers and the customer. Staying in touch means being present in order to listen, learn, and respond.

Today, network technologies link all points of customer support and contact—direct or retail—through supply chain management systems.

The information obtained from sales transactions are recorded, acknowledged, monitored, and moved across the support network where computers and software systems verify, respond, and direct the information for managing the customer's request. These systems are efficient, secure, cost saving, and serve the customer primarily by ensuring the delivery and supply of products and services to the point of presence.

For a business to make its presence persistent, it must create a logistical system that focuses on both physical operations *and* communications: the customer must be ensured of continued—that is, persistent—customer feedback and service. In the coming years, we can expect that these information logistics systems will dramatically improve customer information monitoring and the business's response capability. Computers and software systems can now listen and respond to the ever-changing consumer's preferences more efficiently than people. In effect, these customer dialogue systems will assume more and more of the marketing role by delivering customer satisfaction.

Let's look at each of these forms of presence individually. Some types of "presence" are tangible, such as a producer's outlet in an airport, mall, or grocery store, or at a business or on a campus. Presence can also be more transparent, as exemplified by the embedded software or components in the computer you use, or by services that are offered remotely (through a PDA, GPS, cell phone, or kiosk). A company can also achieve presence by partnering, integrating, or piggybacking its product, service, or message with those carried by compatible businesses, or offering it as an information component of a total access customer solution. A company can have persistent presence via a combination of "hard channels," activities that deliver a tangible fulfillment of the customer need or want, and "soft" channels, which deliver informational sources of reliable reference.

Presence through the Digital Network: Banking at the Gas Station

Historian Michael Kammen has observed that the physical, intellectual, institutional, and social boundaries in American culture are continually shifting. Today's new networked infrastructure gives businesses the capability to move along with those boundaries, and to adapt as society adapts. As technology and society continue changing, underlying computer and network technologies will help businesses understand the consumer-market dynamics and to adjust and respond appropriately. The computer—not people—will best simulate and anticipate wants and needs, for several reasons: First, technology is infinitely programmable and has the ability to learn from past "experiences," allowing it to customize responses, quickly and cheaply. Second, computer systems speed multiple forms of information through diverse forms of media networks to an increasing variety of access devices. Third, information systems and networks are capable of responding consistently twenty-four hours a day.

By connecting all participants in a value network, the rapid flow of information and response changes time and space on demand. Any fixed position or conscious moment can be morphed into a point of presence. The sense of strangeness disappears from novelty as persistent presence absorbs whatever is new into the flow of daily behavioral patterns. The ATM is a good example. Its ubiquity has created a powerful sense of trust. Few consumers realize that the ATM is not a single entity but part of a network of banks and retailers. But that doesn't matter, because we've come to expect to find an ATM when we need one, and we also expect it to perform accurately, reliably, quickly, and consistently. Those expectations come from our past experiences with ATMs, and our unconscious adoption of, and reliance on, the technology reflects our assumption that ATMs will continue to perform reliably in the future. In short, we've developed trust in the ATM—and trust is one thing that all successful brands engender.

A recent study on brand has concluded that "brand awareness is temporary unless accompanied by a strong and memorable customer experience."[1] I'll go a step further: The consumer's experience with a service or product doesn't have to be memorable; the service or product just has to be adequate, affordable, accessible, and convenient. And that means persistent presence. Whether the company is E*TRADE or Starbucks, consumers form perceptions based on personal interactions, how the system of services responds, and, most important, on the persistent presence of an accessible, intelligent interface. Experience with persistent presence offers immediacy, novelty, memory, and simplicity, and in today's fluid real-time environment, it replaces broadcast brand awareness. In fact, the customer's experience of a product or service is the very thing that builds and sustains brand. Any physical location today delivering persistent presence is both an access point and a node on a network. Connecting all the customer access points, synchronizing the information so managers are operating from the same book and page, monitoring sales and inventory and other performance criteria—all present the customer with consistent experiences online as well as offline at various geographic locations. The difference between persistent presence and "place," as defined as one of marketing's Four Ps, is that a digital network provides a coordinated, simultaneous flow of customer support information to and from all points of access. The network enables services that benefit both the supplier and supply chain management as well as the customer. Those services may be inventory and financial management, supply chain integration, distant employee training, or direct customer input. The alignment of operating practices at each point of access demonstrates compliance with the business's strategic goals. The business's IT network must have the same goals as any marketing effort—to develop and sustain customer satisfaction. Even though *place* today can be anywhere, the customer benefits from continuity of experience.

Networks cross the boundaries of diverse but contingent businesses, breaking through and creating new forms of presence. Toyota has entered the telecommunications business because it sees the automobile as a potential medium for delivering content. Just as the cell phone will morph into a multimedia device for voice and data, the gas station will probably become a place where you bank as well as refuel. Over time, Disney and Apple may find that they have more in common than they now think: Both, after all, are looking for new ways to present consumers with products and services that integrate entertainment and information.

From a consumer's viewpoint, information is an integral component of any product or service. Information is a chameleon in its various representations because it can change its meaning and relevance in response to the changing market environment. For example, a "good value" in a booming economy may be "expensive" in a down economy. Because information is intangible and can have many different interpreted meanings, everything and everyone that interfaces with the customer becomes an information distributor. For instance, Tiger Woods is an information distributor for both Nike and the PGA, just as Nike is a distributor for Tiger Woods and the PGA. Every automobile is a distributor of some branded entertainment system. Visa achieved its worldwide presence by using various banks and financial institutions as distributors of information. In short, almost everyone, in one way or another, is an information distributor for someone else. We trust and rely on some more than others. The most effective are those that become part of our daily living pattern and are integrated into places we go and things we do. We trust them because they deliver a reliable experience.

The key to keeping the customer's experience fresh and engaging is connectivity. Although it's best to directly connect with customers, it's not always possible or convenient to do so. Keeping track of the customer's purchases and service activities, as well as providing direct feedback when possible, allows a business to respond quickly to rising concerns as well as to keep the engagement fresh with new products and services. The interactive nature of being constantly connected with all the points of presence gives managements an opportunity to adapt to the changes in the market. Persistent presence, as contrasted with brand, emphasizes the interactive and operational infrastructure necessary to deliver a consistent consumer experience. Presence implies much more than awareness. It also means an intelligent, direct feedback network with embedded services either to the point of presence (the channel) or direct to the customer. The operational infrastructure is what sustains the customer relationship, however, so persistent presence really doesn't rely on a promotional activity but on sustaining a company's brand presence.

As information and marketing continue to converge over the next decade, we'll see more and more new, creative ways to interface with clients and customers.

Physical Presence: Location, Location, Access

Fast-food companies often use the term *point of presence* to describe their outlets in communities. As Professor Merlin Stone, IBM Professor of Marketing at Surrey European Management School, points out, customer "loyalty" is more a matter of geographic convenience than anything else.[2]

Starbucks is a company that certainly understands the importance of physical presence. In fact, its presence established its reputation well before any national advertising did. On a recent trip to Tokyo, I walked outside my hotel and found a Starbucks right next door. I stopped there each morning to get coffee, and I used the location as a temporary office for brief afternoon meetings with my Japanese partner. It was as if I were only a block away from my home in Silicon Valley. Since then, Starbucks has achieved even deeper penetration into our daily lives by introducing coffee stations into office buildings. Now employees no longer need to walk down the block to a Starbucks. They gather around the Starbucks coffee station and brew their own lattés. (As a side note, some think that Starbucks has done a better job developing a brand for stop-and-go coffee establishments than for itself. Many of the small successful cafés that dot the landscape of the United States and Europe are frequented simply because they're geographically convenient.)

Today Starbucks operates more than 3,000 points of presence in Asia, Canada, the United Kingdom, and the United States—in office buildings, shopping centers, airport terminals, and grocery stores, basically any place where consumers gather. The company has become much more than a coffee company; it's really a social phenomenon and a taste bud entertainment company. The Starbucks product line includes thirty or more different types of coffee drinks and coffee beans and a variety of teas, food items, and beverages as well as mugs, coffee makers, coffee grinders, and storage containers. The company sells its beans to restaurants, businesses, airlines, and hotels, and it distributes products through mail-order and online catalogs. You can buy coffee ice cream (made in association with Dreyer's Grand Ice Cream) and ready-made Frappuccino, a bottled coffee drink (produced in association with PepsiCo), which in effect turns Dreyer's and PepsiCo into Starbucks brand distributors.

And what will sustain the Starbucks phenomenon? Persistent presence recreates a familiar experience by maintaining consistency at all access locations. It is best accomplished using an intelligent support management network, which ensures the alignment of operating goals with all points of presence. Ted DellaVecchia, CIO of Starbucks, put it this way: "It's a matter of getting your company in the rhythm. Here's a metaphor for those of you who play golf. It would be like [thinking], 'If I could just get my hands to go right on this grip, everything else would be fine.' But it's an entire rhythm. The whole swing requires everything to work in synchronicity."[3] Such a synchronized system permits the efficient exchange of sales information, inventory control, and operating protocols, and it helps monitor events such as the progress of new product introductions and local competitive promotions. Many networks, such as those operated by Sun Microsystems and IBM, offer sophisticated interactive operational networks as well as companywide broadcast networks of announcements, speeches, and employee training programs.

Not all business and commerce networks need be based exclusively on electronic networks. Nonetheless, for any growth business, scaling an exclusively human marketing network is cost prohibitive. Starbucks relies on its network of managers to ensure that each location complies and maintains consistency with overall corporate objectives and goals. Human response time slows with scale, however, and there are too few good managers to go around. But as Starbucks grows, things are changing. The capability to scale operations is important for any growth business but it is also vital for any business that must continually improve productivity. The growing dominance of Wal-Mart as the world's largest retailer demonstrates how the application of new information and network ideas enables low-cost, competitive operations to scale and to expand with consistency. Starbucks established itself by its innovative persistent presence and uniform processes and business rules. I suspect that in the future we will see an increase in the use of IT to automate and mange their expanding businesses. Starbucks isn't ignoring IT but it has not been using it aggressively as a strategic tool. It does have a PC-based point-of-sale system to track sales and other information, but that kind of system is not unique. DellaVecchia is a firm believer in IT's role in the future of the company. "A company growing as rapidly as we are depends on technology," he says—and the challenge is simply to keep up. "We need new ways to run in-store technology beyond the current client-server, and while our visions would clearly be to have totally thin and Web-based devices, that doesn't work for the size of the network we're going to need to run to connect 20,000 outlets." Next on the agenda? "Things aimed at customer convenience, loyalty, and improvements in business-to-business," DellaVecchia says. "What we call our big, hairy, audacious goal is an enterprise portal on a global scale that allows each user segment to access what they want."[4]

Starbucks is thinking about the use of technology as a way to engage the customer as well. In 2001, it announced a joint partnership with Microsoft and MobileStar to develop services that leverage the power of the wireless broadband network. Customers will be able to download the latest information on local arts and entertainment and shop online while enjoying their lattes in Starbucks shops. In addition, customers who use the MobileStar wireless broadband service will be able to check their e-mail and even access corporate intranets to stay connected to the office. According to Steve Ballmer, president and CEO of Microsoft, "Starbucks' customers will enjoy an even better in-store experience, thanks to our combining Microsoft software and technology with Starbucks' focus on serving its customers' needs."[5] Imagination, innovation, and consistency are the hallmarks of this rapid-rise-to-fame coffee shop network. The challenge will be to maintain novelty and low-cost operations—for in spite of the company's claims about superior coffee beans and processing, its chief offering is coffee-flavored drinks, imitations of which have popped up everywhere. For Starbucks, maintaining its leadership depends on continuing to do what it's been doing so well: expanding its presence and imagination into a variety of new markets and channels. To do so, it will need help from IT.

For businesses relying on only one channel such as the Internet, physical presence can be tricky. For example, the online grocer Webvan invested $1.2 billion before closing its doors. Peapod, a Boston-based online grocery store, was losing money and was acquired by Royal Ahold, a Dutch supermarket chain. Users seem to love the convenience of online grocery service, but the problem is that too few users are spread over a large geographic area. The complexity of the business model and the cost of an efficient infrastructure are very high hurdles for online-only retail businesses to surmount. Amazon.com is as yet not profitable even after seven years of investment.

It's easy for online companies to establish customer access; the hard part is spending the time and money to build the sustaining infrastructure. Online retailers must achieve profitability, maintain low-cost delivery, build the required traffic, and meet customer expectations for cost, service, and timely delivery of products all at the same time. The enormous support cost structure is at the heart of the survival issue. Federal Express and DHL would rather make commercial deliveries than home deliveries because it's not very profitable to deliver packages to widely dispersed homes. On commercial deliveries, they can turn a profit on shipments as low as $15 because single drivers service up to 200 business sites in the same geographic area. The cost of delivering a product to a neighborhood self-service grocery store is well below the cost of delivering goods to the consumer's home.

Some online grocery stores have approached the new Internet channel with caution. Tesco.com (an online operation of Tesco, Britain's largest supermarket chain), for example, has simply added online delivery services to its traditional supermarket operations. By taking a low-cost, evolutionary approach, Tesco.com achieved profitable sales of $422 million in 2000. When I asked a retail executive here in the United States why the traditional grocery store couldn't go online and supply its local market with both walk-in and delivery services, he said that was impossible because the local grocery stores are not set up with Webvan's highly automated operations. "Delivery services that fail to get the math correct," says Lise Buyer, director of Internet/New Media Research at Credit Suisse First Boston, "will come and go in relatively short order. Those that understand and accurately charge for the full cost of the exceptionally complex 3-minute-window delivery systems stand to become incredibly important in retail's future."[6]

Webvan is an excellent example of a well-known brand that didn't "get the math right." Home delivery services are timely, playing into the lifestyle patterns of highly mobile and busy consumers. Their value (or brand, if you will) depends on the timeliness of their service, on the presence of their delivery vehicles in communities, and on the quality of the perishable products they deliver. Sustaining their brand, on the other hand, means making money.

Embedded Presence: Now You See It, Now You Don't

Embedded presence is corporate presence that is transparent to the consumer, such as when one company acts as a distribution channel for another. For example, Intel has persistent presence because its processors are designed into computers and related equipment manufactured by Dell, Compaq, IBM, Gateway, and thousands of other companies. The same is true for Microsoft—even more so when you consider how many PC buyers would choose a computer based on whether it features a Microsoft operating system. In fact, when asked how Dell's brand has changed, company founder Michael Dell said, "A big piece of our brand is being the most efficient and effective way for customers to buy Intel and Microsoft technologies."[7]

Linear Technology and Microchip Technology present two interesting examples of embedded presence. Both companies provide chips that perform functions inside computer keyboards, telephone systems, refrigerators, automobiles, and seemingly a million other applications. But the names of the companies are quite obscure. Linear Technology has a track record of positive growth with fifty-eight consecutive quarters of profitability over 20 percent and twenty-four of those quarters over 50 percent, while Microchip Technology, a bit younger, has had over 20 percent profitability for the past twenty-five quarters. Another company with embedded presence is BEA Systems, a Silicon Valley company that builds software that manages and integrates all Web applications for e-commerce transactions. By continually advancing its technology, using the Web to initiate user trails, and signing up solution partners, the company has been able to maintain the lead in its market space. It has almost two thousand partners (distributors, if you will), which include system integrators, independent software vendors (ISVs), and application service providers (ASPs), which carry the company's message and software to more than ten thousand customers. The general consumer public probably isn't aware of it, but they encounter products from these companies every day, because they are inside (embedded) many of the devices we all use. The "Intel Inside" advertising campaign didn't create Intel's market position—it just made us all aware of an existing situation: that most computer companies were choosing to install Intel microprocessors. The irony is that the standardization of components and computing architecture has limited the number of components manufacturers can choose at the same time that it has expanded consumers' choices of applications and means of access.

Presence through Services:
Tangible Experience of the Intangible

No company can entertain thoughts of mass customization without molding its business into a service model. Today, everything from chips to software, cars to computers, lipsticks to perfumes is a commodity and is forcing price to become the key competitive differentiation. Companies must look for new business models to sustain growth, margins, and customer loyalty. Services offer the opportunity to break out of the commodity price maze. Adding services, however, is not easy either. It requires an understanding of customers' needs and wants, applied imagination, and a constant connection through a consistent, reliable customer interface. All kinds of businesses are now defining themselves as service businesses. IBM has for many years sold hardware to customers, but under Lou Gerstner, who became president and CEO in 1993, IBM's Global Services business has exploded worldwide, with $35 billion in revenues and almost $9 billion in profits in 2000. Services now account for over 37 percent of IBM's business. Global Services helps IBM customers better manage and implement its IT resources and is now the largest e-business services company worldwide, dominating every market area, including Europe, Asia, and the United States.

Other companies must find ways to embed the services they provide into diverse products and distribute them through as many avenues as possible so that customers have a *tangible experience of the intangible service*. In fact, to engage and sustain a customer, a service must have a physical presence or some tangible representation. A service cannot be touched, placed in inventory, or returned with a money-back guarantee. Services rely more heavily than products on symbols, references, and tangible expressions of their presence. A monthly statement, cash, incentive programs, an ATM, a doctor's white smock and stethoscope—all these are tangible, visible things that provide evidence of an intangible service. Yahoo! launched its own magazine, for example, and E*TRADE is opening retail offices (which is a wise move because the companies that will be most successful at online commerce will be those that already have multiple forms of customer presence).

For online services to achieve persistent presence, they must develop other ways to deliver total access and a tangible customer experience. Customer conferences and satisfaction surveys are often valuable not only because they provide crucial feedback to companies, but also because they give customers an opportunity to identify the benefits of the services with specific experiences. Similarly, e-mail or other interactive communications with customers help make a service appear tangible—such contact enhances, sustains, and solidifies the producer-consumer relationship. Lynn Shostack, vice president of Citibank in the 1970s, wrote convincingly on this subject. She saw an inverse relationship between the characteristics of products and services. The more tangible the product, the more intangible its attributes must be. Intangible services, on the other hand, require hard evidence of their value to enable customers to make judgments. Shostack noted that because a service is already abstract, "service realities appear to be shaped to a large extent by the things that consumers can comprehend with the five senses—tangible things."[8]

Because the Internet is a soft channel, providing only visual information, by itself it's not strong enough to sustain consumer loyalty. As synchronized networks take hold, businesses with multiple points of access will be able to offer tangible reinforcement more often and at different access points. For example, when I order a book from Borders online, it would be great if the Web site were to prompt me to choose whether I want to receive the book by mail or go to a local Borders outlet to pick it up. BevMo.com, a wine, spirits, and beer superstore chain in California, gives customers the choice of home delivery or a pickup from a local store. Customer identification and other purchase information is synchronized and available at all twenty-one stores and at www.bevmo.com so shoppers who register free with "ClubBev" can be readily identified and given incentives and rewards across all access media.[9]

But when an investment Web site charts a user's portfolio and updates it in real time, that's also presence through services. However, that presence is reinforced by direct interaction with brokers, investment advisers, or an online or in-person seminar on investing, retirement plans, or government bonds. Bricks and clicks businesses have the advantage of touching the customer in many different ways to make an intangible service tangible, to make the consumer aware of the service through one of the five senses.

Two companies emerged early as recognized leaders of online trading, Charles Schwab and E*TRADE. Thanks to its multiple forms of presence, Schwab has a distinct edge. The company is ready to do business any place, any time, offering client access through its 372 branches, through touch-tone and speech-recognition phone services, and through its Web site. Because of the company's early jump on Internet technology, Schwab can claim the Web's largest encrypted site, where it does more business online than any other firm in the world. In addition, Schwab offers its customers direct face-to-face services through a network of 5,800 independent investment managers. This service now accounts for 30 percent of Schwab's customer assets.

Schwab executives understand that investment in productivity-enhancing systems can lead only to increases in market share, particularly when competitors are cutting back. Despite dismal market conditions in 2001, Schwab announced a long-term commitment to buy BEA Java server software to strengthen its position. Ronald Lichty, vice president of Schwab, said the new software would enable the firm to finish projects 30 percent faster and with fewer people.[10] From a marketing viewpoint, a recession may be an opening, in that it increases the speed of change by giving visibility to companies with weak infrastructures and limited resources while giving the resource-strong an opportunity to invest and build market share.

Being Down Is Never Out: The Role of Presence in Down Cycles

From Coca-Cola, Sears, and Procter & Gamble to Apple Computer, Hewlett-Packard, and Cisco, many well-known companies have experienced hot and cold cycles in recent years. Their problems have stemmed from an anemic economy to outdated strategies, lags in new product introductions, slowness to adopt new technologies, poor management, and even combinations of all the above. Whatever the cause, the result of a corporate cold cycle is that the competition gains ground and customers fall away. This is especially true in business-to-business and financial consumer service markets, where information about a company's financial performance is readily accessible, and where good financials build customers' confidence. You could even say that in today's broad-based online trading marketplace, good financials establish a company's brand.

For most companies, changes in external forces precede the cold cycle; for example, a company may become aware of new competition, or new technology, or new consumer preferences. Internal changes come about because current management has not anticipated or responded quickly enough to the external forces. Overly narrow perspectives and management's lack of confidence in anything new often cause corporate progress to lag. Many companies spend large sums of money researching their customers, subscribing to industry forecasts, and studying the competition, trying to avoid the very mistakes they inevitably encounter. Still others try to justify using outdated business models in new competitive times. Traditional marketing models can't help in these situations. The problem is that marketing is ill equipped to deal with the complexity of technology and the competitive market environment. Companies that experience a cold cycle are unable to invest and exert the corporate leadership required to integrate and coordinate all the functions necessary to deal with change.

When problems begin to arise, marketing's usual response is to focus on message development and some form of broadcast to distribute a newly configured response. More often than not, marketing budgets are cut in down cycles. When brand is considered a distinct entity unto itself, it's of little help in warding off corporate slumps or in providing the creative solutions necessary to address the fundamental ills of the down cycle. Brand has long been viewed as something that's internally driven rather than market-based. That is, it is traditionally developed inside the organization and promulgated by broadcast media, which in turn are expected to change consumers' perceptions and behaviors. In fact, companies often perceive and portray brand as a product unto itself, which they can modify simply by changing the message.

To help a down-cycle company find its way to an up-cycle, marketers usually try to change consumer perceptions, a task that often involves such things as selecting a new ad agency, slogan, or logo, and developing an extensive advertising campaign. Sometimes a company will even decide to change its "corporate identity" to cure its poor image or lack of customers. During the year 2000, a record number of U.S. companies—2,976—changed their names. Most changes resulted from mergers and acquisitions, but 37 percent just felt they needed sexier names.[11] The assumption that any makeover or cosmetic approach will address the fundamentals of creating and delivering value to the customer or alter the customer's perceptions is not well founded.

In addition to changing names, new managements love to let everybody know that things have changed. IBM launched its global branding strategy by consolidating its entire advertising effort under one agency shortly after Louis Gerstner arrived. HP launched its "Garage" campaign only months after Carly Fiorina became CEO, only to find that the changes necessary to implement that vision will take years of investment and process adaptation. And when Steve Jobs resumed leadership of Apple, the company embarked on a 1960s-style image campaign, showing famous people from history with the new tag line "Think Different."

When *Business Week* asked Jobs whether Apple was "getting by" on its slick design and marketing, he replied, "If people think Apple's success is based on candy-colored iMacs that sell because of their colors, they're not seeing the whole story. Making the iMac work without a noisy fan (for example) is not just fit-and-finish, it is hard-core engineering."[12] His response was typical of that of other executives who rely on new images to get their companies out of slumps. That is, when asked whether the marketing is the sum and substance of changes at the company, they downplay the campaign and point to what they consider more substantial and sustainable operational changes.

The iMac's unique design and colorful appearance give the product a distinctive presence, but persistent presence for the iMac is missing. There are too many markets in which Apple products are not considered standard productivity tools. I suspect that Steve Jobs well understands that and will continue to make engineering advances that enable future products to be easily adapted to other technologies, thus extending and achieving persistent presence. Recently Apple opened two retail stores, and it has plans for another twenty-three in major high-traffic centers to give shoppers a "hands-on" digital experience in a world of computing blandness. That's great, but no matter how much advertising is targeted at gaining the iMac acceptance, that acceptance won't come unless Apple fundamentally changes how easy it is to integrate iMacs with other computing products, expands software applications, and establishes more competitive pricing models. And doing all those things will require a considerable number of changes in partnering strategies as well as a different approach to market presence. To really gain ground, Apple has to consider new and different distribution channels; for instance, it might think about embedding iMac technology into the backs of airplane or automobile seats or into other access devices.

In the cases of Apple, IBM, and Coca-Cola, consumer perception changed only when the companies introduced new products and services, cut costs and lowered prices, developed new distribution partners, and began to turn around financially. To accomplish all that, they had to transform and innovate, become more competitive, change market strategies, enter new markets, develop new channels, and much more. IBM's Gerstner went through several years of cost cutting, management changes, and dead-end explorations into areas like consumer electronics before he came back to basics—mainframes and services.

When a company succeeds, the advertising agency and "branding experts" often claim credit, based on the number of awards the advertising received. But the real marketing advantage these companies had wasn't their promotional campaigns, their name, or their logo, but rather their technology and the role it played in their respective industry infrastructures, as well as the legacy of installed products still in place and used by their customers. In other words, these companies had a sustaining presence to carry them through the cold cycles.

Four Steps to Achieving Persistent Presence

A company can achieve presence in many ways, depending on the nature of the business, the market, and the company's competitive position. But a few key points apply to just about any business trying to establish persistent presence.

1. Take a Market Architecture Approach to Total Access

To keep pace with changing technology and corporate evolution, marketing executives must contribute to the overall success of creating and sustaining customers. Marketing can no longer be limited to one perspective or to any single medium; it will become increasingly complex, requiring a much broader vision of the future enterprise than we've seen in the past. Businesses must view and approach marketing as an integrated enterprise activity, and, like all other aspects of the enterprise, marketing must become a network of coordinated information and responsibilities.

When you withdraw money or charge a purchase with your ATM card, the system recognizes your PIN, checks your account balance, debits the charge, and automatically updates your balance and statement. When I order a computer from Dell, the complete system is delivered ready for use, and although some of the components might be from different locations and different suppliers, all the boxes arrive on my doorstep at the same time. I receive an e-mail and a letter thanking me for my order, as well as an online survey requesting my feedback on the service. Dell's operational network links functions and the supply chain partners provide data on sales, returns, inventory, and myriad other things. That's marketing architecture.

Wal-Mart's success is directly tied to its market architecture approach and the resulting financial advantage over competitors. Each Wal-Mart store is linked to others through distribution warehouses that interconnect to a giant database (which is second in size only to that of the U.S. government). Suppliers are linked to the network as well, which enables them to tailor supplies to changing demand. Major suppliers like Procter & Gamble are given ready access to transactional data, which is updated every ninety minutes.

Wal-Mart began its pursuit of industry leadership by envisioning marketing as architecture well before the Internet became a commercial entity. By employing a private network using EDI (electronic data interchange), the company built a system that was so powerful that it eventually became a tail that wagged the dog. In 1987, Procter & Gamble approached Wal-Mart and proposed setting up a joint management and data-sharing relationship. While both claimed the mutual benefits of rapid and predictable stock turns, it was clear, according to *The Economist*, that Wal-Mart ended up way ahead. Within a few years, as other retailers adopted similar distribution systems, P&G began closing plants and laying off employees. Wal-Mart, on the other hand, saw sales rise from $1.2 billion in 1980 to $26 billion in 1990, with 1,528 stores.[13] Today Wal-Mart is the world's largest retailer, with sales of over $165 billion and four thousand points of presence worldwide.

2. Beef Up Your Customer's Support Infrastructure

An operational support infrastructure is key to persistent presence. Once that infrastructure is in place and the volume of users increases to a point of persistent presence, the infrastructure can be scaled, adding new applications, products, and services with increasing efficiencies. Thus, as Geoff Mott, managing partner of The McKenna Group, points out, "Economics directs perception." Of course, consumers must find out about these new services in some way, and advertising and public relations are essential to getting the message out. But we can't assume that "the message" is branding, for it doesn't sustain the value of the customer's experience. The message can only reinforce or reflect branding.

Coca-Cola is a company with an amazing global customer support infrastructure. In fact, without its vast consumer access network, the brand name Coca-Cola would be an empty bottle. But throughout its long history, the company has had its ups and downs. In the mid 1990s, for example, Coca-Cola experienced a decline in prestige. Between 1995 and 2000, "brand Coke" fell from 70 to 64 percent of the sales by volume of the company's 190 other brands. Slowed market growth, decreased earnings, and the death of a very successful leader, Roberto C. Goizueta, took their toll. Reports of contaminated products in France and Belgium forced a shutdown of plants, and a recession in Asia slowed sales. In January 2000, Coke's new president announced the layoff of some six thousand employees worldwide.[14]

This wasn't the first down cycle Coca-Cola experienced in its 112-year history, and chances are it won't be the last. But regardless of the challenges facing this giant, access to its products is almost universal. The company's presence is the result of a process begun just over a hundred years ago when Asa Candler, who owned Coke at the time, awarded a franchise to an independent bottling company for one dollar. Like the open systems software of today, Chandler's franchising approach put hundreds, then thousands, of entrepreneurs to work expanding the market for Coke.

Today Coke has 1,500 bottling companies in 155 countries. One billion people in 200 countries around the world buy Coke products every day. In the New York metropolitan area alone, Coca-Cola has 70,000 outlets and accounts for 50 percent of the soft drink sales in that region.[15] It's been said that you can't walk a city block without finding a Coke. In *The Ends of the Earth*, journalist and traveler Robert Kaplan mentions drinking Coke in such remote places as sub-Saharan Africa and the far corners of the Gobi Plain, bordering China. While in Sierra Leone, he dined on a breakfast of scrambled eggs and Coca-Cola. "In the postindustrial temperate zone, with its myriad juices and bottled waters, I rarely touch Coca-Cola. In the tropics, I live on it," writes Kaplan.[16]

It's taken more than a century for Coca-Cola to develop and manage the network of franchised bottlers, distributors, and retailers that makes Coke available in so many different regions of the world. The company's mission statement sheds some light on the company's know-how by saying that Coke creates "value" by creating not only "superior soft drinks" (value to user), but also "beverage systems that create value for our Company, bottling partners, customers, share owners, and communities in which we do business."[17]

3. Think Total Access

Establishing persistent presence requires vision without the conviction of prediction. In his classic 1960 article, "Marketing Myopia," Harvard Marketing Professor Ted Levitt advised business executives to define their industries broadly to take advantage of growth opportunities. American railroads, he said, illustrated an industry that severely limited itself by defining its business as "railroads" rather than as transportation. Because the industry defined itself too narrowly, it missed out on new and growing forms of transportation and inevitably declined as technology advanced.[18]

Today it's more crucial than ever to realize that retail, distribution, or services have multiple and flexible paths to and from the market. We're not talking about a business defining its goals so broadly that they become meaningless; we're talking about a business expanding its perspective to embrace the technological evolution that drives investment today and leads to leadership tomorrow. While the various forms of media and the bricks-and-clicks establishments benefit from the Internet, each still represents a distinct form of information delivery. No single access channel provides persistent presence on its own. Rather, all access channels must work in concert to deliver a consistent consumer experience.

Most products require "hard channels" to fulfill transactions or to provide tangible ways for the consumer to experience the product or service. A hard channel is a physical location, such as a retail outlet, shelf space, an airport, a FedEx or DHL delivery to your business or home, or a car dealership. It is a place where the customer can touch and feel the product, experience a service, or make assisted choices. Soft channels, on the other hand, are primarily informational. Today's consulting firms act as soft channels, selecting and integrating various software packages into complete solutions. The Internet is also a soft channel. As such, it delivers information and digital content such as software, music, and books.

Companies that use both hard and soft channels need to integrate them. Many "clicks-and-mortar" operations have computerized inventory management, but they haven't integrated their hard- and soft-channel databases, so that the physical location doesn't have access to data from the cyber location. Borders, with an online Web site and 300 retail stores, is an example. My wife and I often browse and shop at a local Borders, but even though we've regularly bought books there for years, the store doesn't track our purchase history. A few months ago, as we made yet another large purchase of books and CDs, the sales clerk jokingly asked, "Do you do this regularly?" Unfortunately for Borders, he had no way of knowing that we do. The company doesn't cross-reference its retail purchases with each other or with a customer's online purchases. Fortunately, though, Borders management is well aware of this limitation and has been busy developing a synchronized channel strategy, which will connect all customer access modes to one database.[19] On a more recent book-buying excursion, the clerk offered me a 10 percent discount if I would give him my e-mail address. Aha! They're beginning to connect online and offline.

Tasks such as the synchronizing of points-of-presence with customer information databases, balancing inventories, and dynamically linking suppliers into a seamless, closed-loop supply chain are extremely difficult and expensive, but they are essential to attaining persistent presence. Amazon.com is trying to establish persistent presence on the Internet by doing just these things. To compete with its clicks-and-mortar competitors, the company is investing significant capital on warehousing, automation software, and distribution infrastructure. In that it doesn't have multiple points of presence, Amazon is at a disadvantage compared to Borders (which has 300 stores) and Barnes & Noble (which has more than 500). It has to rely on encountering its customers exclusively through the soft channel of the Web, something it does do well. Its software "remembers" my purchases and suggests related books, and Amazon sends me e-mails suggesting new books on particular topics. In addition, the range of books is wider than what I can find at many bookstores, and the prices are often lower. Nevertheless, the online experience can't compare with browsing in a bookstore: Leafing through a book and reading a few pages often helps me determine if I will actually read the book. When I want to browse at a bookstore and buy books right then, I often go to a local Borders, even though I make most of my book purchases online from Amazon. On the other hand, I tend to spend more money per visit at Borders than I do online. Although all three competitors have significant customer volume and sales, Barnes & Noble and Borders are profitable, while Amazon.com is not. Now that Barnes & Noble and Borders have online stores, it will be interesting to see if Amazon's one-store approach can survive in the face of its competitors' multiple points of presence. I suspect Amazon.com will ultimately expand into multiple channels of distribution. Customers form strong preferences based on persistent presence, whether that presence is physical or remote. And the combination of both is very powerful.

Some companies deploy a strategy of increasing channels in order to achieve persistent presence. AOL's $183 billion acquisition of Time Warner in 2000 shows that it well understood that the Internet is a limited medium and found it necessary to expand its subscribers' total access options. According to AOL, the combined entity will permit more than 100 million subscription relationships with consumers through the Internet, cable, television, and magazines.[20] As a result, consumers will experience AOL as an entertainment/media company, with services in a wide variety of formats in diverse locations.

Disney has also done a great job of using multiple channels. Anywhere a family seeks entertainment—at the movies, on the Internet, in theme parks, online, via television, or in bookstores and retail stores—they find Disney. Eddie Bauer is another example: Consumers can buy Eddie Bauer clothing through a mail-order catalog, at www.eddiebauer.com, or at one of over 600 retail stores. All those points of purchase pay off. Customers who shop using only one channel typically spend $100 to $200 a year; a customer who uses two channels typically spends $300 to $500 a year; and a customer who uses all three channels typically spends $800 to $1,000 a year, according to Eddie Bauer CEO Rick Fersch.[21]

Finally, Intel, the world's leading microprocessor manufacturer with $37 billion in sales, is developing new strategies to ensure long-term presence, which is a must in a dynamic market. During the past decade, Intel became an active venture investor in start-up companies. The strategy behind those venture activities seems to be to create persistent presence for the company's chips. In 1998, Intel joined Compaq, Dell, HP, NEC, and Silicon Graphics to form the $250 million Intel 64 Fund, the charter of which is to drive new applications for Intel's new 64-bit processor, a powerful chip due to arrive on the market in early 2001. The Intel Itanium processor will power a new generation of computers and other machines whose performance will exceed anything we've seen before. The investment consortium consists of Intel's key customers, as well as its customers' customers. To help ensure the success of its entrepreneurial investments, Intel not only gives them access to its software optimization lab but also orchestrates access to its network of customers, including companies like Ford Motor Company, the Boeing Company, and Procter & Gamble. Intel's partners benefit by gaining access to a wide array of new applications before its competitors do. Les Vadasz, Intel executive vice president and president of Intel Capital, put it this way:

> We invest to accelerate the development of our markets. The way I look at this is that for technology markets to develop, you need a lot of players to deliver hardware and software products. If we can accelerate the development of this market ecosystem by making investments and providing support for innovative technology companies, then we are all ahead. Everybody benefits.[22]

For Intel, this is a strategy of persistent presence. It can be considered marketing by investment. Intel's chips are the ones that will be at the heart of each machine running the new business applications that drive emerging markets. In practical terms, Intel is creating a new generation of distribution channels for its chips. The high tech equity market's collapse in 2001 did not alter the company's strategy to invest in R&D, capital expansion, or new market-creating applications.

4. Invest in Time, Money, and Customer Relationships

Achieving a persistent presence is complex. Terms like CRM and one-to-one marketing are bandied about, and to many companies, these tools have been justification for supply chain automation. Automation is necessary but not sufficient to achieve persistent presence. Persistent presence requires vision and an architectural approach to marketing strategy. It further requires the realization that marketing isn't this month's ad campaign, an article in a popular magazine, or a trade show calendar. Although all those things are valuable strategies, by themselves they cannot sustain the producer-consumer relationship over time, through hot and cold cycles. Nor can they provide the continuous feedback and distribution of customer and marketing knowledge that it takes to satisfy buyers and rapidly adopt innovative ways. Total access will continually alter customers' perceptions, wants, and demands. To get ahead of the curve, to engage and build relationships with customers over the long term, businesses will have to push the edges of technology applications, recreating their form and function as innovation reshapes them.

Developing the architecture for persistent presence takes time—time for management to gain hard-earned and valuable knowledge through trial and error, and time to roll out, adapt, and develop the confidence to innovate new forms of access. This is why only a handful of the million or so new businesses started each year do achieve lasting-market presence. Success requires a distinct and sustained vision, as well as an architectural approach to the business and a relentless drive to reduce transaction costs.

Most important, persistent presence requires a substantial and sustained financial investment. The Yankee Group estimates that businesses will spend $7.53 billion on CRM (customer relationship management) software applications alone, with the expectation of an 8 percent growth in sales revenue within one year of deployment.[23] But despite the cost, companies will have to do what's necessary to develop cost-efficient, helpful, and engaging ways to service, support, and interact with their customers. Brand no longer wields the powerful influence it once did over consumer consciousness. The concept of persistent presence offers a strategic way of thinking about how to employ a coordinated architecture of information and total access resources to be always there for customers.

Chapter Seven

Putting It All Together

The Marketing Architecture

Today's marketing demands that we rethink what we do and how we do it. Building persistent presence is key to that. And the key to that is a marketing architecture.

THE INFORMATION AGE has brought a growing complexity of business interactions and interdependencies. Direct and continuous customer communication, the increasing dependence between products and services, the need for partnerships to complete solutions, the globalization of competition, and more have created demands on organizations that stretch them across new and unexplored managerial and operational boundaries. In this kind of environment, establishing market presence and sustaining brand are more important than ever. Those who hold the keys to doing so therefore also hold the keys to the marketing kingdom.

Achieving Market Presence, Sustaining Brand

There are two key components to achieving a lasting market presence and sustaining brand: points of access and the marketing architecture network.

Points of Access

Points of access (or presence) are essentially multiple distribution channels integrated by a shared information network. The channels can take various forms—they can be retail outlets, embedded and shared presence within alliance partner's applications or devices, Web pages, call centers, kiosks, and so on. Each has a distinct physical presence and elicits a consistent customer experience. Most points of presence are becoming more interactive, providing an immediate customer engagement and opportunity for feedback. A wide variety of U.S. companies offer multiple points of access: Visa and American Express do so through global partnerships and alliances; Microsoft, Intel, and AOL Time Warner are striving to establish diverse places where consumers can encounter their products and services; and Starbucks and Wal-Mart have done this in the U.S. market space.

When customers become so dependent on a product or physical location that they would not consider filling their need or want any other way, that business has achieved persistent presence. AOL e-mail ("You've got mail!"), McDonald's, an ATM, and local convenience stores might be examples. The point of presence has become thoroughly ingrained in that customer's consciousness and is a part of that customer's everyday traffic pattern or routine. It's not brand awareness that has made the consumer so dependent, it's the consumer's actual physical experiences with the point of presence, services, applications embedded within appliances, access devices, and other tangible objects.

As time goes on, we will begin to see more access devices, establishing points of presence for a wide variety of information services, everywhere. IBM calls this ever-present information access phenomenon "pervasive computing." Smart devices such as PDAs and digital wireless devices, as well as fixed transaction locations such as a kiosks, cash registers, or ATM-like counter devices, will contain microchips that will allow direct, simple, free, and secure access to intelligent networks. People will have convenient access to information and services stored on powerful networks, allowing them to easily take action anywhere, anytime, whether the use is business or personal. These same devices and networks will give producers feedback on customer transactions and buying patterns.

There is a close correlation between persistent presence and a company's definition of its market space. (Think AOL Time Warner or Disney.) Some companies seem to move toward persistent presence by identifying unmet customer needs and adjusting (often broadening) their scope of offerings to address the current customer gaps—to go where no one else has gone and to meet customers' needs in a whole new way.

Often a company that has achieved persistent presence has extended its offerings to meet unmet customer needs outside the traditional box of what it has considered to be its primary market space. Such a company creates new access points and physical outlets, but it also creates constant novelty in its products or services. Book publishers, entertainment companies, and television networks understand the concept of novelty and the need to keep expanding their points of presence. The almost weekly changes in the "top ten hits" on music charts or the "bestseller" list of books sustain the demand for novelty in the publishing and music businesses. The variety of access points and devices have also expanded with super retail stores, airport shops, grocery stores, catalogs, and online access points. To keep viewers coming back, television executives change programming every season, but even this may not be sufficient to satisfy the demand for novelty. Blockbuster movies released in the summer of 2001 hit record high ticket sales in the first three days and vanished from the charts just as quickly. "This summer could be measured in days: a huge opening, a rapid plunge, and a few weeks later the hit movie is just a speck in the rear-view mirror," commented Rick Lyman of the *New York Times*.[1] The rapidly changing demand for novelty in the media may well fill the dark fiber if marketers come to understand that marketing is about building the infrastructure for services more than about making promises it cannot deliver on. Staying connected through a marketing architecture may be the only way businesses will be able to keep pace.

The Marketing Architecture Network

Persistent presence also relies on a marketing architecture, an underlying infrastructure that supports and connects all points of customer support, including suppliers, carriers, services, and content providers. The architecture flows from producer to consumer in concertlike fashion, gathering information, learning, adapting, and responding. It is an approach to conceptualizing the total architecture of relationships to enable a perpetual, reliable, and yet creative interaction and response to customers. The response may be as simple as order status or instructions for use or an application for complaints. The architecture is creative, in that it seeks to develop new content and diversify access points, and it seeks to share information in an interactive manner to and from the customer. As broadband access expands throughout the network, remote, live customer education or purely entertaining programs become possible.

Note, though, that the architecture is not simply an expansion of channels and partners; it's a cultural integration of goals and objectives aimed at improving the customer experience and satisfaction, as well as improving everyone's return on investment, which is achieved through sustained customer loyalty. The statistics here are pretty vivid: It takes five times as much investment to obtain a new customer as it does to keep a current one.

Portrait of an Architecture

The *Merriam-Webster Dictionary* defines marketing as "an aggregate of functions involved in moving goods from producer to consumer."[2] While definitions don't necessarily hold up in practice, it's interesting that the dictionary defines marketing in such general business terms. Likewise, a marketing architecture has a broad perspective. It's based on the same idea as network architecture: It interconnects all the relevant players, protocols, access devices, controls, and interfaces, and it defines the rules for participation. It is a relationship model that ties together mutually supporting functions, partners, channels, and services, all dynamically managed via the network.

The Hartford insurance company deploys an IT system that enables a consistent and continuous customer interface across all channels. The system links all customer information across multiple product lines (e.g., auto, home, and life insurance). The network has multiple front-end connections that create total system transparency for the company to understand a customer's complete history, regardless of which channel the customer chooses to access the company. The network also extends to agents, who can use an extranet to access real-time data to help service clients. "Customers now have more freedom to choose how they want to shop for insurance, and carriers must constantly improve their distribution strategy," says David Annis, chief information officer at The Hartford.[3]

In a transactional working environment, participants share information, learn, act, and respond to each other with confidence and assurance in the transaction. With shortened product cycles, increased competition and consumer options, changing technology and channels, and volatile market reactions, everything between the boardroom and the consumer is about moving relevant information faster and more coherently between people so that they make good decisions and are responsive. A marketing architecture spells out the detailed business processes that connect all corporate resources, inside and outside the enterprise, that are involved in continuously delivering persistent presence and customer satisfaction, and for owning your marketing space. However, a marketing architecture is more than an IT network connecting information resources. It is also a culture-changing process that requires a perspective and sensitivity for the human interactions with the architecture. I've spelled out three of these interactions and their effect below:

Shared Creativity

Businesses must constantly develop and deploy new applications and services with adaptable, engaging interfaces. In the past few decades, most businesses found that sustaining better market share demands a parade of new products flowing from R&D, and that the highest percentage of their revenues and profits comes from products and services developed in the previous two to five years.

During my career I've observed many innovations that were developed in concert with customers. Examples of shared creativity include Intel's first microprocessor, which was a response to a Japanese company's need for a low-cost way to integrate all the calculator functions on few chips; the Apple II personal computer, which was Steve Jobs and Steve Wozniak's response to the needs of their hobbyist friends; and Microsoft's MS-DOS operating system, which was a response to IBM's need for an inexpensive operating system. The worldwide quality movement began when customers publicly voiced their dissatisfaction with American-made cars, semiconductors, and other products. Many companies from IBM to GE began to work jointly with their customers, sharing ideas for process improvements.

In the business-to-business marketplace, companies commonly work closely with their customers, adjusting and customizing products and services. Recognizing new opportunities in the process has been rare because customer feedback was often caught up in the maze of bureaucracy and statistical reports, or often ignored. For many businesses addressing large markets, expanding the shared learning environment to include millions of customers was prohibitive until computers, databases, simulation software programs, and networks became economically feasible. Out of this interchange, shared creativity arises because the flow of information is no longer restricted to filtering agents or any one function. Creativity in this environment has no boundaries.

A healthy architecture demands that the planning process include new products and service launches, promotion programs, logistics support, interface design, and preparation for customers' expectations for feedback. These functions and tasks cannot be developed in isolation and must be approached by the enterprise as integral marketing architecture service customers. Customers will eventually rely on a particular experience and location, and they will expect a unique experience within and from the points of presence. In addition, they will seek those locations based on their preferences: choice, novelty, price, and others.

Making these interactions unique experiences for customers demands creativity. Businesses must develop new ways to deploy the network and engage participants, as well as useful and transparent applications for customer-sustaining interfaces.

Keeping the Customer's Trust

Trust is at the heart of marketing. Without it, a business, product, or service cannot expect loyalty. Trust isn't a matter of selling; rather, it's a matter of delivering. To build and sustain customer trust, the marketing architecture must both perform and respond consistently. Customers learn to trust a service, product, or company through consistent, reliable experiences; over time, businesses earn their customers' trust by consistently meeting or exceeding expectations. As the number of players inside and outside an organization grows, and as information systems become integral to meeting customer expectations, building and sustaining consumer trust becomes a much more complex task. Trust can't be won through broadcast messages, which should reflect reality, not try to create it.

The rising cost of providing services necessitates that businesses work at making their response systems to customers increasingly productive. At first, businesses can automate recurring producer-consumer transactions and services to keep costs low. These transactions and services will be absorbed into the enterprise information architecture because networked information is by its very nature decentralized. Businesses will need time to develop, learn, and deploy more complex tasks, such as reporting order status, announcing pricing changes, making new product announcements, responding to inquiries, and even permitting some self-service activities. While many of these marketing tasks are repetitive and are absorbed into the network, their very triviality keeps consumers dependent upon them. Therefore trust is expressed by credibility that comes from consistent, reliable performance. David Annis of The Hartford puts it this way: "I love talking about how we can bring some capability to market that's going to give us an edge. But in order to be effective, a CIO must have first established a sense of credibility and trust. They have to believe that you're going to do your part as a technology organization. You build trust by delivering consistent results."[4]

Nurturing Change: The Organic Factor

Perhaps one of the most important characteristics of a marketing architecture is that it is organic: It's able to evolve, grow, and adapt to changing customer needs and environmental factors. The ability to respond to new customer information and changing environmental conditions is as important as the entities participating in the architecture. The architecture is a complex infrastructure, but its purpose is to deliver a simple customer experience that disappears into the user's intuitive behavior pattern. Its energy comes from shared value building as well as from a continuous flow of applicable information to and from customers. The favorable customer serving, marketing architecture environment happens when the company's leadership establishes the cultural platform and discipline of superior implementation performance.

"Marketing has always been associated with the creative aspects of marketing while the operational details and execution were handed off and expected to be there," says Brian Fitzgerald, former vice president of operations at Intuit. He adds, "You can't get away with that anymore."[5] True enough: A healthy architecture includes the right participants, such as R&D and business development. Everyone participates. Marketing is no longer a spectator sport.

The Marketing Architecture Trumps the Value Chain

A marketing architecture is not a loosely defined alignment of functional players in a value chain. It is, rather, an evolving set of relationships, internal and external to the enterprise, that sustain market presence and customer engagement. The marketing architecture also differs from a value chain in that it creates additional value for all participants, instead of simply redistributing value among existing players. We've seen examples of this value creation developing over the past decade, such as revenue sharing, joint market development partnerships, and jointly financed spinouts.

The value chain has been the focus of automation, integration, and the application of information and networking tools for the past ten years or so. Unfortunately, it's often viewed as a static set of definable relationships and processes. In fact, it's a dynamic, evolutionary process of changing tools, information, and relationships. It is structured differently for each industry and it elicits value in different ways. It's always a "work in progress."

Many businesses' executives recognize that change is coming, and that it will make their existing infrastructure obsolete, force them into a commodity role, or remove them from the process altogether. They are choosing to hasten the demise of the old model, looking to digital technology and networks to break the rules that dictate how goods and services are bought, sold, and produced. They are forming new relationships with customers and competitors by automating expensive processes or giving away proprietary tools others can use to move away from the industry entirely. These organizations hope that by unleashing a "killer app" themselves, they will be able to exert control over how much earth is scorched in the process.[6]

However you define the value chain, it is a direct or indirect integral part of the marketing architecture, linking the support and services necessary to deliver customer satisfaction consistently. To compete effectively in the marketplace, marketing executives must learn how to engage every player, from supplier to all the interrelated partners, in such a way that the network looks and feels like a dynamic nerve center. Retailers, customers, and consumers derive value from the points of presence and the frequency and dependency of use. Too often the value chain focuses on automation and not the interface and the changing and adaptive nature of the various players in the chain. And while simply improving supply chain efficiency by automation may give a short-term advantage to some, it doesn't necessarily sustain loyalty or create new market opportunities.

The Role of IT in the Architecture

Marketing has evolved into an ever more complex cluster of relationships connected by an equally complex information network. Information, customer expectations and satisfaction, and brand must operate as inseparable, closely interrelated partners. The goals of these relationships and networks must be allied with the customer experience both at the point and time of delivery, and during the use of the product or service. The common unifying thread is information.

That said, CRM and IT can't solve all of a business's problems alone or in isolation from marketing or the customer. An estimated 60 to 80 percent of the companies that have installed a CRM solution are not fully using the capability of that software, simply because many companies don't have adequate workflow processes in place before they implement a CRM package.[7] If the company's underlying processes are flawed and inefficient to begin with, implementing a software package won't fix the underlying inadequacies—it will only result in a similarly bad process that is automated.

"Information existed long before computers," says Jim Cates, a highly respected information researcher and CIO of Brocade, an enterprise network data storage company. "If you have a bad work-flow process and you don't automate it, you'll die a slow, cheap death. And if you automate it, you'll die a fast, expensive death. In either case, you'll be just as dead." During his many years as a researcher at IBM, an IT consultant, and CIO, Cates has developed an evolutionary view of deploying information systems within an enterprise, a view that begins with an understanding of business and work process rules. "Choosing an architecture and software support system is not generic but must be applied within the constraints and openness of a particular cultural and business model. That is to say, 'one size doesn't fit all.'"[8]

Business processes and rules—objectives, goals procedures, schedules, operational or financial parameters, and customer responsiveness—are, after all, independent of technology and existed long before automated information systems, Cates observes:

> These business rules create information, and the value of this information is equal to the ability of the person looking at the data. One might say, the DNA of the human doing the viewing, plus the experience of that human, plus their communication skills becomes paramount. That's the value of any particular information within a domain of that company. All three of those things are important. And of course, different humans will be able to do all three of those things differently. Sometimes it makes no difference if I can move the data through the pipes faster, because humans can't comprehend the information or make the damn decisions any faster.[9]

Cates's ideal organization evolves, learning as it moves through six evolving levels of IT business applications. The bottom rung of Cates's "Ladder of Business Intelligence" is disparate data sources or facts. Data are organized facts, information is organized data, and knowledge is organized information. Understanding is organized knowledge. When, after investing considerable money and time, you have achieved knowledge, then that "allows you to do the ah-ha stuff." "Because now," says Cates, "you've got all this stuff in your head and events start occurring for you in your universe that allow the greatest insights. Insights normally occur not through planning but from brains that are experienced and prepared and can observe what's happening around them and hence draw the right conclusion."[10]

A marketing architecture must evolve in similar fashion. As the applications and use of enterprise-wide marketing information expand, managers will use it, change it, adapt it, and integrate it into their work-flow processes and eventually arrive at the "ah-ha stuff." Many marketing applications today are function-specific and used for lead tracking, scheduling, telemarketing data input, expense reporting, order entry, and prospect/customer segmentation. These tools are the equivalent of Cates's first or second level of development. Over time, these specific function-automation tools will be integrated into the enterprise-wide marketing architecture, expanding the customer and market knowledge throughout the business.

E.piphany, a leading provider of CRM solutions software, offers a big step in this direction. The E.piphany enterprise-wide approach blends all inbound and outbound marketing, sales, and service customer inter-actions and data with analysis capability, enabling a marketing architecture with a single, enterprise-wide view of each customer. The limitation of these systems is that they still regard the customer as a data point and "target of opportunity," rather than as a partner in the equation. Data are entered into the system when a customer transaction occurs, but the feedback from that customer, such as satisfaction with the service or product, is limited by the abstract nature of the data. Competitive pur-chase behavior is not in the model, and often follow-on service informa-tion is also not cross-referenced. The other limitation is that too often the R&D, production, distribution, and field support people are not encouraged to use the data for improving their processes. E.piphany, however, is a pioneer of marketing architecture systems and their soft-ware is evolving and integrating more and more of the enterprise-wide customer response information requirements.

These systems involve an investment in money and management time. I haven't found a company that actively uses enterprise marketing architectures across the enterprise. Most applications are partial; many use some of the marketing automation tools. I believe most IT enterprise smart businesses are on the ladder rising from analyzing data to total management and customer access and finally to an intuitive marketing architecture.

Why is an enterprise architecture approach to marketing important? Because service is now being shifted from the distributor or retailer, par-ticularly for information-related services, directly to the producer. The Internet has changed everything in terms of how a business approaches customer support, education, logistics, services, and partnerships. Companies are expected to be responsive, and marketing must shift its traditional focus from promotion to customer response. A marketing architecture integrates the company's support and service capabilities and focuses on sustaining customer relationships. Living and surviving in this new environment means learning to open databases, share customer information, work off the same plan, add value cooperatively, standardize where necessary, and be creative all the while. A marketing architecture grows by learning how to better interact within itself in response to its environment and in concert with customers' needs and wants.

Customer Satisfaction

In contrast with the "push" and distribution role marketing played in the early part of the twentieth century, marketing's new role is to develop and integrate a network of resources available to the corporation; to provide customers with continuous access to those resources; and to manage the systems for interacting with, responding to, and managing the interactive customer transaction process. I can't say it enough: Marketing must become more engaged in delivering customer satisfaction.

But there's a conundrum here. Marketing today is a balancing act that requires solving complex business problems with equally complex information systems—but while those systems give us more data more quickly, the people using the systems don't assimilate the information any more quickly. In other words, Moore's Law does not apply to people. Even with the new information tools, we don't double our efficiency every eighteen months. Add more people and partners to the "satisfy customers" equation, and not only does the whole thing get more costly and complex but people need more time to learn and adapt.

Achieving customer satisfaction takes a team approach. It requires a combination of different corporate functions and often third-party fulfillment businesses. Abandoning a linear chain of functions, today's ideal marketing architecture has a network of interrelated functional capabilities directed toward one end—satisfying a customer. Establishing standards of performance, quality, business goal compatibility, and constant process improvement are key not only for realizing improved service costs but also for gaining better knowledge of the customer requirements. Service industries such as insurance and financial services interact directly with customers and address specific needs or a community of needs. Services rely heavily on the knowledge and skill of the person who directly interacts with the customer. Because pure-play service businesses are more subtle or abstract in nature, they demand a higher degree of trust between the customer and the business.

Intuit: Building Marketing Architecture

"Brand today lives and dies on the quality of information, service, and product logistics execution," says Brian Fitzgerald, former vice president of operations at Intuit.[11] He knows what he's talking about. Intuit holds the number-one market share in financial software and has the distinct position of having "outmarketed" Microsoft in this category. During Fitzgerald's tenure, company revenues rose from $200 million to over $1.3 billion, and the retail business grew from 700 outlets to over 3,000. In 1999, Intuit's Internet sales were approximately $500,000; in 2000, they jumped to $90 million.

The critical, event-driven nature of Intuit's products and services adds to the company's challenge. Many of its products and services (TurboTax, for example) are financial management and tax-planning and reporting tools for consumers and small and medium businesses. The expectations and needs of those consumers and businesses are high—and Intuit perceives them as urgent. "When the web page tells the customer, 'immediate delivery,' and the customer clicks the order button, expectations go through the roof. That customer is on his or her way to the front door to see if it's there," jokes Fitzgerald.[12]

More and more of the marketing relationship between retailers and companies take place at the operations, information, and logistical levels; less and less of the relationship involves promotion and incentives. Building a marketing architecture from the internal marketing and operations function down to supplier relationships and then farther down to the grass-roots level is an evolutionary learning process. Bill Campbell, chairman and former president of Intuit, was always a different sort of marketing person. Although he was VP of sales and marketing at Apple in its heyday, he knew and understood brand at the level of operational detail. At Intuit, he set the strategy, developed the partnering culture, and brought in top-notch operational people to handle the implementation.

Extending your intellectual capital to a network of partners and even to customers is important because business models today require multiple partners to build value jointly by serving the same customers with a common solution or service. The company has a goal of out-sourcing 90 percent of its operations to a network of business partners. However, according to Bill Campbell, "Signing a laundry list of alliances is not the starting point or the way to ultimately service your customers. The starting point is your corporate culture."[13] In some instances, Inuit encouraged suppliers to merge or work together to develop the best possible business model; in that way, the supplier and Intuit were able to build value together. Fitzgerald sums up with this perspective:

> And this is just the retail side of the Intuit business. The retail business is still very relationship-oriented, but taking the distributor out of the middle and developing a closer relationship with the retailer. We end up managing at the store level. Each store is an individual B2B transaction. You have to look right down to the grass roots level. Supporting one store is not much different from supporting an individual consumer or small business. Operations at Intuit became much more involved in what goes up on a marketing campaign. We have to look closely at content, so we know exactly what we're telling customers and whether we can really do it. All the operations stuff—we have to be able to articulate clearly, and be careful what we promise. There's a lot to manage. We're talking about 200 million components in 17 to 18 million deliveries per year. In an extended model, the only thing that's binding is information flow.[14]

Different Channels for Different Needs

From the customer's point of view, world-class marketing rests on the details of execution. Depending on the type of industry, product, or service, and on the nature of the market infrastructure, different types of businesses perfect different types of channels. Most retail organizations have highly tuned logistics systems, for example; Wal-Mart is perhaps the most sophisticated in that business. Many other companies are leading in their respective industries, including FedEx, Citibank, Harrah's Entertainment, and Charles Schwab. Each of these businesses has unique marketing architectures supporting their customers through their particular points of presence—online, ATM, casino, and retail locations.

Industries today can learn from one another. Consumer businesses have long worked on the development of their distribution channels, adding technology to run their channels efficiently and to gather the much-needed information necessary to keep the supply chain flowing. Cost, margins, and shelf space are priorities for success. Business-to-business industries are most adept at direct interface, developing close relationships with key customers, modifying or adjusting products and services and evolving products and solutions from that interface.

The Internet and various types of interacting networks and devices disaggregate the information channel and fulfillment channel. According to Forrester Research, 68 percent of American car buyers go online to gather information before they purchase a new car, a phenomenon that is growing and expanding to every category of product regardless of price. In both direct interaction and fulfillment channels, marketing programs find *their* fulfillment. Increasingly, the information exchanged between businesses and customers in all industries—automobile, financial, healthcare, technology, and others—is direct, while the fulfillment channels continue to expand in multiple ways.

Businesses must see the brand experience at the various points of presence, as well as via the direct communication channel, as delivering a consistent and coordinated customer experience. Direct access raises expectations and thus the need to synchronize all forms of information with the fulfillment channels. For purely information-based products such as research reports, news, or books, access and fulfillment as well as service are often combined in the same medium through the same access point. On-demand entertainment is an example.

The Internet is an access and fulfillment point of presence, although the business models for most services other than certain software products have yet to be defined and proved. Eventually, the Internet will deliver a customer experience much like that of the ATM; customers will access the Internet for specific reasons but not really think about the network that coordinates and enables the transaction. The synchronized informational relationships among the various players and supporting members of both the information and fulfillment channels constitute a marketing architecture. Like an ecosystem, it is ever-expanding, adapting, and interdependent.

The character and meaning of distribution channel has changed radically with the application of the Internet and shared access to information databases. The concept of automating the supply chain is now thought of as integrating a network of resource partners. Information and value is increasingly shared among the partners who collectively constitute a customer-supporting marketing architecture. Business to business relies more heavily on its direct sales force and distributors, while retail and services rely on location, location, location. Traditionally, in all past distribution models, information was integrated with the fulfillment channel. When I bought a new car, I had to spend time shopping, talking with sales representatives, gathering specifications and prices, and interacting with the point of supply. And if I were selecting a financial service, I might talk with several brokers at competitive firms. While all businesses used broadcast as a means of disseminating information, consumer business rely more heavily on it because they reach millions of people, in contrast to business-to-business companies, where customer interfaces are limited and salespeople usually interact at the channel levels. Intel, for example, may advertise to influence millions of potential computer buyers, but the number of personal computer manufacturers that must buy into the Intel (and Microsoft) standard and deliver PCs with "Intel inside" is relatively small.

Customers now have access to information channels, separate and distinct from the product or service fulfillment channels, to make comparative buying decisions. The preferences for choice and better price encourage the use of the new Internet medium. For the marketers, however, this phenomenon adds a new complexity to the marketing task and, as a result, we are seeing more partnering and alliances for joint market development and distribution of both products and information.

The Value of Connected Partners

A marketing architecture goes beyond the corporate walls that encompass the resources that engage, develop, fulfill, and satisfy customers' needs and wants. A healthy architecture includes a variety of partners. For those partners to participate, they need to believe that the architecture can and will create additional value for them, that it will expand their horizons for business development, that it will create a distinct competitive advantage for them, and that it will build market share. Building a supply chain automation program is the first step, but in and of itself, it is not an architecture, which achieves healthy growth from shared network resources. Vertically integrated companies can deploy a marketing architecture because the network encompasses much more than just the supply chain. Integrated companies often have more difficulty aligning goals and objectives with sister operations because they usually have a long history of independence and because they base their financial measurement criteria on interdivisional pricing models. Operations within companies frequently compete for the same customers' business with different solutions.

The marketing architecture must encompass partners who are on the same wavelength, who mutually support the same goals and objectives, and for whom the benefits of participating in the system are mutually rewarding. Toyota provides an impressive example. At a recent meeting, I heard Toyota's senior management speak with pride about the company's financial performance in 2000—the best in the company's history—but they seemed most proud of the fact that 2000 had been a banner year for their suppliers as well. In other words, Toyota gets it.

Businesses must keep innovating in order to sustain their relationships with their partners, who are the supporting cast of characters, and ultimately with their customers. To work well with their partners, they must interlink all the customer-relevant functions in order to create an efficient process that can respond rapidly and satisfy customers anywhere on the globe. And they must use specialized software systems and networks to automate all systems that can be defined and mapped as workflow processes.

Developing the Strategic Framework

Judging by the way futurists and proponents of end-to-end managed business networks talk about it, we could assume that marketing architectures are neatly packaged solutions. They're not, of course. Applying technology solutions to any task requires a change in the behavior of the people who do the work.

The first step toward building a marketing architecture is to cultivate a coordinated service vision of an information resources network that continuously interacts with customers transparently. The Hartford case cited above, illustrates an application of a comprehensive approach to a marketing architecture strategy. The architecture is geared to support their customers but it takes into account the need to make the information accessible and complete for those who interface directly and indirectly with their customer. With the basics of a foundation in place, The Hartford is assuring persistent presence because the various places and sources of information, product, and service fulfillment are all coordinated—and they operate from the same knowledge base. This kind of comprehensive architecture doesn't spring up overnight, and I have to say that very few businesses have achieved nirvana.

To begin, developing a competitive marketing architecture requires the following:

1. Executive leadership willing to make the commitment and investment necessary to rethink and reinvent marketing as part of an information-based, enterprise-wide, value-added agenda.

2. A buy-in from senior management who commit to a customer-centered learning culture. Within the enterprise, management must think through all the elements that encompass the marketing challenges of the business, set objectives and goals, champion the process, and create the cultural and financial incentives necessary to revitalize the self-centered functional thinking and transform it to shared network thinking.

3. An assessment of present marketing systems. How integrated are they with IT and R&D? Is there a continual flow of transactional information from channels or customers back into the appropriate areas of the organization for knowledge, planning, response, and measurement?

4. A codification of the business rules: processes, standards, timetables, targets of customer satisfaction, outsourcing requirements, channel efficiencies, inventory management goals, and new product service requirements. If the business rules are not codified and put into the work processes, adding

automation or new tools of network information services will cause much organizational pain and be more costly.

5. A conceptual framework and systems information architecture that spell out the various components, relationships, and possible points of customer interface, as well as the information requirements of each component. Phase one of this step is making each of these interactions more efficient. But don't stop there.

6. A map of the flow of information to and from the points of presence, as well as the response system required to deliver unsurpassed customer service. It's essential to take this step before applying the tools, systems, networks, databases, and layers of applications.

7. Definitions of the responsibilities and processes for continuously delivering innovative content through the system, to present customers with an engaging experience through a creative interface.

8. Methods to engage R&D, IT, operations, outside resources, and key customers in pilot programs. Architectures do not begin in full bloom. They require experimentation and trial and error.

9. An evaluation of present branding expenditures. While many executives may agree in theory with what I've said in these pages, my fear is that, in practice, they'll spend most of marketing's money on promotion rather than on an interactive knowledge infrastructure. An organization's responsibilities, attention, and power will gravitate to where the budget is allocated.

10. A reevaluation of the roles of existing functional responsibilities. Businesses should also begin to define broader responsibilities for marketing, IT, operations, and R&D. They need to bring the various responsibilities together to interact more frequently, seeking new ways to improve the marketing architecture and deliver a persistent customer presence.

Expecting marketing people to build and deploy a marketing architecture may sound like a utopian dream. But the idea of total quality management was also considered next to impossible twenty years ago.

Too many executives settled for less than perfection in design or reliability and, as a result, were content to pay for increased service or high customer losses. Clearly the task is bigger than the marketing department.

By combining the best of the consumer, business-to-business, and services industries with information technology and networks, businesses can plan, develop, nurture, and sustain a marketing architecture. From consumer and retail, we learn the value of efficient logistics and cost management; from business-to-business the value of direct relationships and adaptation to customer needs; from service businesses the value of personal interaction; and from the franchise business, the value of uniform knowledge networks. This may seem like a simplistic way to look at each of these business specialties, but by combining the best features of each of them, a business can envision and create a marketing architecture that delivers a persistent presence.

There may be no one business that incorporates the best of all these various practices. But we can well see that product businesses are adopting more and more of a service approach to business, and that technology is allowing everyone to interact on a more personal level. Interacting with millions of people in any other way but via information systems, self-serve software programs, and interconnecting support and response networks is still too costly and complex from any business viewpoint. I expect that within the next few decades over half of all services, and their marketing interactions, will be handled either by people-to-computers or computer-to-computer systems.

We need a new definition of marketing, one that encompasses not only the new network technologies but the many enterprise players necessary to attract, satisfy, and sustain customer loyalty as well. Here is my take at such a new definition:

> *Marketing is an integrating architecture that enables the continuous process of organizational learning, whereby the enterprise gains knowledge by continuously interacting with customers and the marketplace in order to learn, adapt, and respond creatively and competitively.*

Chapter Eight

Total Global Access

Act Globally and Connect Locally

A decade ago, some businesses promoting globalization tended to repeat the phrase "think globally but act locally" like a mantra. Few businesses really paid much attention to it, other than to repeat the phrase in speeches and annual reports. I contend that we should resurrect the phrase with a different focus today: "Act globally and connect locally."

G LOBAL MARKETING is the business and process of developing local presence in distant places, in the interest of leveraging existing resources, growing revenues, optimizing distribution, addressing logistics, preempting competition, and engaging and satisfying new customers. Companies succeed at global marketing by engaging people, and the only way for a company to do that is by becoming part of the community. "Culture does not reveal itself in five-star hotels," says *Globalization and Culture* author John Tomlinson, "but in the streets, the houses, the churches, the workplaces, the bars and the shops that lie beyond the business or tourist centers."[1]

Some of the most well-known and successful companies today have built their global brands by focusing on their customers' experience;

companies like Coca-Cola, Starbucks, Visa, Sony, IBM, L'Oréal, McDonald's, Nokia, Toyota, and Disney are all good examples. But it's no easy task; even companies with long and successful track records find managing multiple operations and marketing within diverse countries difficult and increasingly complex.

Globalization, Marketing, and Economic Development

Globalization is the commercial operation of business activities across multiple national boundaries. It often takes something of a bad rap. In less developed countries, globalization is sometimes viewed as an exploitation of the countries' human and physical resources; developed countries, on the other hand, tend to see the expansion of operations into less developed countries as a way to gain competitive market share. Without question, both governments and corporations have exploited foreign resources. But over time, we've also seen the good side of globalization. For one thing, global commerce has promoted the evolution and natural flow of economic development throughout the world.

Most companies begin their early marketing efforts by reaching beyond their own borders to establish relationships with local suppliers, distributors, representatives, and license and market development partners. This coin has two sides. On the positive side, the global companies can use local companies' intellectual and physical assets as leverage in a new market. On the negative side, intermediaries are placed between the business and the customer, which often obscures the real dynamics of the daily market interaction. Information technology in the form of global networks promises to turn both sides of this coin into a positive situation by establishing knowledge networks with both the intermediaries and the end customer.

According to Peter Weill and Marianne Broadbent, authors of *Leveraging the New Infrastructure*, international business organizations fall into one of four categories: multinational, international, transnational, or global.

The basis for identifying a company as one of these types is the extent to which it deploys and manages company assets, and whether information within the company is centralized or decentralized. *Multinational* firms manage information predominantly at the local level, where the local firms have a high degree of autonomy. *International* firms tend to disperse their information management and develop a certain amount of cross–business unit infrastructure services. *Transnational* firms evolve to a "federated approach," with some IT services managed across the firm and others managed locally. *Global* firms centralize IT management in order to "deliver the consistency and extensive range of infrastructure required to match a firms' centralization of operations and assets."[2]

Advances in global communications technologies—in particular, the World Wide Web—are changing those definitions. Until recently, global commerce has relied on proprietary communication networks for internal logistics with local and somewhat autonomous representatives interacting with the customers. Thanks to technology, the world's communications infrastructures are becoming increasingly linked, giving a growing proportion of the world's population access to vast amounts of information.

The World Wide Web is key to these changes. From a global perspective, it offers an entirely new way to interact with distant markets and people. Hundreds of millions of people worldwide will have access to information sources separated from their local gained knowledge base, which means that people from many different economic levels and cultures can access information unimpeded by the regulatory and political controls often placed on broadcast media. When controls are applied, many users seem to find ways of circumventing them.

Our understanding of the communications nuances of this new technology, other than as corporate operational tools, is less clear. As George Lipsitz points out, "The capacity of mass communications to transcend time and space creates instability by disconnecting people from past traditions, but it also liberates people by making the past less determinate of experiences in the present."[3]

In addition to advances in communications, competition in every industry is intensifying in mature markets, and there are new opportunities for reaching customers in China, parts of Eastern Europe, Latin America, Africa, and Southeast Asia. Early players in these new markets may well have the "first mover" advantage by developing an understanding of the local market and the nuances of government regulations, by adapting business processes, by usurping relationships with local partners and distribution channels, and by developing the information infrastructure necessary to better use, manage, and integrate global assets.

Little discussion and thought have been applied to the impact of cross-border, interactive marketing and communications and their effects on the development of global markets, cultures, and customers. But these things have a great deal to do with the quality of a company's marketing on a global scale. For the company entering a new territory, the market, experience, and lessons learned may be entirely new. But the global market has a history, much of which carries undesirable baggage.

Traditionally, many people have viewed marketing as the exploitation of the masses; I have long believed that marketing executives must reach beyond their narrow functional confines to become engaged in the larger issues of the enterprise and the marketplace. By doing so, the marketing executive's stature, perspective, and role will gain far greater credibility. The agent that forces marketing's enlightenment may well be the global customer's access to diverse local sources of information. For example, someone can obtain information about a new pharmaceutical on the Web, then contact a friend or visit Japan or Europe, say, to obtain a prescription drug that the FDA has not yet approved in the United States. The U.S. government's clamp-down on Napster has not prevented people around the world from exchanging or illegally purchasing copyrighted music titles online. Even though customers differ from one part of the world to another, producers tend to develop ideas, styles, and products that easily adapt and appeal to customers in many countries. Quite often, enthusiastic customers in distant markets seek out and buy products for reasons we do not quite understand. Marketers must be sensitive to the needs and wants of the local consumers in order to guide the adaptation of those products and services.

Global Commerce: From Exploitation to Economic Development

While local commerce has existed for thousands of years, global commerce has a shorter history. It has evolved alongside new forms of enabling technology. As civilizations evolved, governments and business interests pushed the advancement of technology when it helped them expand their power and influence, and global commerce followed. Soon after fifteenth-century explorers found a way around the tip of Africa in search of a faster route to the spices and silks of the Far East, regular trade between distant points became a means for increasing wealth and power. As trade expanded, bigger, faster, and better-armed ships were designed to meet insatiable appetites for profits and growth.

Until the nineteenth century, global information traveled at the speed of ships, which meant that delivering a message from a distant land to London or Amsterdam could take up to half a year. While the invention of the telegraph and then the telephone shortened that time dramatically, the cost of delivering information still remained high. For example, the cost of sending a hundred-word telegram in the 1860s was $700, in today's dollars.[4] As a result, only the wealthiest companies and the most powerful nations could rapidly expand trade.

The invention of the telephone and the expansion of its network brought costs down enough to stimulate new visions of global commerce, once again for those who could afford it. Noted economist John Maynard Keynes foresaw the kind of network the Internet would make possible more than half a century later. In 1919, he wrote, "The inhabitant of London could order by telephone, sipping his morning tea in bed, the various products of the whole earth, in such quantity as he might see fit, and reasonably expect their early delivery upon his doorstep; he could adventure his wealth in the natural resources and new enterprises of any of any quarter of the world."

Notwithstanding Keynes's foresight, the practicality of e-commerce was then but an economist's dream. The free flow of goods and the rapid deployment of physical presence were severely limited, partly by the logical complexity of long-distance communications and partly by the high cost of such communication. In 1930, a three-minute phone call from New York to London cost about $300 in today's dollars, but it would cost less than 20 cents today.[5]

Recent historical events have increased the potential for global business dramatically. The end of the cold war shifted the global battle of ideologies to a battle for commercial world market share; since then, world trade in goods and services has expanded, as evidenced by its almost 6 percent growth over the past decade. While the United States and Europe still accounted for 60 percent of world trade in 2000, almost every region of the world benefited. Regional trading "networks" such as the North American Free Trade Agreement (NAFTA) and Mercosur have helped hasten trade liberalization, as well as industry privatization and lower tariffs. As we move into the twenty-first century, the world's political, economic, and social structures are entering a new interconnected theater accelerated by economic restructuring and self-interest. Businesses are driving a new economy and possibly a new economic order based on business-to-business and social networks that supply and support an interconnected global community.

Global commerce dominated by business self-interests may sound like an inhuman, mechanistic, all-commercial world, a blight rather than a benefit. But increasing the standard of living for more peoples of the world is an economic and social necessity. The growing disparity between rich and poor nations will not decrease until all nations embrace economic development, market economies, and a long-term perspective.

The foes of globalization would do well to study a bit of history. The U.S. semiconductor company Fairchild set up assembly operations in Hong Kong in 1963 and became the progenitor of today's huge Southeast Asian electronics industry. U.S. investment in manufacturing plants not only increased the area's standard of living but also helped establish a technology presence in Southeast Asia. Eventually many semiconductor companies from the United States, Europe, Japan, and Korea used the low-cost labor and skills of that region to pursue Moore's Law. One of the unforeseen consequences of technology and trade is that the low-cost labor assembly regions have benefited from the transfer of knowledge and new skills and the increased wealth flowing into the region. Over time, many Southeast Asian companies have applied what they've learned by designing and manufacturing their own products and brands for global markets.

By participating in the economic development of those regions, businesses can help foster a new "global middle class" capable of absorbing the output of ever-prolific production capabilities. Ireland is a recent example of such a transfer; its successful economic development over the past twenty years exemplifies this self-interest. That success is the result of several factors: European Economic Community investments; the development of industry-friendly regulation and tax policies; and the placing of Irish Industrial Development Authority (IDA) regional marketing offices in Silicon Valley, Tokyo, and other world centers of industry. Early companies such as Apple Computer, Amdahl, and Japan's NEC participated in the promotion of the region by encouraging others to follow them in setting up assembly and manufacturing operations. Early participants added local employment, new skills, and communications infrastructures, as well as advisers to the IDA on needed changes in policy and infrastructure.

Over 1,200 companies have taken advantage of the low-cost labor, tax, and export benefits and the growth of the Irish market. And more than 1,000 new home-grown entrepreneurs have launched their own businesses. According to the World Trade Organization, the average annual rate of increase in the Irish GDP has been 9 percent over the seven-year period from 1993 to 1999. Ireland is one of the most open trading economies in the world; the value of exports and imports combined amounted to over 16 percent of its GDP in 1999.[6]

The Global Market Opportunity

The growth in market economies, deregulation, privatization, and the awakening of the new global consumer are major stimulants for the growth of global commerce. In addition, the efficiencies of communication and transportation methods have collapsed time and distance in such a way that the geographic location of suppliers and production plants is less and less important. Modern plants are highly automated, and the huge increases in productivity in recent decades have given most operations the capability to outproduce market demand. And automation, logistics, and other applied production technologies give us an overabundance of goods.

In the world of high tech, the oversupply of everything from capital to telecommunication infrastructure equipment and personal computers helped bring on a recession in 2001. Production efficiencies also push companies' marketing efforts to find and compete for new markets and customers—which is why many businesses expanded their channels by selling into private-label markets. It has also led to much industry consolidation, such as Daimler-Benz's acquisition of Chrysler. According to the authors of *Taken for a Ride: How Daimler-Benz Drove Off with Chrysler,* Chrysler CEO Bob Eaton struggled with this problem before seeking a buyer:

> *Eaton sat alone at his desk one morning in June 1997. Spread out before him were documents detailing the size, products, and profits of the world's forty automobile manufacturers. About ten, Eaton figured, were making money. Even fewer earned a decent return on investment. The industry landscape seemed to be shifting in ways unimaginable, he thought. An astonishing number of new assembly plants were going up around the globe, way more than needed to meet current demand. Eaton started scribbling calculations. He tallied up the industry expansion in Korea, Southeast Asia, Central Europe, Latin America, and elsewhere and came to the stunning conclusion that by the year 2002, demand would lag production by the equivalent of eighty assembly plants. The overcapacity would equal the size of six Chrysler Corporations. Eaton shuddered.*[7]

With most major competitors in any major market category operating at high efficiency and cost parity, we've seen a marked decline in the prices of almost everything manufactured. The WTO's 2001 annual report points out that in the year 2000, prices of manufactured goods fell for the fifth consecutive year, causing average prices to fall to their lowest level in ten years.[8] Even though the developed countries command well over half the world's trade, the WTO reported that export countries of the world had a faster nominal trade growth, "with exports and imports of developing countries expanding by more than 20%, lifting their share in world merchandise trade to the highest level in the last 50 years."[9] Over all, global trade in goods and services exceeded $6.5 trillion in 2000, up from just $2.4 trillion in 1980.

That's the good side of globalization. On the other side, 54 of the 176 countries monitored by the IMF (International Monetary Fund) in 1999 had per capita GDPs under two dollars a day.[10] This disparity demands that global business leaders begin to think seriously about economic market development beyond "making and selling" and is important for self-interest reasons. People who enjoy a high standard of living buy more goods and services than those who don't. To keep factories producing and corporations growing, new consumers with purchasing power must enter the marketplace. Otherwise, businesses will find their brands devalued, as price declines accelerate and the battle for market share is dominated by competitive low-price bidding for the same affluent customers.

The positive aspect of the constant pressure to improve productivity, lower costs, and encourage competitive pricing creates an opportunity for the developing as well as the developed regions of the world, enabling all to participate, both as producers and as consumers. China's rapid growth in both exports and imports is an example; its markets have become the hunting ground for every type of product, from computers and cell phones to textiles, paper, and chemicals.

Since 1992, when the U.S. government lifted its trade ban with China, the enormous market opportunities for that region of the world have become a reality. China is the fastest-growing IT and telecommunication market in the world today; it is also fraught with political, social, infrastructure, and cultural market differences that can present huge obstacles to market penetration. With 1.3 billion people spread over 3.7 million square miles (slightly larger than the United States, which is 3.6 million square miles), China obviously has a need and a market for communications as well as environmentally sound transportation. The country has been investing heavily in the infrastructure of telecommunications, putting some $25 billion into equipment in 2000 and thus becoming the second largest IT market in the world, behind the United States. Yet China's highway infrastructure is inadequate, and low-cost auto loans are practically unavailable.

The need for a communications infrastructure is evident from the country's significant investment commitment to telecommunications and IT. Since 1992, many companies, from Macy's and Bloomingdale's to AT&T and Applied Materials, have established manufacturing operations, sales offices, and local partnerships. In 1995, IBM set up a research lab in Beijing. Recently, AOL Time Warner invested $100 million in a partnership with Legend Holdings, a personal computer company. Legend will develop "consumer interactive services" and AOL Time Warner will own 49 percent of the new company. China is well along the path toward a total access marketplace.

The Network-Forcing Agent of Organizational Change

While globalization is not a new business phenomenon, managing global operations and interacting with distant peoples via the networks is very new. Network technologies are the means of communicating, but they also carry information that empowers those who use it. Shifting "local knowledge" to the network is one thing. Assuming that a manager in one part of the world can use that information to make judgments is something quite different.

Corporations have long struggled with how to manage distant operations. Most tend to send home-office executives to initiate and manage distant operations to make sure that local practices conform to the company's standard operating processes. Eventually, local nationals replace those executives, but the problem of communication between different geographic regions continues because opinion and individual perspectives dominate the exchange of information.

The battle over "centralized" or "decentralized" management took place largely in the late 1980s and early 1990s. The model that has been emerging since then combines both centralized and decentralized operations by structuring business activity around a "network" that is accessible to all managers and stakeholders. Everyone has an opportunity to learn by continuous engagement. Senior executives can "see into" operations from different locations, manage inventories, and track sales, with far more accurate and current information. The open standards of the World Wide Web allow for applications and content to be deployed rapidly and adapted locally. Network-based information gives us the best of both centralized and decentralized worlds, while vastly improving the efficiency, adaptation, and lower cost of both deployment and maintenance.

The modern organization is a network of interconnected responsibilities. No corporate function today is an island. Decision-making executives (or anyone who has the right to access) across the enterprise can monitor changes and develop relevant programs to respond to market conditions, something that does a lot to sustain customer presence because it's "listening and responding" anywhere, anytime. The network is forcing a redistribution of responsibilities, allowing many more executives to participate in local and global opportunities and issues.

As globalization matures, companies are relying on information-based networks to create value both from and in diverse markets as they exchange goods, services, and capital within their enterprise and between partners in a production or distribution chain. Few businesses have the financial or management resources required to effectively develop and operate complex global operations. It takes long-term investment in local markets, information systems, and people. *Globalization and Culture* author Tomlinson has defined globalization as "complex connectivity."[11] Complexity increases with every new node in the chain and local adaptation, which means that a company can't gain value by simply managing data in a highly efficient logistics network.

Global strategies demand knowledge and timely information as well as experienced management capable of defining the market's threshold for innovation, novelty, new services, and value. They also require knowledge about how and when to adapt to local competition and cultures. Today's networks can deliver data and information, but they can't deliver insight, understanding, or judgment. Rather, those who access the information, and make decisions about how to deploy and use it, are the ones who must discern the significance of that information.

Total Global Access versus Total Cultural Conformity

Today's global marketplace is vastly different from what we've known. It's a place of paradox, in that common technology and protocols operate across social, geographic, and political boundaries, while individuals of uncommon ideas and aspirations increasingly use the technology for expressing individual preferences. In an ideal world for most traditional businesses and marketers, uniform tastes and cultures converge, and customers buy into and consume globally branded products and services. That's a much easier marketplace to deal with because nothing has to change, but that world is vanishing along with mass production. And its disappearance is certainly a challenge to today's businesses.

The idea that the world's population is becoming one like-minded global citizen is a myth. The reality is that the world is becoming more culturally diverse all the time. In California, for example, there is no ethnic majority. "It may be that only Western nations interpret Asian consumerism as 'aping the West,'" says Louise Williams of the *Sidney Morning Herald*. Middle-class Asians see themselves as part of a modernization process, not "a look-alike version of Western society."[12] Networks encourage individuality while also giving users an opportunity to share in their chosen communities. One of the network's effects may well be to encourage cultural dichotomy. People can buy into a common community perception regarding some activities and issues, and they can act individually in regard to others.

A mass-market approach to global marketing hasn't faded from practice; many marketing executives still believe that television has the power to turn everyone in the world into a model of an American consumer. There is some truth to this view. IBM, Microsoft, Levi's, Coca-Cola, and *Seinfeld* are all globally recognized American-based products. And while other names such as Toyota, Sony, Armani, and Chanel are also internationally recognized for their brand presence, those businesses all had to adapt to local requirements; some changed their products and others adapted to local distribution and sales channels, pricing requirements, regulations, and variations in the meaning and delivery of service. Logos are banned from broadcast media in China, so businesses must build identity around their presence and relevance to the market. To isolate brand from any local considerations is to lose touch with those customers. The concept of global brands also fosters a certain "brand arrogance" that often undermines the maintenance of competitive vigilance, as well as the sensitivity to local customers' concerns.

If consumers were the same regardless of their geographic locations, it would be much easier for businesses to base strategic models on their own home markets. Companies in the United States would then assume that response to images and messages is identical throughout the world. American "values and culture" are both admired and despised around the world; U.S.-based television programs are held up as examples of both good and bad influences. They are praised for their diversity and choice but universally condemned for their reliance on violence and consumerism. Broadcast may be universal, but interpretation and response are local. After all, we derive meaning from the context of our daily lives.

In many local markets today, the old ways are practiced right alongside the new. Marketing for most companies on a global sphere is a mixture of centralized and decentralized functions and responsibilities. I believe this is changing for two reasons: Marketing executives have had to take a comprehensive world-market view to respond to the increasingly competitive environment, and global customers with universal access to information looking for local sources and solutions.

The Mobile Global Consumer

Well before the Internet came on the scene, business-to-business (B2B) connectivity existed via private communication networks. Companies from Procter & Gamble to GE, from Toyota and Ford Motor to Intel, connected distant operations, suppliers, and manufacturing locations in an attempt to manage the supply chain and keep tabs on operations and sales. Over the past decade, the transition to Internet-based communication provided a much cheaper way to gather and exchange information, and it gave access capability to many more managers in all locations. In fact, it's changing the quality of B2B communications.

But the most significant change the Internet has introduced is universal customer access. For the first time, large numbers of consumers and customers have access to corporate and public databases via Web sites. This access is adding a new layer of complexity to management and marketing. While global businesses gained a new tool for faster and more efficient intracompany communications, little conversation has taken place about the nature and intricacy of communicating with and satisfying customers in diverse parts of the globe simultaneously. Communication is two-way, and it involves much more than simply developing Web sites in different languages.

As a group, global-Net consumers are on the rise. They are a paradoxical group, existing in a hybrid of local and global cultures. These consumers are well aware of their national identities, but they also have a thirst to expand beyond the boundaries of their tradition-bound culture. Ann Cvetkovich and Douglas Kellner have observed that "the intersection of the global and the local is producing new matrixes to legitimize the production of hybrid identities, thus expanding the realm of self-definition."[13] We may well see an entirely new response to the mass marketing approaches from this new hybrid generation, presenting global marketers with the challenge of figuring out the "self-definition" and "identity" of individuals who are steeped in their local cultures yet equally in touch with global trends.

While in Brazil recently, I met the son of a friend, along with three of his classmates, all of whom were studying business at a university in Rio de Janeiro. Thanks to the Web—which they could access through their school computers—they had an amazing grasp of what was happening with businesses throughout the world, particularly what was going on in high tech in the United States. While they updated me on which companies were hot in Brazil and the status of local Internet access, they also offered opinions on Napster, Yahoo!, AOL, Microsoft, and Amazon.com, and the ill-fated dot.coms. From time to time I meet other young professionals from many parts of the world, and like my friend's son and his friends, all are fluent in "Internet-speak" and are well aware of the changing world marketplace, particularly in the high-tech arena.

Because the cost of accessing the Internet is still prohibitively high for most people in the world, these young people are only a small representative group. With more and more countries deregulating their telecommunications industries and altering trade rules, however, the cost of communication access as well of PCs, cell phones, and other communication devices will decline. Brazil, for example, deregulated application service providers (ASPs) in 1995. In 1999, AOL entered the market, creating a lower-cost competitive access market. More than 4 million people are now online, with growth estimated at 50 percent per year. The cost of bandwidth to a Brazilian ASP is still five to six times higher than in the United States.[14] Despite expensive access service in many parts of the world, over 50 percent of the online community originates from outside the United States.[15]

To date, the computer has been the primary access device to the Internet. But over the next few years, we will see an increase in the variety of low-cost devices used for personal data storage, voice communication, and Internet access. DoCoMo of Japan, which many see as a marketing model for the mobile connection, is taking a lower-cost and more consumer-friendly approach to access. In 1992, the deregulation of NTT (Nippon Telegraph and Telephone) split the company into four operations, freeing its wireless operation to determine its own future. Despite its regulated and bureaucratic heritage, since deregulation DoCoMo has acted like a hot entrepreneurial start-up. Thanks to its innovation, imagination, and grasp of its customers' context, the company can claim 60 percent of Japan's cellular market, and 70 percent of the local wireless Web market. In the summer of 2000, DoCoMo was Japan's most valuable company.[16]

Subscribers to DoCoMo's always-on "I-mode" service pay only for the information they access. In Akihabra, a DoCoMo cell phone costs about 100 yen—around a dollar. The user pays 300 yen per month, plus a fraction of a yen for each packet of information—about 4 yen for sending an e-mail or 20 yen for obtaining a detailed news report. Users can send and receive e-mail, handle banking and stock transactions, obtain travel and entertainment information, read daily news, make reservations, and so on—basically, they get all the services that come with the Internet. And DoCoMo has figured out how to make the embedded services transparent: The interface is so simple that the consumer isn't aware of the technology at all.

While DoCoMo's present services don't require much bandwidth, company executives are betting on the continued expansion of bandwidth, the value of ever-expanding connected users, and the power of Moore's Law to provide a continuing array of online novelty. Subscriber growth has been nothing short of phenomenal. For example, the number of subscribers to I-mode, the wireless Internet service, grew from 1 million in August 1999 to over 17 million by the end of 2000.

Perhaps more than any other market activity, global-scale communications technology must be aligned with other standards and business interests. Many European and U.S. companies, including Ericsson and Motorola, for example, are promoting an approach that differs from DoCoMo's, one that allows competitors to design their own products using a universal communication standard called the wireless application protocol, or WAP. Global standards are essential to connect economically via any type of access device to databases anywhere in the world. This standard is compatible with the Internet Protocol and will allow, for example, a wireless phone to access the same information as a home-connected computer.

The development of the standard, and its adoption by telecommunications infrastructure and device suppliers in different countries, is a study in the global relationship market. For a standard to be successful, many market players (or at least the major ones) must adopt it—and each wants a say in its design and each wants the benefits of market opportunity and profitable growth. According to Scott Goldman, CEO of the WAP Forum, "By aligning its technology closely with the IP (Internet Protocol) and the web, WAP is designed both to meet the needs of the largest number of users and to benefit services providers, software developers and device manufacturers while still allowing for differentiation between various devices." Goldman also addresses why this is good for the customer. Interoperability, he says, "requires a standard non-proprietary wireless communications protocol so that the devices, infrastructure, applications and browsers can all 'interoperate' with each other, assuring that the user has a good, consistent experience regardless of which service or hardware they use."[17]

DoCoMo's approach gives Japanese consumers a useful, entertaining, and valuable experience at low cost. Expanding this idea to the rest of the world will require a network of international players adopting their proprietary approach as the standard, so as to deliver services to the new mobile consumer. I expect we will see this infrastructure evolve and take shape over the next decade. However, DoCOMo's success will require that they enlist global partners who buy into their standard and help to propagate it.

Almost two billion people from around the world are expected to be using cellular phones by 2005. Today more than 400 million people use the World Wide Web—50 percent of them outside the United States—with more than 100 million people joining them each year. And an estimated 600 million additional people will gain access to the World Wide Web sometime in the next five years. In this ever-connected world, every individual has increasing access to a common network, a fact that's hardly good news for the mass-minded marketer, whose ideal is to turn everyone into like-minded consumers. If and when the physical and economic barriers to cross-border marketing and selling really do come down, Web surfers will have an almost infinite choice of commodities and will be on top of whatever is new and hot.

As more access media become available and as more of the world's population gains access to the Web, people will express more and more of their preferences: what kinds of choices they want, what prices they want to pay, what services they prefer, and so on. The Web, in this scenario, is educating a global consumer and building expectations that may or may not be within the economic or physical reach of that consumer. Local as well as global competitive firms will try to adapt and respond to those new-found consumer preferences by developing appropriate local services. To achieve universal customer satisfaction, global marketers must become sensitive to local cultural and economic markets. While people outside the United States voice their complaints about the limited choices they have in their own countries, they are tied to the cultural context of their homelands. They don't want to become mirrors of America; they would much rather use the technology and know-how developed here to make improvements at home. "The U.S.," says The McKenna Group's Geoff Mott, "is culturally unsuited as a model for how the rest of the world operates."[18]

Global E-Commerce

Global commerce is a complicated endeavor, and one that few global enterprises have the resources to engage in well. It is so complex that you might say it's global commerce cubed: It involves not only the factors mentioned earlier, but also logistics, marketing, and customer-support technologies. Exactly how global e-commerce will fit into global marketing schemes is difficult to project, given the diversity of users around the world and the lack of sound business models for making money.

Global infrastructure issues will make it difficult for most new e-commerce businesses that rely on only one channel such as the Internet to succeed without acquiring companies or getting significant help from local partners. New ways of governing global trade must be established along with new global business networks. The political and social infrastructures of most countries have not kept pace with the rapidly advancing sophistication of IT and telecommunications business infrastructures. And although technology is pushing regulators to come to terms with economic development, progress is slow. A report by the Internet Society to UNESCO put this in perspective:

> As Internet use in business activities substantially contributes to economic growth in general, the gap in economic development will widen between those countries where end users enjoy the benefits of the Internet, without financial or any other obstacles, and those where they do not. This difference largely coincides with different national telecommunications regulatory regimes, i.e., those countries that are open to competition and others that are not, as the regulations create costs to Internet

users and service providers. Thus, telecommunications regulations create a "digital divide" in economic development on a global scale.[19]

Governments rarely lead technology or social change. They prefer to follow at a safe distance and respond only when the economic need becomes evident.

Global e-commerce marketing, perhaps more than anything we've seen in marketing history, requires an understanding of local regulations, as well as political, economic, social, and competitive market dynamics. Telecommunications and the Internet are, of course, two key players in global e-commerce. Anyone who has traveled to different countries and tried to connect to the Internet knows that not all areas are on a par with the relatively few countries that are advanced in telecommunications. Wireless digital systems, which are already enabling many countries to adapt rapidly to advanced communications systems, will help change many of the incongruities. The problem is that most of the world's telecommunications continue to rely on old technology. For example, while most phone systems in the developed world are considered advanced, most still rely on an analog infrastructure (designed to support voice) and not digital (designed to exchange data) and analog switching technologies.

Digital technology revitalized that aging copper infrastructure by changing its content from analog signals to bits and bytes, and the global economy is being buoyed by nations' rising investments in their telecommunications infrastructures. Worldwide telecommunication equipment and services sales now exceed $2.1 trillion a year, with much of that spent on updating the older analog infrastructure.[20] For business, the change to a digital infrastructure is like the switch to automated container ships for the shipping industry, making it easier to load and transport almost anything while adapting to different modes of carriers. Likewise, music, books, insurance, securities transactions, self-service, banking, education, or any other type of "content" can take digital form and be adapted to various "digital carriers." Those carriers may be cell phones, PDAs, televisions, airplanes, automobiles, kiosks—any number of gadgets and devices.

Global telecommunications works surprisingly well considering much of it is still not modernized and the various infrastructure players promote so many different competing standards. According to Robert Morris, director of IBM Almaden Labs, "The Internet is far less coherent as a global uniform network than is the reality."[21] As Morris points out, the Internet is only a "loosely connected" network of networks. That looseness is demonstrated by the fact that today's limited search engines reach only 30 to 40 percent of the total data available on any single subject.

Global e-commerce still faces old-world regulations, taxes, and entrenched patterns of behavior. The day that consumers in China, India, and the United States can shop freely from a world directory and obtain their purchases securely is a long way off. International advertising restrictions illustrate differing privacy and consumer protection initiatives from country to country. China, for example, closely regulates Internet businesses, requiring all content to be from state-approved sources. Violators risk lengthy prison terms. Vietnam, which the United States recently gave "favored nation" trade status, established regulations forbidding "data that can affect national security, social order, and safety or information that is not appropriate to the culture, morality, and traditional customs of the Vietnamese people." Further, "the directorate reserves the right to define what information falls under those categories."[22] In Europe, Denmark bans advertising to children, France bans advertising in English, and Germany bans comparative advertising.[23]

In most parts of the world, access costs are a big limiting factor. In some European countries, telecom charges can be five times higher than they are in the United States, where there are too many standards but access is almost "free."[24] In the United Kingdom, access charges are 25 percent higher than they are in the United States. Tax issues are also a major concern for governments dealing with cross-border commerce. As the result of much lobbying by the high-tech industry, the Internet is tax-free in the United States. But because local small businesses are not happy with this situation, the tax-free status may well change in the future. A small bookstore in Carmel, California, asks customers to write to the state's legislators to stop the unfair tax of local sales while giving the very same transactions tax-free status over the Internet.

How will global e-commerce affect us? We can start to answer that question by looking at history. Global commerce has had a far-reaching impact on the political, economic, and social makeup of the world, beginning with the exploitation of foreign people and their resources, which led to colonialism. In fact, the world is still reacting to the political effects of early attempts at global commerce. Global e-commerce will have effects as far-reaching or more so. Even though we don't yet know what their long-term effects will be, we're seeing some effects now. Expense is one; the "Love Bug" global virus cost businesses and governments hundreds of millions of dollars. Another is complexity, which is inherent in international business strategies because of country-to-country differences in technology and government regulations. Other potential effects of unlimited global Internet access range from a worldwide gridlock of complexity to increased cooperation between sovereign governments on communication standards, intellectual property protections, trade, e-commerce, privacy, and security.

On the other hand, as access spreads, the Internet may also be a medium enabling the spread of discontent. For example, people who have no choice will be more aware of those who have excessive choice. Unfortunately, we in the United States have already witnessed what can happen when dissident groups use open access to exchange ideas easily with similar groups around the globe. The rise of dissatisfaction may spread faster than the benefits of the new information tools. Global GDP expanded sixteenfold in the past fifty years, owing mostly to trade and more recently to information technology-based products.[25] Still, more than four-fifths of the world's people still have little control over their own economic destinies. Some 40 percent of the world's population, for example, has little or no access to health care, and a third of the world's population is technologically disconnected, neither innovating at home nor adopting foreign technologies.[26]

Establishing Global Persistent Presence

So how does a business establish global persistent presence? Global brands get to be global by learning from "being there" and by adapting products, services, and business practices to the local market. Today, a business must establish local production operations for many different reasons: to overcome regulatory requirements, for political reasons, to head off trade issues, or to have convenient market access. A business must also consider locating in regions where economies are expanding and competitors might establish an infrastructure beachhead. A company might also establish a market leadership position by aggregating and consolidating smaller competitors within a geographic region.

Although fraught with risks, a company's strategy for market expansion might include global acquisitions and partnerships and worldwide logistical support for fulfillment and services. Carrefour, the giant European retailer, is challenging Wal-Mart around the globe. Like Wal-Mart, Carrefour uses its buying clout, according to *Business Week Online*, "to extract deeper discounts from suppliers, undercutting rivals and accelerating a push toward consolidation in the industry." Carrefour is now the number-one retailer not only throughout Europe but in Brazil, Argentina, and Taiwan. It has had regional setbacks, but it has also successfully challenged Wal-Mart in the global marketplace.[27]

Mere knowledge about a local market isn't enough—companies must learn to adapt economically to various channel and service customs and to customer expectations. And, perhaps most basic, companies need to focus on building a global brand by building a local community-participating presence. A word of caution is in order here, though: The cost of building a truly global presence is high, so high that right now the prospect of establishing global presence is within the means of relatively few large and powerful companies. Most exclusively Internet-based businesses will remain local entities until cost and cross-border commerce issues are resolved, or until large global players with established infrastructures and global experience move into their territories. Few will ever become global players. Even in Silicon Valley, only a very few of the tens of thousands of start-ups have emerged from their niche businesses and become global enterprises in the past fifty years. Internet growth won't change that. Instead, it will increase the pressure on new companies to merge or partner with larger ones to gain the resources they need to build their global infrastructures.

At a time when technology had yet to develop the capability to supply variations in product choice at low cost, Henry Ford said, "Any customer can have any car painted any color that he wants, so long as it is black."[28] Automobile manufacturers soon addressed that limitation by innovating in both production systems and consumer marketing. My friend and mentor Ted Levitt, a professor at Harvard Business School, highlighted the idea of "one brand fits all" or "global brands" in a *Harvard Business Review* article in the early 1980s. Levitt argued that well-managed companies are those that offer the world's markets standardized products with advanced functionality and low price. He pointed to the ubiquity of Coca-Cola, McDonald's, Hollywood movies, Revlon cosmetics, and Sony television as examples of "standardized products" that had achieved global brand status, and he stated that treating the world as "one or two distinctive product markets" is simply much more economical than serving multiple markets. "Different cultural preferences, national tastes and standards, and business institutions are vestiges of the past," he wrote.[29]

Levitt's article stimulated new thinking about marketing by pushing then-current thinking beyond the borders of the home market. His viewpoint had a big impact on marketing organizations because many had assumed that marketing was a local initiative. In fact, most international companies I worked with in the 1970s and 1980s gave foreign operations autonomy in local marketing and sales. Whereas I disagree with Levitt's general thesis (chiefly because it doesn't allow for local differences in culture expressed in individual needs and wants), consumers in various world markets do seem to accept brands more readily when they have a limited choice. Even when products are identical from country to country, consumers have different perceptions of price/value, service, and response time and delivery channel. My wife likes to drink caffeine-free Diet Coke, but she finds it almost impossible to find outside California. But the concept of adapting to customers' wants goes well beyond the idea of product variation and choice. Addressing customers as individuals builds loyalty in any country of the world.

Building Global Brands

Managing what's needed to sustain the customer satisfaction necessary to achieve global presence or global branding is almost a business of its own. Building a global brand that addresses multicultural preferences is even more expensive, time-demanding, and complex than building a brand in any home market, owing to the variations in consumer behavior, the need and demand for service, local laws and customs, and the capability of the infrastructure.

Marketers must first *understand the market beneath the surface*. A thorough understanding of the subtleties of the marketplace is difficult to achieve, but it's important to identify the context within which to operate and communicate. Developing this understanding requires time spent in the area and "feet on the ground"—not just exploratory visits by executives or customer surveys. As John Tomlinson points out, "Distant places are culturally close for the business executive because they are carefully negotiated. . . . The orientation of business travel is actually to minimize cultural difference so as to allow the 'universal' practice of the international business culture to function smoothly."[30] People form assumptions during every kind of business activity; executives often make judgments about local cultures based on frequent business visits.

The pressures and pace of business today too often push executives to move rapidly by applying existing business models to new market areas. Partnering and patience are two essential components of the learning process. Joint ventures, alliances, and other partnering activities allow close interaction and exposure to business processes, channels, and customers. Acquisition is another alternative. But managements and investors often lose patience with merger-and-acquisition approaches, demanding rapid integration and immediate improvement in operating efficiencies.

Federal Express and Wal-Mart are two companies that ran into trouble by not thoroughly understanding the territory. Although both had sophisticated infrastructures, they had problems adapting their business and market models to local markets. Federal Express learned that neither its name nor its business model traveled well when it launched into the European market. Wal-Mart, the largest retailer in the world and considered the "best-case" model for that business, learned the same lesson in Germany a few years later, when it chose to control its own U.S.-modeled distribution to the stores, disregarding the German retail distribution infrastructure. As a result, it had a higher incidence of out-of-stock items than competitive German retailers, and it ended up ranking lowest in customer satisfaction of all retailers in Germany. Trying to navigate Germany's planning and social regulations, meet higher labor costs, and face an already low-margin, low-cost retail marketplace, Wal-Mart was reported to be losing as much as $300 million a year.[31] The company can claim only about 2 percent of the German retail market. It will have to find a way to generate substantial growth to reach critical mass. As an experienced international retailer with stores in many other countries, Wal-Mart will probably get it right eventually, but its case illustrates that even the largest retailer in the world doesn't always think locally.

A Vision for the New Consumer

The hope and vision for the "new global consumer" is that new technologies based on information and digital communications will not only bring nations into closer harmony but also give the "have-nots" greater access to new tools for self-empowerment and growth. The United States experienced rapid economic growth in the twentieth century partly because of the emergence of an affluent and consuming "middle class." The value of the "consumer" is often overlooked in economic development, but it's as important to the growth and prosperity of a nation as is a solid technology base. Henry Ford's idea was not only to mass-produce an automobile but also to pay his workers enough for them to afford to buy the product of their labor.

For both the advanced nations and those who strive to be advanced, the development of human resources is key to progress and successful trade. And that's more important than ever in the Information Age. Intellectual capital and the progressive shaping of the marketplace through innovation and efficient implementation are keys to economic progress. The hope for emerging nations is that they move from being exploited to being interactive, beneficial participants in the global economic network. For global businesses to succeed in the twenty-first century, they will need to reevaluate their infrastructure investment priorities to encompass the education and development of developing nations' people. Borders must open to allow access to flourish and to allow for investment in people (or potential consumers) on the global stage.

One of the most difficult challenges facing marketers in the future is to develop the capability to interact and respond to the new global customers, and to adapt and respond to a diverse and constantly changing global marketplace. An understanding of marketing per se won't help them meet the challenge; rather, they must understand local markets—the people as well as the social, economic, and political environment in which they live. This understanding will enable marketers to develop strategies that will help them communicate better with those local markets and link ideas, applications, knowledge, and know-how on a global scale.

Finally, global brands, if they are to be truly global, must rely on a coherent, responsive information network that is capable of gathering information from distant locations and minimizing the cost of responding or deploying resources while maximizing customer satisfaction. That's a big task. Little wonder that twenty-first-century marketing organizations must step up to new challenges.

Chapter Nine

Managing It All

Roles and Responsibilities

Sustained, innovative marketing will continue to evolve as an

integrated, seamless part of the enterprise information network.

It will become an infinite loop of intelligence and learning, gaining

knowledge as it connects and encompasses more participants. The

value of a brand can now be defined as the number of active

participants in a company's total access network.

M ANY YEARS AGO, when I was in the advertising and public relations business, my company researched customers' experiences with a large client's new product. The feedback was mostly negative. I advised the client's vice president to hold off on the product promotion until his company addressed the problem. He replied that fixing the problem was not my concern—that all we were paid to do was achieve the goal, not solve the company's problems. His company's marketing people, though aware of the negative feedback and of the product's problems, nevertheless forged ahead and set a goal "to change the perceptions of the marketplace."

As surprising as it may sound, this sort of thing happens often. Most advertising and public relations people could tell many similar stories.

Economist John Kenneth Galbraith once commented, "Man has become the object of science for man only since automobiles have become harder to sell than to manufacture."[1] Driven by the economic necessity of production, businesses push marketing to convince consumers to buy ever more branded products and services. But the nature of both the enterprise and the market is changing rapidly. More and more businesses are defining themselves as services, and services now constitute a larger part of many company's revenues. As choice and novelty become more and more prevalent and total access constantly shifts consumers' behavior, we must abandon traditional marketing models.

Marketers are too obsessed with the behavior models of customers and push media in a marketplace where consumers are looking for responsiveness. We must work to broaden marketing's role in the enterprise, changing it from a "push" function to a responsive service. Total consumer access, along with increased competition, is changing the nature of the marketplace by shifting it from creating demand to responding to and for customers. In 1973, economist E. F. Schumacher characterized the need for a shift from production for the masses to one of production by the masses in this way: "The technology of production by the masses, making use of the best of modern technology and experience, is conducive to decentralization, compatible with the laws of ecology, gentle in its use of scarce resources, and designed to service the human person instead of making him the servant of machines."[2]

Schumacher must have anticipated the rise of the Internet and total access. Both give rise to user-configured information services or transparently configured self-service. "Production by the masses" means giving consumers access to the information database and allowing them to design their experiences consistently and reliably. In some ways, this concept is not new to marketing. For years, marketers have talked about achieving market "pull" rather than "push," of getting customers to "buy" rather than to "be sold."

How Marketing Came to Be Everyone's Job

Several business concepts popularized over the past few decades—total quality management (TQM), the value chain, and customer relationship management (CRM)—have led businesses to realize that marketing should be a corporate-wide responsibility. In addition, the Internet and total access are having an enormous impact on how companies deploy their marketing resources.

Total quality management requires organizations to focus on improving quality by enlisting everyone from the chairman of the board to the shipping clerk to support its tenets. The very idea of TQM was considered next to impossible twenty years ago. Too many executives settled for less than perfection in design or reliability and, as a result, were content to pay for increased service or high customer losses. Today product and service quality programs are basic essentials for businesses hoping to compete in any market. TQM programs have demonstrated the benefits of improving the customer experience; they've also improved organizational competitiveness through better, more efficient design and production processes, as well as communications. TQM has also spawned a spinout business practice, that of cross-functional teams empowered to address complex, multifunctional challenges and issues within the organization. Teams that integrate and reach across the boundaries of various corporate specialties are now commonplace.

The value chain concept has also contributed to the evolution of marketing thought and practice. A value chain is a model of how businesses systematically add competitive advantage (value) throughout business processes, starting with input materials and progressing through design, production, and product fulfillment. Michael Porter introduced the concept in 1980 in a book titled *Competitive Advantage: Creating and Sustaining Superior Performance.*[3]

Porter's approach is an outside-in approach to business strategy, which he sees as competitively driven while directing all the interrelated corporate functions toward the ultimate goals of customer satisfaction and market leadership. His approach leads an enterprise to a distinctive market presence and a valued brand. Porter's work evolved over the years, and by 1995 he was espousing the idea of "complementary activities." He described this approach in *CIO Magazine*:

> *Rarely does sustainable advantage grow out of a single activity in a business. A company doesn't get sustainable advantage simply because it has some unique product design or a unique sales force. Those kinds of*

advantages tend to be visible targets to imitate. If it relies on one activity as its key strength, all its competitors are going to work very hard to match that—especially if it is dubbed a best practice against which everybody else is benchmarking.

Sustainable advantage comes from systems of activities that are complementary. These "complementarities" occur when performing one activity and gives a company not only an advantage in that activity, but it also provides benefits in other activities.

For example, if a company has a very good inventory management system, it can also offer faster delivery and do so cheaper than a company without the inventory management system. Companies with sustainable competitive advantage integrate lots of activities within the business: their marketing, service, designs, and customer support. All those things are consistent, interconnected and mutually reinforcing.[4]

Since the publication of *Competitive Advantage*, it's rare for a marketing or strategy session not to include a discussion of the value chain. In fact, the value chain is one business concept that has sustained its merit since the 1980s, when a number of "customer-centered" theories and practices, emphasizing the value of the customer as partner rather than as target, became popular. Today the value chain model—or, as I prefer to call it, the value network—remains an excellent way to map the most essential components of corporate value, even though it doesn't take into account the recent developments of total access and interdependent network relationships.

Customer relationship management, or CRM, is a network-enabled way to manage customer relationships by automating various tasks of traditional sales and marketing support activities. With the advent of CRM and other enterprise networks and programs, the diverse functions of the enterprise connect and directly interact with customers in new, unprecedented ways. Although CRM can't replace direct management-to-management contacts, it does provide a way to better manage the important day-to-day details of maintaining customer satisfaction.

Despite the limitations of CRM today, it does help manage business relationships, in particular the complexities and details that are so costly and people-intensive yet still necessary to sustaining good customer service. The issues and challenges that this sort of interconnected enterprise creates are apparent in the evolution of functional roles within today's organizations. And while it's true that great advances have been made, we are still at a very early stage in the evolution of designing and deploying CRM applications that truly manage customer relationships.

Over the next decade, we'll see the evolution of CRM networks that are increasingly intelligent and that offer higher-level human interface, real-time reporting, analysis, simulation modeling, and anticipated responses to customer needs. Higher-performance computers and increased bandwidth will expand the ability of these customer-centric applications to act as intelligent surrogates for management. CRM will also be increasingly interconnected to various databases, functions, and activities, a development that will permit the efficient management of the flow of new products and services to customers.

CRM will further pull marketing into the responsibilities of the CIO and other functional operations. As network-based management tools improve and their contributing value is recognized, such tools will become the standard means of interacting with customers. The IT research firm IDC projects that the CRM market will reach $19 billion by 2005. The market for software licenses is expected to grow from $3.5 billion in 1999 to $24.4 billion in 2005. Companies are committing to CRM because they see it as both a cost-saving measure as well as a way to manage the customer service interface efficiently. As customers use these systems, they too will come to expect the immediacy and responsiveness they encounter with them.

A New Definition, New Roles

The Internet, total access, CRM, supply chain management software, Web sites, and marketing automation tools have helped forge a new marketing, one that insists on a revised definition that will encompass not only the new network technologies but the many enterprise players necessary to attract, satisfy, and sustain customer loyalty as well. Marketing must be recognized throughout the enterprise as a coordinating, value-building architecture that integrates people and resources with the mission to serve customers. By mediating and expanding access to the knowledge network, continuously interacting with customers and the market-supporting infrastructure, marketing empowers everyone in the enterprise to participate in the process of sustaining customer relationships.

Owing to total access and the interactive nature of the new media, the enterprise will receive more information from the marketplace than it will send out. Marketing, then, must shift gears and become a responsive function rather than a *brandcast* one. This kind of marketing differs dramatically from the "push" marketing of years past. Marketing as a push activity is easy to execute, while marketing as an interactive and enterprise-learning architecture is difficult. Marketers will need to develop and integrate the network of resources available to the corporation; to provide customers with continuous access to those resources; and to manage the systems for interacting with, responding to, and managing the various transactions. They will need a lot of help, because all these tasks are clearly beyond the scope of today's marketing charter and capabilities.

Adopting this new definition requires not only a different mind-set but a cultural change in the management of the enterprise as well. Today marketing is everything, and it includes everyone.

Over the years, I have had the opportunity to meet and befriend many CIOs and directors of R&D. In each of these relationships, I've been impressed not only by these specialists' breadth of knowledge of the technologies but also by their knowledge of business models, market development, and their customers. We often discuss their role in the marketing process. In the past, most technical specialists would disclaim any knowledge or expertise in the area of marketing. Many still disclaim any knowledge of marketing but their conversations about their role in the enterprise now includes phrases such as "satisfying customer," "brand leadership," and "value creating." My conclusion from these conversations is that, like TQM, marketing is permeating the enterprise, and more and more executives feel a new tide of market interaction pulling them ever closer to the customer. It's also becoming more clear that marketing is everyone's responsibility and that the current charter for most marketing organizations has yet to recognize the impact that networks are having on their role and responsibilities.

Marketing today is a matrix or network of responsibilities shared by the CEO, CIO, director of R&D, vice president of operations and logistics, vice president of marketing, and others:

- *The President/CEO as Chief Strategist.* The CEO is the one responsible for seeing that everything becomes a unified, integrated strategy. He or she is ultimately viewed as the person responsible for defining and successfully implementing the business model and market strategy. As such, the CEO is also the chief marketing officer, because he or she is the only one who has the power and perspective to integrate all the resources the enterprise needs to invest, design, and build a global infrastructure strategy.

- *The CEO's Alter Ego: Vice President of Business Development.* In recent years, a new position has assumed the task of building major corporate alliances, seeking out acquisition and merger opportunities, and forging key customer and supplier alliances. Usually titled "vice president of business development" and already a separate role within many organizations, this function is responsible for building a market leadership position, as well as for overseeing rapid expansion into new markets.

- *The CIO as Chief Total Access Architect.* In a total access environment, information must be managed, distributed, and appropriately applied—and secure. An enterprise information network handles all these tasks. Marketing information is constantly feeding into that knowledge base, touching all those who share that information. The CIO has the technical and network management skills to be the interface between the customer's need and the company's response. As the marketing system's architect and implementer of the interactive supporting infrastructure or marketing architecture, the person responsible for the information network is in the best position to integrate the various players and resources.

- *The Chief Novelty Officer: The Director of R&D.* Traditionally seen at the opposite end of the spectrum from marketing, the director of R&D is now responsible for the development of "game-changing" products and services. With novelty a consumer preference, the head of R&D is essentially a "chief novelty officer." For him or her to be efficient, research and development people must be engaged with customers, with the goal of investing in and bringing market-driven innovations to market.

- *Operations Logistical Support Vice President.* The logistical support function has emerged as an essential and critical element of customer satisfaction. If, as some say, a brand is a promise, this function is critical for satisfying a major part of that promise: meeting the customer's delivery expectations.

- *Vice President for Service and Self-Service.* An officer charged with these responsibilities will develop and manage the use of networks and interface software to design and build efficient customer response—which will become increasingly important as customers gain easy-to-use access. Understanding the service business and function is both an art and a science, requiring experienced executives who know how to implement processes and metrics, as well as interface with customers.

- *Vice President of Advertising and Public Relations.* The person in this role is responsible for the traditional functions of advertising, public relations, and promotion. Paradoxically, in this age of easy and cheap access, diverse media, and overabundance of networking resources, communicating to the market and customers is more difficult and complex than ever. More demands for knowledge and systems expertise, performance, and measured results will be levied on this function. Continued innovation will be demanded.

Because of their critical importance, we'll look at the first four roles in detail.

The CEO as Chief Strategist

I have a question for you: Who is responsible for the marketing strategy of Intel, Apple, Microsoft, Cisco, IBM, Federal Express, AOL Time Warner, or Procter & Gamble? The answer, which may surprise you, is the same across the board. It's the top person: Craig Barrett at Intel, Steve Jobs at Apple, Steve Ballmer and Bill Gates at Microsoft, John Chambers at Cisco, Lou Gersner at IBM, Fred Smith at Federal Express, Steve Case at AOL, and now Alan G. Lafley at P&G. Each of these companies has a top marketing executive, but in terms of the market—the company's strategic partners, investors, analysts, media, and customers—the person unifying the company's marketing strategy is the top person in the company.

A study by the Silicon Valley Chapter of the American Marketing Association found that while 90 percent of the CEOs of technology companies considered marketing critical to the success of their companies, over 74 percent of them rated the effectiveness of their marketing programs as poor, fair, or average.[5] Apparently CEOs are taking matters into their own hands these days—or maybe shareholders are demanding a change. In any event, it's becoming increasingly clear that the caretaker of the corporate strategy is the CEO. Changes in the top spots at IBM, HP, Intel, GE, Procter & Gamble, Coca-Cola, Apple, NEC, Microsoft, Lucent, PeopleSoft, and Mattel were viewed with the kind of anticipation that you'd expect in response to major changes in corporate strategy. Only a few of the changeovers I've mentioned were transitions that resulted from a succession plan; most came about via stockholder and board pressure on the CEO, caused by declining revenues and the lack of a clear, competitive market direction.

So what's the role of today's CEO? Certainly he or she must rely on the executive team for specialized advice and counsel. And most CEOs want and need to communicate with Wall Street, investors, and customers on the progress of their business—which is why so often one of the first things a new CEO does is to command a new advertising campaign. New ads present a visible symbol of change. The new message hits the market, which in turn builds anticipation for rapid improvement. Unfortunately, too often the new CEO's vision for change as projected in the advertising is far ahead of the organization's ability to respond. As a result, more often than not the market suffers "postpartum blues."

To reinvent or reenergize the company, the new CEO must turn to the people who can cut costs; improve productivity; develop new products, services, and markets; divest or acquire operations; engage untapped customers; develop new alliances; expand geographically; and integrate everything with an information network. These activities can change the substance of a company and build greater value for customers and shareholders alike. Today CEOs are engaged in major customer relationships, alliances, contracts, acquisitions, and the hiring of key executives. All these activities are more fundamental to the marketing process than any form of promotion because they address the bottom line, which has a direct impact on the company's leadership position. They must fit a common strategy that translates into increased customer and market value.

Here are the three most significant marketing assets a company can put forth, along with what they entail:

1. Growth versus the competition (you're doing things right)

   - New products/services
   - Industry infrastructure alliances
   - Acquisitions and/or mergers

2. Market share increase (you're satisfying customers)

   - Major customer agreements
   - Positioning in growth markets
   - Total access, points of presence
   - New channel expansion
   - Multiple-channel synchronization and customer access
   - CRM systems deployment

3. Profits (you're doing things well)

   - Improved productivity
   - Asset management
   - Focused strategies
   - Clearly defined business model
   - Innovative competitive differentiation
   - Value-creating novelty
   - Efficiency of services
   - Quarter-to-quarter incremental earnings

In a complex, uncertain, and noisy information environment, the one clear message that management has the right strategy and vision will come from growth and positive financials. Those two things—growth and positive financials—compose a company's best marketing face because they instill confidence both in the company's capabilities as a business and in investors' decisions to buy from the company. The marketplace of the 1990s was one of vision, and of promise with high expectations of return. The marketplace of the present decade is more pragmatic and demands "show-me" financial performance. Profitable companies have the capacity to exercise more freedom of action. They can acquire, invest, deploy resources, and attract new employees and partners. Companies that cannot invest, build infrastructure, expand services, develop efficiencies, and continually deliver novelty at the lowest competitive costs

A Model Marketing CEO

Managements are struggling today to find the right mix of talents and organizational flexibility to manage and grow the business. Experienced executives in marketing—indeed, in all management roles—are scarce. Perhaps this is why we find so few models of superior performance. Marketing needs models as well. Bill Campbell is the chairman and former CEO of Intuit and former executive vice president, group executive of the United States for Apple Computer. Bill joined Apple in 1983 as vice president of marketing and sales. He was a driving force not only during Apple's high-growth period but also through some turbulent times. Bill was dedicated to learning about the total business not from within Apple but from out in the marketplace. By spending time with customers, dealers, software developers, and even competitors, Bill quickly earned a reputation as a leader in the personal computer industry. During Apple's bleak days after Steve Jobs left and Mac sales declined, a former Apple executive told me, "Bill personally saved Macintosh one dealer at a time."

Bill refers to the time he spent interacting with the market as "my education." Because of that "education," he is knowledgeable about all the various players in the market and actions within the marketplace, but he is also highly attuned to the operational details of the business. He can analyze a financial statement as well or better than most CFOs. At Apple and at Intuit, when boards and management pushed for growth, Bill fought for profitability. Rather than building Apple's image in the media, Bill spent more than half his time in the marketplace with customers, sales people, and dealers, and he spent the other half in the office, fighting for changes in products, pricing, and policies. When Bill first met Steve Case, then vice president of marketing at AOL, in 1986, Bill wanted to license AOL's technology to create an Apple network to service dealers and then extend it to customers. He became president of Claris, the spinout of Apple's software business, and proceeded to convince management that to be a software developer, Claris would also have to develop applications for the PC market. In a consequential decision, Apple management chose to keep the operation proprietary. Bill left the company. (*continued*)

Bill's first task at Intuit was to ensure the long-term viability of Intuit products by having all the basic code rewritten so it could be easily updated in the future. His early moves enabled the company to maintain its leadership in the face of intense competition from Microsoft, Oracle, and IBM. Intuit is now the leading provider of financial software and Web-based services for consumers, small businesses, and accounting professionals.

Perhaps there is no better way to illustrate the breadth and success of this CEO marketing executive than to quote a company profile written by JobCircle.com, an employment and information Web site for information technology job seekers:

> Intuit promotes a culture of "hard work and hard play," insiders say. The company stresses teamwork, and employees remark that their ability to complement each other's strengths and weaknesses is one of Intuit's leading assets. Employees describe the office atmosphere as "casual and sometimes quite playful," with "no dress code—written or unwritten—to speak of." While employees often work long schedules when a project nears completion, they say that Intuit "recognizes that its employees have lives outside of the office." "At Intuit," says an insider, "the firm considers their employees 'internal customers' and those who call for support 'external customers.'"*

* See <http://www.jobcircle.com/career/profiles/108.html>.

ultimately lose their customers. These issues are at the heart of marketing because they ensure lasting relationships with customers.

The CEO is the one who must take the leadership position to express the vision, champion the changes, and lead the organization through the difficult task of transformation. It is unlikely that traditional marketing or management will take on the heroic task of challenging the status quo or reinventing legacy systems. A coherent strategy demands a coherent information network. Preparing the enterprise for an open environment where access is the norm, where information is shared, and where decisions are disclosed requires a CEO of uncommon capability with extensive market knowledge.

The CEO's role in today's marketplace is much more complex than it has ever been. Businesses and relationships are more labyrinthine and the marketplace is more demanding. The CEO must be an inspired visionary, a market strategist, an articulate spokesperson, a leader, and a successful author. The role carries high visibility with high expectations, while the marketplace continually places hurdles in front of already existing obstacles. Opportunities abound for those who step outside the boundaries and exert bold but deliberate moves. Early retirement awaits those who fall short.

The CEO's Alter Ego: The Vice President of Business Development

The vice president of business development is both strategist and implementer of major customer alliances, market-oriented resource partnerships, and mergers and acquisitions. Once under the management of the marketing operation, this big role demands much of the CEO's time as well.

The leveraging of financial strength—equity or cash—is an important part of any aggressive market growth strategy. Even during the 2001 market slowdown, companies with cash or reasonable equity valuations continued to take advantage of the lower valuations of potential acquisitions as well as those seeking refuge in consolidation. During its high market valuation period, Cisco Systems, a networking technology and solutions company, grew to the industry's leadership market position by acquiring small leading-edge technology companies. Between 1993 and November 2000, Cisco used more than $400 billion of its market capitalization to acquire seventy technology companies for approximately $11.6 billion in stock.[6] These acquisitions gave Cisco the strategic opportunity to lock up key parts of the Internet infrastructure, jump ahead of competition, and establish a marketing architecture that gives the company persistent presence. Lucent, one of Cisco's major competitors, had its eyes on many of the same properties but either moved too slowly or was outbid. And Deutsche Telekom, to expand its global reach, spent $80 billion in a little over one year under CEO Ron Sommer.[7] The same strategy enabled AOL to acquire Time Warner, which expanded AOL's presence and market leadership. In light of the collapse of the equity markets in early 2001, these moves by AOL and Cisco seem prescient and visionary.

The role of business development is to assess the competitive landscape, guide their company in selecting opportunities for developing a competitive infrastructure, acquire valuable intellectual property, and expand and position the company in new markets. It's easy for companies to miss the window of opportunity to use their market valuation or cash to build operational or market-expanding infrastructures. Amazon.com and Yahoo! missed an opportunity to buy and build their infrastructures during the boom years of the market. AOL did not. The only way these and other businesses will have a shot at addressing the competitive and rapidly changing environment is to go back to basics and show tangible results, thereby rebuilding stockholders' trust.

The age of total access will bring many more unprecedented issues and opportunities. It will require all managers to evaluate their functional position thinking and perhaps redefine their roles within a network of shared responsibilities. Many executive staffs are already doing this in practice, if not by title or charter.

The CIO as Chief Total Access Architect

In addition to planning and managing the information assets of the enterprise, the chief information officer is taking a greater role in the marketing process by acting as the architect who plans connections with distributors, retailers, and major customers, by developing self-service programs, Web-based programs and services, and many other activities. Trained to understand and develop complex computer and software systems, the CIO today must manage such functions as customer relationship management and logistics. At FedEx, for example, IT specialists work with customers alongside salespeople.

Today the CIO must be a chief marketing architect, someone who can align all the diverse goals of the enterprise into one coherent structure that provides total access. Thomas Ajuba, entrepreneur and former CIO of Kraft Foods, Dell, and 3Com, said, "At 3Com, [I] was expected to be involved in discussions of how to improve the business, build better products, take the air out of the supply chain, and which markets to attack first. Smart CEOs are looking for CIOs to be a business partner."[8] The CIO is drawn into all areas of the business, which also happens to be an excellent training ground for future CEOs in this age of information. CIOs now see their role as serving customers by making information useful and actionable.

Networks have the capability to marshal diverse and distant resources, enabling them to act in concert for a common goal. Tying together all the vested-interest players to achieve a job is a much bigger task than the vision or power of current marketing departments suggests. Market presence and customer continuity demand a vast network of resources acting in unison. Exploiting the interactive network, not broadcasting messages, is a process of learning through implementation, feedback, and experience, and also of innovating and relearning. Everyone agrees that the market is progressively moving toward a more service producer–consumer relationship. Nonetheless, a "mass-market" mentality still permeates the marketing mind-set—although it is gradually giving way to the idea that marketing must rely on enterprise resources to become more customer-centric.

Marketing solutions, from gathering information to fulfilling customers' needs and wants and sustaining producer-consumer communications, are evolving to an enterprise-wide, integrated network of information resources designed and managed by the CIO. Someone has to oversee the proliferation of applications, to make sure they are compatible, reliable, distributed, accessible, and integrated into other work processes. Many marketing software applications today are stand alone workgroup applications. Over the next few years, individual applications and narrow marketing automation tools will be integrated as network-enabled, enterprise resources.

Egg, the leading U.K. e-commerce bank, changed its entire technology platform because, as IT director Pete Marsden says, "Customer experience dictated a change in IT strategy." This change was driven by the need to give its customers "fast and easy access." The *Financial Times* observed, "Never before has the IT department found itself so close to the frontline of brand creation."[9]

In business-to-business marketing, we can find many models of marketing in which the function disappears into the network and, as such, comes under IT's control. Cisco and Intel are two highly successful models for product businesses that develop and manage online commerce. Both companies do over $1 billion of business a month using the Internet. The healthcare company Baxter International lists "leveraging the Internet within the company" as one of its top five priorities. The company is using the Internet to deploy consumer Web sites, improve productivity, automate 401(k) plan administration, and automate the procurement of goods and services.[10] IBM is another example. Not only has a major portion of its business become services, but in 1999 it reported 42 million self-service customer transactions, with savings of $750 million in support costs. IBM is a huge buyer of goods and services, and by encouraging its suppliers to use e-procurement, it bought about $13 billion in goods and services over the Web, saving another $270 million.[11] And the company handled 25 percent of its internal training remotely, at an additional savings of $200 million. Businesses from steel and automobiles to healthcare and finance are finding that when they improve distribution and sales efficiencies, they must immerse themselves in the IT and services businesses.

Enterprise software solutions are seen as integrating architectures driven by senior IT officers. Many marketing people believe that the IT function is capable of building and managing the network, but not applying the "creativity" necessary for doing the marketing job. IT people are typecast as "nerds" or "data types." Pigeonholing any person or organizational function into a "personality category" is perhaps the result of overspecialization. Putting people in boxes is the surest way to inhibit the development of human resources. In my experience, advertising people tend to retreat to the realm of psychology when defending their turf, when in fact reliable interfaces and tangible support systems will do more for sustaining customer loyalty than the latest ad campaign. The most important element of marketing is the logistical and information infrastructure, which reliably delivers persistent presence to the customer. And that's the CIO's job.

The Chief Novelty Officer: The Director of R&D

The world of research and development is one of paradox. Highly acclaimed R&D centers such as Xerox PARC and Bell Labs have generated revolutionary technologies, only to see others successfully implement their work. R&D has a long tradition of maintaining its independence from the day-to-day demands of the marketplace, and yet it's R&D that spawns new markets and provides the competitive edge for a whole array of businesses, from high tech to pharmaceutical, chemical to food processing, cosmetics to clothing.

Whether it is Pfizer's Viagra or IBM's one-gigabyte miniature Microdrive storage device, R&D has been at the heart of many market creations. In recent years, more corporations are linking their R&D investment more closely to the competitive needs of their customers and business. GE's corporate research and development mission statement states that the company's goal is to "develop innovations that 'change the game' by creating entirely new business opportunities." To carry out that mission, R&D must embody GE's corporate value to "act in a boundary-less fashion . . . [and to] always search for and apply the best ideas regardless of their source."[12] (The key word is *apply*.) Corporate networks can only facilitate the linkages between the lab and the marketplace, between an idea and its implementation. Innovation is never born perfect. It must evolve and be shaped by the marketplace.

We often see the scientist and engineer as focused only on the technology or nuances of product features, but I believe that view is outdated. I've spoken to many research organizations about marketing, and I've found that scientists and engineers are universally eager to see their work expressed by profitable, competitive market-share growth and to see that their customers are satisfied. They are eager to develop useful, market-oriented products and services. Jim Gosling, fellow and chief scientist at Sun Microsystems, exemplifies this sort of thinking, as do many R&D people I've met at IBM, Intel, HP Labs, Eli Lilly, Procter & Gamble, and other companies. Here's how Gosling expressed his views on the Web's impact on marketing:

> *People don't want to be controlled, owned, labeled or pigeon-holed. People are individually unique with their own wants and desires. This, for me, is the bedrock of the power of the Web. People want to know what they want to know, not what someone else wants them to know. This turns marketing around: it's not a service to the company, it's a service to the customer of the company.*
>
> *It's been very fashionable to look down on "brochure ware," but I think it is often the most powerful commercial use of the Web. Marketing is often about the controlled disclosure of the information the company wants to get out. But all too often that doesn't include what I want to know. If you shop for anything sophisticated like a car or a piece of stereo equipment, company brochures and salespeople are almost never satisfactory sources of information. Diffusing "marketing" throughout an organization is the only way to get it all out. If you look at the material on java.sun.com very little of it is actually created by "marketing." A huge fraction of it comes directly from the engineers and designers who create the stuff.[13]*

Researchers have the ability to see the evolution of technology and imagine what is possible. Far from being the common nerds in a lab, most are dreamers at heart. Joel Birnbaum, recently retired as HP's senior vice president of research and development and director of HP Labs, is now serving the company in a consultancy role as chief scientist. He expresses his vision of persistent market presence this way:

> *For many years now, I have dreamed of the day when computers would become a pervasive technology—that is, a technology more noticeable by its absence than its presence—in just the way that cars, television sets, and telephones have become part of everyday life for most people.*
>
> *Electric motors are a good example of a pervasive technology. The average American home contains about two dozen or more electric motors; because those motors are buried in consumer appliances like vacuum cleaners, electric toothbrushes, washing machines, and VCRs, we have trouble identifying all of them, and we don't know or care how many are inside each appliance. In the next generation, the same will be true for computers, most of which will be embedded computers hidden in information appliances, enormously powerful because their parallel architectures will be tailored to particular tasks and inexpensive because of huge production volumes.*[14]

For marketing to become a systemic corporate force sustaining a company's leadership, it is important not only to listen to R&D people but to partner with them as well, as vital forces sustaining the process of market and customer development. Science and technology are the sources of imagination, which, together with knowledge, can lead to the creation and sustenance of market leadership. To see the validity of that view, just consider the sustaining examples of diverse companies from IBM to Procter & Gamble.

The recent trend in R&D organizations is to reach outside their corporate boundaries, open their labs, and establish relationships with corporate customers. Over the past fifty years, the time span from basic research through development and onto the market has steadily decreased. This shortening of the process is partly the result of increased collaboration between universities and industry, as well as between corporate labs and end-use customers. Today, service and retail organizations, as well as industrial companies, are meeting with R&D organizations not only to seek new ways to sustain business-to-business relationships, but also to search for new ways to solve problems and address new opportunities for their customers. High-tech research organizations are also trying to bring what they do into sync with consumers' needs, wants, and behavior, as you can see from the following employment ad placed by Intel's R&D organization:

> *The End User Driven Concepts Group at Intel Corporation has a position possibly opening up for an anthropologist or similar researcher with ethnographic field experience. The position would include ethnographic research of varying degrees of intensity and duration, in a variety of settings. The research is "applied" with an emphasis on generating ideas for new uses of computing power. We are looking for someone who has the ability to work on multi-disciplinary teams, interacting with engineers, marketing professionals, and others who do not have experience with ethnographic methods, theory or perspectives, and whose goal is the design of new types of computing products.*[15]

Ethnography is a little-known branch of anthropology that analyzes the behavior of individual cultures. At Intel, these human factor scientists seek ways to incorporate computers and other technology products more naturally into people's lives. "The whole point of it is to make technology work for people, rather than the other way around, of making people work to understand technology," says Jack Whalen, a member of a nine-person ethnography team at Xerox's Palo Alto Research Center.[16] "Everything we do is targeted at reaching out . . . and facilitating the entry of new technology into the marketplace," says Greg Barrett, president of Intel.[17] This Intel program may be experimental, but designing technology products to fit into the patterns of people's lives seems to be a better investment than trying to change behavior to adapt to technology.

Over the next decade, R&D organizations will find it essential to interact with the marketplace—with corporate customers and end users alike—to better match what they do with real-world applications. Without a continuous linkage to the market, R&D investment is blind.

A New Marketing Paradigm

Network-based information solutions integrate more than just data. They also connect all the customer-critical support people in the enterprise and stimulate creativity in those who have been bound by old notions of functionality. Focus group reports cannot substitute for "seeing" first-hand the way customers respond to and use products and services.

The exchange between producer and consumer is significantly different in the network marketplace than it was in the broadcast-dominated marketplace of the past. Regardless, academics and marketing practitioners alike cling to the outdated view that the quick-fix, broadcast model builds awareness, converts consumer behavior, and establishes a brand. It's difficult, if not impossible, for most marketing organizations to venture beyond this limited sphere of concentration because their responsibilities and empowerment end with the traditional boundaries of the function.

That view is fading into the past. Sustained, innovative marketing will continue its evolution as an integrated, seamless part of the enterprise information network. It will become an infinite loop of intelligence and learning, gaining knowledge as it connects and encompasses more participants. The value of a brand can now be defined as the number of active participants in a company's network. The participants include consumers and producers, as well as the supporting cast of suppliers and partners. In this scenario, a brand obtains value not from its reach or people's awareness of it, but rather from the dynamics of continuing connections and interactions. In effect, we see Metcalfe's Law applied to marketing: The value of a brand grows by the square of the number of active participants connected to an enterprise network.

I once described the role of marketing as a "systems integrator" responsible for pulling together all the resources of the enterprise to serve the customer. For marketing to achieve this role, businesses need executives with a new vision for marketing's expanding role and with greater depth and breadth of information and market knowledge. In recent years I've received an increasing number of calls from CEOs who ask for help finding a "great marketing" person. Last week, a board director of a large company said, "We need someone who understands the new information technology, who can command the respect and attention of top executives at [the companies of] customers and partners." Sounds to me like the CEO's role.

The new marketing will demand creativity in developing new ways of deploying the network, as well as new ways of interacting both internally and with customers. That means sustaining relationships with both customers and the supporting cast of characters necessary for a complete solution, and interlinking all the customer-relevant functions of an enterprise to achieve an efficient process capable of responding rapidly and satisfying customers anywhere on the globe. Specialized software systems and networks will automate all systems that can be defined and mapped as workflow processes. To remain competitive and keep costs low, businesses also will need to automate recurring producer-consumer transactions and services, and because networked information is, by its very nature, decentralized, these transactions will be absorbed into the enterprise information architecture.

Marketing is a basic corporate activity demanding the skills and talents of many functions, organizations, and people. The shift in organizational management from a hierarchal structure to that of a shared enterprise network of responsibilities enables a new vision for the concept of marketing. In much the same way that the Ages of Reach and Push gave rise to new ways for corporations to interact with the marketplace and customers, the unfolding Age of Total Access will change everything. For marketing, the Age of Total Access is a work in progress.

Chapter Ten

The Magic Touch

Corporate Creativity

When many of us think of corporate creativity, we tend to think chiefly of a company's ad campaign. Creativity, however, plays a far more expansive role in business today. How a company presents itself in the marketplace reflects its creativity, not only its creativity in marketing but the creativity it brings to its entire approach and strategy. The more creative a company is throughout its entire enterprise, the more successful a company will be in sustaining its presence in the marketplace.

W E ARE LIVING at a time when the competitive environment has a steep and rapid learning curve. It's also a time of unprecedented change, change that's intensified by factors such as market impatience, competitive intensity, volatile market reactions, and high expectations from customers and investors. Although some like to compare current trends with historical trends, in fact today's business climate is significantly different from that in the past—the Information Age involves much more complex issues than did, say, the Industrial Revolution. Our challenge today is to live and manage businesses through *this* period of change.

Doing so requires focus, planning, and a high level of cooperation. No one part of the organization can be isolated or out of sync from another, and nowhere is that more true that in marketing. That's a real change; almost from its birth in the early part of the twentieth century, marketing has been isolated in the extreme. In the early part of the twentieth century when marketing became a separate function within the corporation, it was a mere stepchild of management. It wasn't its own cost center, and it never really fit into neat definitions or had clear criteria for improving its productivity or quality. Of course, such "fuzzy marketing" does have its advantages if everyone in marketing sees his or her role as part of the overall responsibility to achieve such broad and nebulous goals as brand awareness, differentiation, and positioning. Managements expect marketing to sustain the consumer's attention, and overcome a product or service weakness by creating a new message or image. Most of all, marketing is seen as selling a new or refurbished idea to implant in the consumer's mind a desire to buy the producer's wares. I began this book by saying that most businesses view marketing as more important than ever. Indeed it is! However, for the role of marketing to meet management's expectations, it must become more than a broadcast function and take on the responsibility for creating value, developing the market, and building the market support infrastructure, as well as maintaining customer satisfaction. That's a tall order for any one organization or function. Thus, I return to my view of the marketer as an integrator of all the enterprise resources with the goal of servicing customers.

By compartmentalizing marketing and viewing it as a "push" function, we lose sight of the vital role played by other market-creating functions: research and development, product design and engineering, quality manufacturing and reliability programs, software application innovations, network-supported market presence, self-service information systems, customer feedback systems, supplier and other partnering alliances, automated and efficient fulfillment systems, and unique customer interface presentations. These capabilities will sustain brand loyalty and persistent presence.

Today, with the exception of advertising and promotion, marketing is no longer an isolated function; rather, it's being dispersed throughout the business. The information network is the mainspring. Every advancing enterprise today depends on an information network, a network that more and more often is digitally connected, defined and refined, improved and advanced. From healthcare to financial services, retail to professional services, high tech to low tech, businesses are redefining and reinventing every work process through the application of network processes.

Managing businesses through this time of upheaval also requires creativity. But we can't isolate creativity any more than we can isolate marketing. Today businesses need to be creative throughout the enterprise, taking an expansive approach that touches every part of the business.

The Creative Challenge

Ask the person on the street where creativity resides in a business, and chances are that the answer will be "Advertising." And that's true: Advertising is a creative profession because it employs artists and writers and idea people who can develop entertaining and provocative ads that attract and distract our attention. (Too often, however, the ad is so entertaining that the message is lost in the fun.)

Several years ago, when many businesses were adopting TQM, the president of a large corporation told me that his company was adopting quality performance measurements with the goal of vying for the Malcolm Baldrige National Quality Award. Every part of the organization had met the Baldrige requirements of defined goals and measured results—every part except marketing, which the company had been unable to define well enough to clarify its boundaries. His comment points to one of marketing's facts of life: that the results of advertising and promotion are very hard to quantify in terms of increased revenues, customer satisfaction, and profits.

Businesses spend a great deal of money researching advertising effectiveness, but I think we already know that advertising is most successful when it reflects a competitive service or product that continually gains market presence through efficient distribution. In other words, promotion works if it reflects a total marketing architecture that integrates product and services, the designed-in services and feedback mechanisms, the supporting network of partners and suppliers, the fulfillment channels and feedback information systems, and the creative ways to interface with customers.

Yes, advertising is without a doubt a creative endeavor. But it's not a company's *only* creative endeavor. Creativity has no margins, no rules, and it should have no bounds in an enterprise. Rather, it should be applied everywhere: to the uniqueness of a user interface, the responsiveness of a network, an adaptive service application, a new product or service idea, a distinctive and pervasive community presence, and an imaginative use of computing power.

In fact, encouraging creativity throughout the enterprise is more important now than ever. Life for the consumer is more complex than in past eras. Today the consumer is overwhelmed with information, choices, media messages, and every kind of social and entertainment attraction or distraction. Breaking through all that market noise, creating a brand, and sustaining a dialogue with customers can no longer be addressed by sending out repetitive, entertaining messages. In this new market environment, a more prolific and pervasive concept of marketing is needed. A company that allows creativity to permeate its entire approach and strategy will differentiate itself better in the marketplace. Creative approaches must reach well beyond the traditional marketing function to encompass the talents of R&D, IT, logistics, partners, and other functional areas. The more creativity is present throughout the enterprise, the more successful the marketing.

A Network for Creative Vitality

Nike exemplifies creativity at work. Many assume that Nike is a pure idea company because it doesn't manufacture its own products, but that's a long way from saying that Nike survives only by its ideas. Nike is a technology pioneer, and it survives because it uses the latest materials and designs, consistently turning ideas into reality. The Nike Sports Research Lab and the Materials & Mechanical Test Lab have come up with great innovations, such as Nike Shox, which the company put on the market in 2000 after sixteen years of development.

Nike has persistent presence because of its vast distribution network, a network that took many years to develop and deploy. A long-time jogger, I've been a loyal Nike consumer ever since Nike Air running shoes came on the market. I'm loyal because the company offers a wide variety of choices, but mostly because it continues to come out with new designs that provide better cushion and comfort. Michael Jordan certainly is a powerful brand-building reference, but Nike already had a strong market presence before Michael started showing up in company ads. Like the "Intel Inside" advertising campaign, which was initiated when Intel already held a commanding share of the microprocessor market, Nike's hiring of Michael Jordan was merely the icing on the cake. The company's existing market presence was already bringing success.

I recently asked John Chappell, head of Nike's Japan operation, whether he viewed Nike as a pure marketing play. Here is his response:

> The real substance of Nike is the pervasive evidence of their cultural bias and commitment to performance enhancements that transcends all aspects of product design and development. This goal produces a very collaborative relationship between the designers, biomechanical engineers and athletes—with lots of product prototyping and testing and refining. I think casual observers are often unaware of the widely diverse intensity of customer requirements that Nike performance sports apparel seeks to address.
>
> For serious athletes, there is a much greater physio/psychological involvement with the Nike brand than that experienced by consumers of other branded merchandise. The application of technology in this case must not only produce a better functioning shoe or garment but also a better athletic performance. The quest to achieve the top possible performance advantage often leads the Nike R&D effort to study very quirky and non-apparel applications, materials, designs and technologies. (Like racing cars and reptile ecto-skeleton).
>
> The marketing challenge for Nike is in translating the high performance message into a mainstream marketing offer that will produce the volumes to cover the costs associated with this level of R&D. That's where the appeal of charismatic athletes like Michael Jordan is so important, to give a face to the performance benefits.[1]

Too few executives recognize that technology alone is impotent without corporate-wide creative vitality. Corporate creativity is what empowers an organization to imagine and pioneer new ways of delivering and sustaining value to customers, and it's necessary for successfully applying the new tools of information in a competitive and distinctive manner. But top management has to champion creativity in research and development, in IT, in sales, in HR, and in all areas of the enterprise—not expect it only from marketing.

Ideas into Gold

The *Financial Times* tells us that "today's marketplace is a war of ideas." New ideas are plentiful; the problem is that it's hard to tell if an idea can be sustained or if it's just another short-term fad. Too few ideas become sustaining value-creating businesses. Most executives far underestimate how difficult it will be or how long it will take to turn a good idea into a sustained reality. Xerox PARC made some of the first breakthroughs in personal computer innovations but then never exploited them. This failure was not the fault of the scientists but rather of the company as a whole, which lacked creative vitality.

Despite all the wonders of technology, organizational knowledge and creativity take time to evolve. Nathan Rosenberg, professor of economics at Stanford University, has written extensively on the relationship between innovation and economic growth. He points out that "technology is by nature cumulative: major innovations constitute new building blocks which provide a basis for subsequent technologies, but do so selectively and not randomly."[2] Of course, this concept applies to all business processes and practices. We learn by doing. When you're creative, you recognize the uniqueness of what you discover in the learning process. For organizations to learn, and thus to be creative, they need to allow time but also to establish a pervasive, open culture. Networks are opening up a new way for people to share discoveries across the enterprise. Total access opens the doors, further allowing customers to share in and stimulate the development of new, creative approaches to service.

Most businesses arrive at places they had not anticipated when they started out as new ventures. Successful ventures are led by people who listen to the market, adapt, apply creative imagination to a new vision, and learn from experience. Dell Computer made the move into direct marketing, developing a leading logistical support system along the way, because it could not compete effectively in the overcrowded PC retail space. Dell had established an early direct-market business, but its managers believed that they had to move into the retail channel in order to compete with the likes of Compaq, IBM, and Apple. The direct-market channel for PCs wasn't at all clear to anyone at the time. Dell simply "pushed" the channel and evolved its advanced logistics operation as it was in the process of implementation. And while the company did have both management leadership and the flexibility to change, market conditions "encouraged" the redefinition of the business model. The result was market and marketing leadership.

We don't lack ideas; we lack applied creativity. Successful new markets and market positions, new products and services, extending opportunities—all these come about through innovation. Creativity cannot be relegated to the marketing function or any one-enterprise role alone. It's more likely to arise when all the functional resources of the enterprise interact by sharing knowledge and capabilities.

To build a lasting enterprise, a business needs to establish a continuous learning process for turning ideas into tangible reality for the customer. What's "in" and what's "out," what's cool and what isn't—trends appear quickly and fade just as rapidly. Somewhere around 80 percent of all new businesses—Internet-based as well as bricks and mortar—fail in the first five years of life.[3] I have been reviewing new business plans for more than twenty-five years, as have many of my friends in the venture capital business, and I've found that while a new idea may capture my imagination, what I really focus on is the management's experience, the financial strategy, and key alliances that can assist the start-up with infrastructure development. But more and more of my colleagues are evaluating new deals on the basis of the start-up's accessibility to distribution channels. I've watched businesses deemed "innovative" or "a good idea" come and go. Applied creativity is found in the implementation of the idea.

Vulnerability to failure and market changes isn't limited to small, entrepreneurial companies. According to *The Economist*, "Big companies come and go at lightning speed: one third of the giants in America's Fortune 500 in 1980 had lost their independence by 1990 and another 40% were gone five years later."[4] Thirty-nine of the top 50 companies on the Fortune 500 list in 1998 had either completely disappeared from that elite 50 list or had fallen to the lower ranks by 1999.

We can look to the history of the arts as models, at great artists like Bach and Beethoven, Picasso and Michelangelo, Shakespeare and William Faulkner, individuals who worked hard at developing their talent and evolved by applying their talents with prolific creativity, not sporadic ideas, and whose work has stood the test of time. Great corporations must go and do likewise by being innovative and creative all the time, and by commanding sustained innovation throughout the enterprise, using technology's tools—television, the computer, the Internet—for applying creativity. That's the real challenge.

Where Are We Headed?

In his book *The Age of Spiritual Machines: When Computers Exceed Human Intelligence*, author, inventor, and entrepreneur Ray Kurzweil offers his view of life in 2009:

> At least half of all transactions are online. Intelligent assistants which combine continuous speech recognition, natural language understanding, problem solving, and animated personalities routinely assist with finding information, answering questions, and conducting transactions. Intelligent assistants have become a primary interface for interacting with information-based services, with a wide range of choices available. A recent poll shows that both male and female users prefer female personalities for the computer-based intelligent assistants. The two most popular are Maggie, who claims to be a waitress in a Harvard Square café, and Michelle, a stripper from New Orleans. Personality designers are in demand, and the field constitutes a growth area in software development.[5]

Impossible? I don't think so. After spending nearly forty years in marketing and technology, I think Kurzweil's views seem rather tame. A very different world—indeed, a very volatile business world—is in our future. The sudden change in the economy that we saw in early 2001—which surprised many observers and analysts and was probably hastened by the interconnectedness of the financial and business marketplace—may have been a prelude to that volatile environment.

And how will marketing be affected? Nearly totally. As this book has made clear, marketing functions will be absorbed into the network simply because neither the enterprise executives nor the customers will tolerate anything less than active, efficient, real-time participation in the marketplace. Business functions will be increasingly integrated, the network will require more and more collaboration within and outside the organization, and marketing will be increasingly dominated by software development and network activities.

Management's roles will have to change to adjust to this hyperconnected, total access environment. Because of the new information tools, the enterprise will be defined as an integrated network of customer value–creating resources driven by a combination of clear, competitive strategies. Companies that want to remain ahead of the curve will have to invest and learn how to apply networks to all operations and functions.

Marketing creativity in the future may take the form of conceptualization and implementation of network-enabled, closed-loop communications and services. Marketers may be called upon to come up with new formats, new kinds of cross-industry ties, unique channels, and diverse ways of providing and responding to consumer access. Marketing will also involve creating new ways of interacting with the consumer and developing visualization, mobile services, simulation models, and a host of other information and computer-based services.

And creativity will come from those who know how to apply the new tools and languages to design engaging applications. A "Michelle" or a "Maggie" may well represent the "personality" of a commercial relationship in the future. But a lasting commercial relationship, even with a cyber-personality, must have a payoff. Tiger Woods, Howie Long, and Michael Jordan can command attention. They cannot satisfy customers beyond the moment of entertainment.

Customers in the future will be overwhelmed with access capabilities, which will enable them to choose the place, time, and nature of commercial relationship that addresses their needs and wants. Corporations will not find the future marketplace an easier place to compete— only different. The marketplace will become ever more crowded with competitors and the noise level will amplify. Total access will place increasing demands on corporations to develop automated-response systems and economically viable service business models. Its influence will shift behaviors and responsibilities and redefine the producer-consumer relationship. Only the few businesses that energize all the resources of their enterprise by sharing and applying imaginative intelligence to new ways of engaging the total access customer will sustain market leadership.

Notes

Chapter 1: Introduction

1. "Keeping the Customer Satisfied," *The Economist*, 14 July 2001, 9.
2. McKenna Group Survey, January to June 2000.
3. McCann-Erickson World Group, "Bob Coen's Insider's Report," June 2001, <http://www.mccann.com/insight/bobcoen.html> (accessed 27 September 2001).

Chapter 2: The Three Stages of Marketing

1. Sears, Roebuck and Co., "Sears History," <http://www.sears.com> (accessed 14 February 2001).
2. The DMA (Direct Marketing Association) Interactive, "The United States of America: Land of Opportunity," <http://www.the-dma.org/library/landofopportunity .shtml#1> (accessed 8 October 2001).
3. Robert Bartels, *The Development of Marketing Thought* (Homewood, IL: Richard D. Irwin, Inc., 1962).
4. Ibid., 32.
5. Ibid., 4–5.
6. Thomas H. White, *United States Early Radio History*, <http://www.ipass.net/ ~whitetho/> (accessed 8 October 2001).
7. Michael Kammen, *American Culture, American Tastes* (New York: Knopf, 1999), 85.
8. Donna L. Halper, "Radio in 1931," <http://www.old-time.com/halper/halper 31.html> (accessed 8 October 2001).
9. Ibid.
10. Information on Edward Bernays is from Stuart Ewan, *PR! A Social History of Spin* (New York: HarperCollins, 1996) and Larry Tye, *The Father of Spin: Edward L. Bernays and the Birth of Public Relations* (New York: Crown Publishers, 1998).
11. David Aaker and Erich Joachimsthaler, *Brand Leadership* (New York: Free Press, 2000).
12. Ibid., 6.
13. Sun Microsystems, "Company Information: Sun History," <http://www.sun .com/aboutsun/coinfo/history.html> (accessed 8 October 2001).
14. Stuart Ewan, *Captains of Consciousness* (New York: Basic Books, 2001).

15. Sam Walton with John Huey, *Made in America: My Story* (New York: Bantam Books, 1993).

16. Simon Romero, "A Cell Phone Surge Among World's Poor," *New York Times*, 19 December 2000, C1.

17. eMarketer, "Global Internet Usage Has Come a Long Way," 20 April 2001, <http://www.emarketer.com/estatnews/estats/eglobal/20010420_global_usage_itu.html?ref=wn> (accessed 17 October 2001).

18. "Survey: Telecommunications," *The Economist*, 7 October 1999, 6.

19. John W. Wright, ed., *The New York Times 2000 Almanac*, Millennium Edition (New York: New York Times, 1999), 809.

20. Dennis Kyle, "Deploying IVR/IWR To Meet Customer Self-Service Needs," March 1999, <http://www.tmcnet.com/articles/ccsmag/0399/0399next.htm> (accessed 8 October 2001).

21. Harry H. Crosby and George R. Bond, *The McLuhan Explosion* (New York: The American Book Company, 1968).

22. James A. Martin, "The Net Goes Up and Down: Cyberspace Is Coming to an Elevator Near You," *PC World*, 9 December 1999, <http://www.pcworld.com/news/article.asp?aid=14246> (accessed 8 October 2001).

23. Regis McKenna, *The Regis Touch* (Reading, MA: Addison-Wesley, 1985).

24. Theodore Levitt, "Marketing Intangible Products and Product Intangibles," *Harvard Business Review* 59, no. 3 (May–June 1981): 94.

25. Peter Lyman and Hal R. Varian, "How Much Information?" School of Information Management and Systems at the University of California at Berkeley, <http://www.sims.berkeley.edu/research/projects/how-much-info/index.html> (accessed 17 October 2001).

26. "Japan-IIJ, Sony, Toyota Telecom Carrier Receives License 12/24/98," *Newbytes*, 24 December 1998.

27. "Clarity's Voice Is Heard Loud and Clear in Silicon Valley at AVIOS Speech Tech Expo," *Business Wire*, 23 May 2000.

28. "Wireless Wonders All Set to Change the Way We Live," *Financial Times*, 5 April 2000, xiv.

Chapter 3: New Technologies, A New Marketplace

1. Jared Diamond, *Guns, Germs, and Steel: The Fates of Human Societies* (New York: Norton, 1997), 243.

2. "Technology and the Economy: An Attempt at Pattern Recognition," in *The Technology & Internet IPO Yearbook: 7th Edition—21 Years of Tech Investing . . .* (New York: Morgan Stanley Dean Witter, 2001), 7.

3. "IDF: Diabetes on the Rise World-Wide," Doctor's Guide Publishing Limited, 2 November 2000, <http://www.pslgroup.com/dg/1e929a.htm> (accessed 8 October 2001), and ADA data.

4. U.S. Public Law 106-229, 106th Congress, *Electronic Signatures in Global and National Commerce Act of 2000*.

5. See <http://www.fedex.com>.

6. Matisse Enzer, "Glossary of Internet Terms," <http://www.matisse.net/files/glossary.html#B> (accessed 8 October 2001).

7. Olga Kharif, "The Fiber-Optic 'Glut'—in a New Light," *BusinessWeek Online*, 31 August 2001, <http://www.businessweek.com/bwdaily/dnflash/aug2001/nf20010831_396.htm> (accessed 9 October 2001).

8. Simon Romero, "Once-Bright Future of Optical Fiber Dims," *New York Times*, 18 June 2001, 1.

9. Peter Heywood, "Bandwidth Bonanza 'Won't Happen,'" *Light Reading*, 12 July 2000, <http://www.lightreading.com/document.asp?doc_id=1142> (accessed 8 October 2001).

10. Gary Stix, "The Triumph of the Light," *Scientific American*, January 2001, 82.

11. Telcordia Technologies, <http://www.netsizer.com/> (accessed 9 October 2001).

12. George Gilder, *Telecosm: How Infinite Bandwidth Will Revolutionize Our World* (New York: Free Press, 2000).

13. George Gilder, "Telecosm: Feasting On The Giant Peach," *Forbes ASAP*, 26 August 1996, 85.

14. Robert Clark, "The NTT DoCoMo Success Story," *America's Network*, 1 March 2000, <http://www.americasnetwork.com/issues/2000issues/20000301/20000301_thentt.htm> (accessed 17 October 2001).

15. Dr. Robert Morris, Director of IBM Almaden Research Labs, is the source of the data described by Dr. Joseph Gordon of the IBM Storage Research Center.

16. Peter Lyman and Hal R. Varian, "How Much Information?" School of Information Management and Systems at the University of California at Berkeley, <http://www.sims.berkeley.edu/research/projects/how-much-info/index.html> (accessed 17 October 2001).

17. Ibid.

18. Salomon Smith Barney Report, "Computer Storage," *Disk Drive Quarterly* 31 (December 1999): 9.

19. Jupiter Communications cited in "Internet Usage Worldwide," Cisco Systems, <http://www.cisco.com/warp/public/779/govtaffs/factsNStats/internetusage.html> (accessed 8 October 2001).

20. Regis McKenna, "When Marketing Disappears," *Business Technology Journal* Millennium Issue, 44.

21. Robert Morris, e-mail to author, 14 September 2001.

22. Paul M. Horn, "Information Technology Will Change Everything," *Research Technology Management* (January–February 1999): 42–47.

23. Ibid.

24. Robert Morris, e-mail to author, 17 January 2001.

25. Ibid.

26. Object-oriented programming is a higher-level software language or code that uses self contained "objects." Objects are reusable classes of components, each

of which represents a distinct concept as well as all its intending relationships. Thus, the software designer need not bother with the content of the object but only the interfaces with the object. The object's "behavior" is kept intact as the "object" moves from application to application.

27. Jim Gosling, e-mail to author, 20 December 2000.

28. John Chambers, personal conversation with author, 15 February 2001.

29. I use the word *revised* because although the statement is commonly ascribed to Darwin, extensive research could not identify him as the source.

Chapter 4: Forget about Loyalty

1. Robert D. Putnam, *Bowling Alone* (New York: Simon & Schuster, 2000), 244.

2. Ibid.

3. Ibid., 226.

4. Michael Lewis, "Boom Box," *New York Times Sunday Magazine*, 13 August 2000.

5. See <http://www.domainstats.com/> (accessed 2 October 2001). Domain-Stats.com is powered by the NetNames Global Domain Name database. See also NetNames Statistics, <http://www.cisco.com/warp/public/779/govtaffs/factsNStats /internetusage.html> (accessed 28 December 1999).

6. Sirkka L. Jarvenpaa and Noam Tractinsk, "Consumer Trust in an Internet Store: A Cross-Cultural Validation," *Journal of Computer-Mediated Communication* 5, no. 2 (1999), <http://www.ascusc.org/jcmc/vol5/issue2/jarvenpaa.html> (accessed 9 October 2001).

7. Putnam, *Bowling Alone*, 177.

8. Charles Steinfield, Robert Kraut, and Alice Plumer, "The Impact of Interorganizational Networks on Buyer-Seller Relationships," *Journal of Computer-Mediated Communication* 1, no. 3 (1995).

9. Frederick F. Reichheld, *The Loyalty Effect* (Boston: Harvard Business School Press, 1996).

10. "Online Trading and Finance Trends," in *Plunkett's Online Trading, Finance & Investment Web Sites Almanac.* See <http://www.plunkettresearch.com/finance/ financial_websites_index.htm> (accessed 9 October 2001).

11. John Chappell, conversation with author, 12 July 2000.

12. Michael G. Kammen, *People of Paradox: An Inquiry Concerning the Origins of American Civilization* (New York: Cornell University Press, 1990).

13. "Television Takes a Tumble," *The Economist*, 20 January 2001, 59.

14. "First Scarbourgh National Internet Study Reveals Changes in How Online Consumers Use Traditional Internet Media," Scarborough Research press release, 9 May 2001, <http://www.scarborough.com/scarb2000/press/pr_internet study1.htm> (accessed 9 October 2001).

15. Robert M. McMath, "New Product Failures: The High Cost of Forgetfulness," *Exec* (March 1999), <http://www.unisys.com/execmag/1999-03/journal/ viewpoints2.htm#top> (accessed 9 October 2001).

16. Terry Hanby, "The Concept of a Brand: Definition and Development for Brand Planning and Valuation," *Journal of Market Research Society* 411, no. 1 (January 1999): 7.

17. Putnam, *Bowling Alone*, 139.

18. Ronald Alsop, "Survey Rates Companies' Reputations, and Many Are Found Wanting," *Wall Street Journal*, 7 February 2001, B1.

19. "Y&R Fins Buzz Words for Success," *Wall Street Journal*, 8 June 1994, B8.

20. "Direct Hit," *The Economist*, 9 January 1999, 55.

21. "Can You Spot a Fake?" *Wall Street Journal*, 16 February 2001, W1.

22. The Gallup Organization, "Nurses Remain at Top of Honesty and Ethics Poll," 27 November 2000, <http://www.gallup.com/poll/releases/pr001127iii.asp> (accessed 9 October 2001).

23. Peter Drucker, personal conversation with author, 1998.

24. "America's Most Admired: Eight Key Attributes of Reputation," *Fortune*, 19 February 2001, 104.

25. Drennan Group, "The Unofficial, Unedited, Unaudited History of Electronic Banking," <http://www.drennangroup.com/History/history.html#Seven> (accessed 9 October 2001).

26. David Teece, "Capturing Value from Knowledge Assets," *California Management Review* 40, no. 3 (1998): 55–79.

Chapter 5: The Transformation of Today's Consumer

1. Michael Kammen, *American Culture, American Tastes: Social Change and the Twentieth Century* (New York: Knopf, 1999), 42.

2. SRI International, "New Study by SRI Consulting Maps Consumer Use of New Media," 4 February 1997, <http://www.sri.com/news/releases/2-5-97.html> (accessed 9 October 2001).

3. "Internet Usage Worldwide," Cisco Systems, <http://www.cisco.com/warp/public/779/govtaffs/factsNStats/internetusage.html> (accessed 8 October 2001).

4. Television Bureau of Advertising, "Time Spent Viewing—Households," TVBasics, <http://www.tvb.org/tvfacts/tvbasics/basics6.html> (accessed 9 October 2001).

5. Juliet Schor, "The New Politics of Consumption," *Boston Review*, <http://bostonreview.mit.edu/BR24.3/schor.html> (accessed 9 October 2001).

6. Kammen, *American Culture, American Tastes*, 108.

7. This is an arbitrary scale based on comparing news articles, ads, and market data gathered by the author.

8. Regis McKenna, "Marketing in an Age of Diversity," *Harvard Business Review* 66, no. 5 (September–October 1988).

9. The market decline in high-tech products in 2001 is forcing the failure of many suppliers as well as the consolidation within many sectors of the business. We have seen a similar, albeit not as severe, recession in the high-tech sector over the past forty years. Historically, these consolidation periods are followed by expansion and diversification.

10. Ira P. Schneiderman, "More Major Stores Offer Loyalty Programs: Stores Say Plans Are Working, Outside Experts Question Long-term Success," *Daily News Record* 28, no. 50 (27 April 1998).

11. Indrajit Sinha, "Cost Transparency: The Net's Real Threat to Prices and Brands," *Harvard Business Review* 78, no. 2 (March–April 2000).

12. Evie Black Dykema, "Customers Catch Auction Fever," *The Forrester Report*, March 1999.

13. "This Year, It's Chic to Shop Cheap," *Business Week*, 16 November 1998, 215.

14. National Public Radio, *Morning Edition*, 13 October 1999.

15. Emily Nelson, "Too Many Choices," *Wall Street Journal*, 20 April 2001, B1.

16. Bob Greene, "The Unthinkable Becomes a Casualty of War," *Chicago Tribune*, 10 October 2001, <http://chicagotribune.com/news/columnists/chi-0110100008 oct10.column?coll=chi%2Dhomepagenews%2Dutl> (accessed 17 October 2001).

17. Auto Junction, "Parts of an Automobile," <http://auto.indiamart.com/auto-consumables/parts-of-automobile.html> (accessed 9 October 2001).

18. Regis McKenna, *Real Time: Preparing for the Age of the Never Satisfied Customer* (Boston: Harvard Business School Press, 1997).

19. A. Campbell McCracken, "Security: From Firewalls to Hackers," June 1999, <http://www.madscotsman.freeserve.co.uk/articles/security/security.htm> (accessed 9 October 2001).

20. Bill Crowell, interview with author, 24 August 2001.

Chapter 6: The Customer Experience

1. "Online World Changes All the Business Rules," *Financial Times* IT Review, 2 February 2000, xv.

2. Merlin Stone, "CRM Today—'Viral Marketing' Tomorrow," *Financial Times* IT Review, 1 September 1999, iii.

3. Sarah D. Scalet and Lare Low, "Come Together," *CIO Magazine*, 15 December 2000/1 January 2001 <http://www.cio.com/archive/010101/together.html> (accessed 4 October 2001).

4. Cheryl Rosen, "Talent Scramble Heats Up," *Information Week*, 14 December 2000, <http://www.informationweek.com/803/hospitality.htm> (accessed 17 October 2001).

5. Jay Wrolstad, "Starbucks, Microsoft Brew Wireless Coffeehouse," <http://www.newsfactor.com/perl/story/6435.html>, 3 January 2001 (accessed 22 October 2001).

6. Lise Buyer, "Shopper's Paradise," *World Link*, June 2000, 24.

7. Joan Magretta, "The Power of Integration: An Interview with Dell Computer's Michael Dell," *Harvard Business Review* 76, no. 2 (March–April 1998).

8. Quoted in Lynn G. Shostack, "Breaking Free from Product Marketing," *Journal of Marketing* (April 1977).

9. See <http://www.BevMo.com>.

10. Quoted in Jim Kerstetter and Spencer E. Ante, "Software Makers Hit the Endangered List," *Business Week*, 22 January 2001, 44.

11. Kenneth Bredemeier, "A Corporate Identity Crisis?" *The Washington Post*, National Weekly Edition, 19–25 February 2001, 20.

12. "Yes, Steve, You Fixed It. Congrats! Now What's Act Two? Apple," *Business Week*, 31 July 2000, 112.

13. "A Survey of Retailing," *The Economist*, 4 March 1995, 6.

14. "Debunking Coke, Douglas Appointment as Chairman of Coca-Cola," *The Economist*, 12 February 2000.

15. Frederick G. Harmon and Garry Jacobs, *The Vital Difference: Unleashing the Powers of Sustained Corporate Success* (New York: AMACOM, 1985).

16. Robert Kaplan, *To the Ends of the Earth* (New York: Random House, 1996), 65.

17. See <http://www.coke.com>.

18. Theodore Levitt, "Marketing Myopia," *Harvard Business Review* 38, no. 4 (July–August 1960).

19. Bob Tedeschi, "E-Commerce Report," *New York Times*, 24 July 2000, C9.

20. Sandeep Junnarkar and Jim Hu, "AOL Buys Time Warner in Historic Merger," CNET News.com, 10 January 2000, <http://news.cnet.com/news/0-1005-200-1518888.html> (accessed 9 October 2001).

21. Quoted in Jason Anders, "Sibling Rivalry," *Wall Street Journal*, Special Section on E-Commerce, 17 July 2000, R16.

22. Les Vadasz, e-mail to author, 15 August 2001.

23. "Leaders Target CRM in Attempt to Boost Revenues," *Financial Times*, 15 December 1999, 11.

Chapter 7: Putting It All Together

1. Lyman Rick, "Even Blockbusters Find Fame Fleeting in a Multiplex Age," *New York Times*, National Edition, 13 August 2001.

2. See <http://www.m_w.com>.

3. Quoted in Steve Marlin, "Non-Traditional Distribution," *Insurance & Technology* 25, no. 9 (2000): 51.

4. Ibid.

5. Brian Fitzgerald, telephone interview with author, 20 June 2001.

6. Larry Downes and Chunka Mui, *Unleashing the Killer App: Digital Strategies for Market Dominance* (Boston: Harvard Business School Press, 1998).

7. CRM system purchases have been optimistically forecast at almost $150 billion by 2005. Too often we equate use with the purchase. Discussions with various industry IT people have indicated that they are skeptical about the full use of the CRM capabilities, owing to management's slow adaptation to new work processes and methods as well as integrating current products into the existing IT systems.

8. Jim Kates, interview with author, 15 January 2001.

9. Ibid.

10. Ibid.

11. Brian Fitzgerald, interview with author, August 2001.

12. Ibid.

13. Bill Campbell, interview with author, 28 March 2001.

14. Brian Fitzgerald, interview with author, 20 June 2001.

Chapter 8: Total Global Access

1. John Tomlinson, *Globalization and Culture* (Chicago: University of Chicago Press, 1999), 7.

2. Peter Weill and Marianne Broadbent, *Leveraging the New Infrastructure* (Boston: Harvard Business School Press, 1998), 195.

3. George Lipsitz, *Time Passages: Collective Memory and American Popular Culture* (Minneapolis: University of Minnesota Press, 1990).

4. "Survey of the New Economy," *The Economist*, 23 September 2000, 8.

5. Ibid.

6. IDA Ireland, "Facts about Ireland—Vital Statistics," <http://www.idaireland.com/docs/faivs.html> (accessed 10 October 2001).

7. Bill Vlasic and Bradley A. Stertz, *Taken for a Ride: How Daimler-Benz Drove Off with Chrysler* (New York: Morrow, 2000).

8. World Trade Organization, "WTO Secretariat Releases 2001 Annual Report," 23 May 2001, <http://www.wto.org/english/news_e/pres01_e/pr226_e.htm> (accessed 10 October 2001).

9. Ibid.

10. Mark Weisbrot, Robert Naiman, and Joyce Kim, "The Emperor Has No Growth: Declining Economic Growth Rates in the Era of Globalization," Center for Economic & Policy Research Briefing Paper, September 2000.

11. Tomlinson, *Globalization and Culture*, 2.

12. Louise Williams, "The Rise of Asia's Middle Class," *Sydney Morning Herald*, reprinted in *World Press Review*, August 1993.

13. Ann Cvetkovich and Douglas Kellner, *Articulating the Global and the Local* (Boulder, CO: Westview Press, 1997), 10.

14. Thad Dunning, Christian Gebara, Karen Han, and Antonio Varas, "Brazil: Internet Development for Whom?" 6 December 1999, <http://www.stanford.edu/~muse/brazil/access.html> (accessed 10 October 2001).

15. The Internet Economy Indicators, "The Global Internet," <http://www.internetindicators.com/global.html> (accessed 10 October 2001).

16. "World Domination on the Cheap," *Business Week*, 28 August 2000, 62.

17. Scott Goldman, "WAP on the Attack," *Telecommunications Online*, March 2001, <http://www.telecoms-mag.com/telecom/default.asp?journalid=2&func=articles&page=0103i33&year=2001&month=3&srchexpr=%22WAP+on+the+Attack%22#hls1> (accessed 10 October 2001).

18. Geoff Mott, conversation with author, September 2001.

19. Christine Maxwell, ed., "Global Trends That Will Impact Universal Access

to Information Resources," submitted to UNESCO, 15 July 2000, <http://www
.isocmex.org.mx/frmderunescopaper.html> (accessed 10 October 2001).

20. Telecommunications Industry Association, "2001 MultiMedia Telecommunications Market Review & Forecast: Key Findings & Forecasts Through 2004,"
<http://www.mmta.org/research/market_findings.cfm> (accessed 17 October 2001).

21. Robert Morris, interview with author, 17 January 2001.

22. Mike Yamamoto, "Vietnam Issues Internet Restrictions," c|net news.com,
4 June 1996, <http://news.cnet.com/news/0,10000,0-1005-200-311453,00.html>
(accessed 10 October 2001).

23. "First America, Then the World," *The Economist*, 24 February 2000, 49.

24. Ibid.

25. "Time for Another Round," *The Economist*, 3 October 1998.

26. Jeffrey Sachs, "A New Map of the World," *The Economist*, 22 June 2000.
See also Robert Kaplan, *To the Ends of the Earth: From Togo to Turkmenistan, from Iran
to Cambodia, a Journey to the Frontiers of Anarchy* (New York: Vintage, 1997).

27. Carol Matlack, "En Garde, Wal-Mart," *BusinessWeek* Online, 13 September
1999, <http://www.businessweek.com/1999/99_37/b3646129.htm> (accessed 10
October 2001).

28. Don Lochbiler, "I Think Mr. Ford is Leaving Us," *Detroit News*, <http://det
news.com/history/ford/ford.htm> (accessed 10 October 2001).

29. Theodore Levitt, "The Globalization of Markets," *Harvard Business Review*
61, no. 3 (May–June 1983).

30. Tomlinson, *Globalization and Culture*, 7.

31. Bertrand Benoit, "Wal-Mart Finds German Failures Hard to Swallow,"
Financial Times, 12 October 2000, 21.

Chapter 9: Managing It All

1. Quoted in Jean Baudrillard, "Consumer Society," in *Consumer Society in American History: A Reader*, ed. Lawrence B. Glicjman (Ithaca and London: Cornell University Press, 1999).

2. E. F. Schumacher, *Small Is Beautiful: Economics as if People Mattered* (New
York: Harper & Row, 1973), 163.

3. Michael Porter, *Competitive Advantage: Creating and Sustaining Superior Performance* (New York: The Free Press, 1985).

4. Richard Pastore, "Competing Interests," interview with Michael Porter,
CIO, 1 October 1995, <http://www.cio.com/CIO/porter_100195.html> (accessed
17 October 2001). Reprinted with permission.

5. Stuart Elliott, "Silicon Valley Executives Don't Seem to Feel They Are Getting Much for Their Marketing Buck," *New York Times*, 27 November 1995, D9.

6. Cisco Systems, "Acquisition Summary," <http://www.cisco.com/warp/pub
lic/750/acquisition/summarylist.html> (accessed 10 October 2001).

7. "Sommer's Crunch," *Business Week*, 4 December 2000, 144.

8. James E. Gaskin, "Moving from CIO to CEO," *Inter@ctive Week*, 17 July 2000.

9. "Online World Changed All the Business Rules," *Financial Times* IT Review, "Brands in the Internet Age," 2 February 2000, xv.

10. Ram Chran, and Geoffery Colvin, "Managing for the Slowdown," *Fortune*, 5 February 2001, 79.

11. IBM 1999 Annual Report, <http://www.ibm.com/annualreport/1999/let ter/letter_04.html> (accessed 17 October 2001).

12. See GE's corporate Web site: <http://www.ge.com/news/podium_papers /ourvalues.htm> (accessed 10 October 2001).

13. Jim Gosling, e-mail to author, 30 November 2000.

14. Joel Birnbaum, speech at the American Physical Society's 1999 Centennial Conference, Atlanta, GA, 22 March 1999, available at <http://www.hpl.hp.com /speeches/birnbaum_aps.html> (accessed 17 October 2001).

15. From an advertisement found on the Tufts University Human Factor and Ergonomic Society Web site, <http://www.tufts.edu/as/stu-org/hfes/thfes/jobs/1998/ mar/intel.txt> (accessed 22 October 2001).

16. Quoted in John G. Spooner, "Inside Intel: Betting on the Future," *ZDNet News*, 24 July 2000, <http://www.zdnet.com/zdnn/stories/news/0,4586,2600824, 00.html> (accessed 17 October 2001).

17. Ibid.

Chapter 10: The Magic Touch

1. John Chappell, e-mail to author, 18 December 2000.

2. Nathan Rosenberg, *Exploring the Black Box: Technology, Economics, and History* (New York: Cambridge University Press, 1994), 15.

3. Small Business Administration Office of Advocacy, <http://www.sba.gov/ advo> (accessed 17 October 2001). Note: Failures variety by type of business and industry. For analysis of data see reference site.

4. "The World's View of Multinationals," *The Economist*, 29 January 2000, 22.

5. Ray Kurzweil, *The Age of Spiritual Machines: When Computers Exceed Human Intelligence* (New York: Penguin Putnam, 1999), 195.

Index

About the Author

Regis McKenna is Chairman of The McKenna Group, an international consulting firm specializing in the application of emerging information and telecommunications technologies to business strategies. For the past thirty years, McKenna's firm has been helping clients develop creative approaches to emerging and rapidly changing market environments. The McKenna Group is an alliance partner with the Cantanas global professional business services network and with OC&C, a pan-European strategy consulting firm. McKenna is included in the San Jose Mercury News Millennium 100 as one of the 100 people who made Silicon Valley what it is today.

McKenna and his firm worked with a number of entrepreneurial start-ups during their formative years, including America Online, Apple, Electronic Arts, Genentech, Intel, 3COM, and many others. In the last decade, McKenna consulted on strategic marketing and business issues to industrial, consumer, transportation, healthcare, and financial firms in the United States, Japan, and Europe.

McKenna has appeared on the television *NightLine* special on "Time," the *Jim Leher Report* on technology at the millennium, and on *The Today Show* on venture capital. He has written and lectured extensively on the social and market effects of technological change advancing innovations in marketing theories and practices.

McKenna is Chairman of the Board of the Santa Clara University Center for Science, Technology and Society, and was a founding board member of Smart Valley. He is a trustee at Santa Clara University, and on the advisory board of the Haas School of Business, University of California Berkeley, and the Economic Strategies Institute.

McKenna is the author of four other books—*The Regis Touch*, *Who's*

Afraid of Big Blue?, *Relationship Marketing*, and *Real Time*—and numerous articles on technology, marketing and social change. Currently, he lectures and conducts seminars on marketing and information technology throughout the United States, Europe, and Asia.